Bob Vila's
Complete Guide to
Remodeling Your Home

Bob Vila's Complete Guide to Remodeling Your Home

Everything You Need to Know

About Home Renovation from the

#1 Home Improvement Expert

Bob Vila **and Hugh Howard**

Principal Photography by Michael Fredericks
Line Drawings by Nancy Hull

A V O N   B O O K S   ◆   N E W   Y O R K

AVON BOOKS, INC.
1350 Avenue of the Americas
New York, New York 10019

Copyright © 1999 by B.V.T.V.
Line drawings © Nancy Hull
Principal photography © Michael Fredericks
Cover architectural drawing by Gregory Rochlin
Interior design by Richard Oriolo
ISBN: 0-380-97673-0

Library of Congress Cataloging in Publication Data:
Vila, Bob.
    Bob Vila's complete guide to remodeling your home : everything you need to know about home renovation from the #1 home improvement expert / by Bob Vila and Hugh Howard ; principal photography by Michael Fredericks, line drawings by Nancy Hull. — 1st ed.
        p.   cm.
        1. Dwellings—Remodeling.   2. Buildings—Conservation and restoration.   I. Howard, Hugh, 1952– . II. Title.
TH4816.V53797   1999   99-25410
643'.7—dc21   CIP

First Avon Books Printing: October 1999

AVON TRADEMARK REG. U.S. PAT. OFF. AND IN OTHER COUNTRIES, MARCA REGISTRADA, HECHO EN U.S.A.

Printed in the U.S.A.

FIRST EDITION

QPM 10 9 8 7 6 5 4 3 2 1

www.bobvila.com
www.avonbooks.com

This book is dedicated to America's remodelers,

from enthusiastic novices to practiced preservationists.

Acknowledgments

Many people made invaluable contributions to the creation of this book. Among them are Michael Fredericks, who took most of the photographs, and Nancy Hull, who executed the bulk of drawings. In those instances where the photographs are the work of others, the caption credits the photographer and, thus, to Melissa Marchand, John Eberle, Sam Gray, and Paul Warchol we extend our thanks. In a few instances, antique line drawings or woodcuts have been used to give certain architectural styles or details a period feel.

Many architects, designers, and builders helped directly or indirectly. Special thanks to Ian J. Cohn of Diversity: Diversity & Design, who provided the set of plans featured in Chapter 5, and to Gregory Rochlin, Architect, who provided the architectural drawings in the Introduction as well as the design work for my Cambridge home. Our appreciation to Asher Benjamin, Thomas Bitnar, Andrea Clark Brown, Tom Goffigon, David Hall, Kate Johns, James Volney Righter, John Tittmann, Denis Wedlick, and Malcolm Woollen, whose work is represented by images in this book. Architects Tyler Donaldson, Paul Eagle, and Professor Duncan G. Stroik at the University of Notre Dame each offered important guidance. Builder Steven Anderson made available to us a work site where not a few of the work-in-progress photos you see in this book were taken. Other contributors of ideas, anecdotes, images, and photogenic homes include Richard Bennett, William Blitzer and Heather E. Whiting, Donald Carpentier, the Columbia County Historical Society, Michael Dunn, Tom and Loree Goffigon, Jerry Grant, Robert Haldane, Robert Herron, James and Susan Jensen, Maarten Kooij and Lynn McLaren, Willam McMillen, Ann and Evan Maxwell, Old Sturbridge Village, Diane and Braxton Nagle, the National Park Service, Mr. and Mrs. Nicholas Potter, Michael Polemus, John Pope, the Red Rock Historical Society, Randle Robinson Bitnar, Jeremiah Rusconi, Alan Schoen, George and Cathy Shockey, Strawbery Banke, the Trustees of the Reservations, and Martin Van Buren.

At Avon Books, Lou Aronica helped develop the original book idea and had the patience to see it through and Senior Editor Jennifer Brehl has lent her high enthusiasm and energy throughout. Robin Davis Gomez did a superb job of getting the words right and Richard Oriolo's design truly brought the elements together.

Thanks, as well, to agents Jonathan Russo, Barry Weiner, and Lydia Wills, of Artists Agency, Inc., and Dominick Abel of the Dominick Abel Literary Agency, Inc., as well as attorney Ron Feiner. Thanks, too, to the people who help make BVTV run, Michael Ferrone, Jeanne Flynn, and Sheila Morris, and to Jack Hill at *www.bobvila.com*.

Finally, a few words of thanks to the many designers, contractors, suppliers, home renovators, and interested others who have shared with us their experiences and expertise over the years in the making of *Home Again* as well as this book.

Foreword

Since I began remodeling houses, there's been a sea of change. In the seventies, a lot of us do-it-ourselves guys figured prominently in the demographics of home renovation. Today, with two-career families, the aging of the baby boomers, and increasingly sophisticated building techniques, the *do-it-yourself* tactic has, for most people, been superceded by the *buy-it-yourself* strategy.

That change is what made this book necessary.

My goal in the pages that follow isn't to tell you how to do your own remodeling job. There are already entire shelves of references books devoted to every detail that can do that. In no way am I discouraging a hands-on approach—I know from experience there's little else in life that delivers the satisfaction that a completed I-did-it-myself job can. But people who have neither the time nor the inclination to do the work themselves can buy fine workmanship on a finite budget.

This is the book to help you do just that.

Better than three out of four homeowners launching a remodeling project today don't plan to lift a hammer. If you're one of them, your task requires good business sense rather than tool sense. Americans spend tens of *billions* of dollars on residential remodeling every year and you may know from first-hand experience or from visiting the newly renovated homes of friends that sometimes that money isn't well spent. Thus, one major goal of this book is to enable you to get the most for your remodeling dollars.

Yet even before you start writing checks, you need to understand very clearly what it is you want in order to communicate it to the professionals. Thus, this book begins with several chapters devoted to considering your house in ways you probably never have before. In Part I: Looking at Your House, we'll look closely at its condition (Chapter 1: Examining the Existing House); consider larger matters of style and detailing (Chapter 2: A Matter of Style); and then begin to synthesize that knowledge into a larger understanding of how buildings look and evolve (Chapter 3: Looking at Buildings).

Part II: Making Plans begins the implementation process. Chapter 4: Thinking Through the Design explains how to apply what you learned in general to the particulars of your house. Chapter 5: The Working Plans focuses on how to work with an architect, designer, or contractor to put your vision on paper. Chapter 6: Contractors, Contracts, and Costs is about the business of building.

In Part III: Making Changes, the work begins. Chapter 7: Building the Box concerns the skeleton. Chapter 8: Wiring, Plumbing and Insulation is about the working systems. Chapter 9: Finishing the Job is about completion, from the finish carpentry and setting the fixtures to settling in and setting up.

As you can see, this book follows the logic of the renovation process—the more logically you approach your renovation, the happier you will be with the result. I recommend you read this book start to finish *before* you hire a designer or commit to a contractor. There are a lot of sections you will want to come back to later as the process unfolds, but understanding the entire process from inception to completion will be invaluable. Construction is a continuum, and having an appreciation of the whole sequence of events will offer you a valuable perspective for understanding what a designer is trying to do in the early stages and what the tradespeople are working toward at the end.

Renovation is about making the right hiring decisions, so much of this book is concerned with profiling the professionals; you'll encounter different pros in every chapter. Even a small renovation job such as the installation of a new half bath might involve a designer, carpenter, plumber, electrician, tile setter, and painter. Or, in some instances, a single person will wear each of those hats in succession. One focus of this book is to help you identify, hire, and work effectively with the designers and contractors best suited to your needs, tastes, and budget. Still another will be to help you think about design and material choices—there'll be a great many decisions to make, and I'll try to provide you with a framework for making them. I will also guide you about managing the entire process with efficiency and economy.

If this all sounds complicated, let me assure you it doesn't have to be. After all, the goal of this book, simply stated, is to help you to get the most for your money, in an orderly fashion that disrupts your life as little as possible—*and* to be happy with the result.

So let's get to work.

Contents

Bob Vila's Complete Guide to Remodeling Your Home

Introduction

I have been remodeling houses for most of my life. I've been doing it in on television for twenty years. Before that I did renovation work as both a homeowner and a contractor and, earlier still, as a Peace Corps volunteer in Panama. As a boy, I helped my father around the house. You might say that buildings, especially *homes*, have become my life's work.

Perhaps that's why the remodeling job I did in Cambridge in 1996 for my television show *Home Again* gave me so much pleasure. Not that it was the biggest, newest, or fanciest house I've ever done. What I liked about the job was that the assignment was to renovate a house for *me*, the home that is now the primary residence for my wife, Diana, our younger daughter, and me. We needed room, too, for my son and older daughter for vacation visits.

Home sweet home on a quiet Cambridge street, a lovely place to return to.

The task was in part a restoration since much of the interior had been gutted during a 1970s renovation. But our goal wasn't to turn the place into a house museum. It was a top-to-bottom job, involving a good deal of demolition and the rearrangement of some spaces, especially upstairs. We shored up the structure and installed essentially all new heating, ventilation, and air-conditioning systems (HVAC), as well as plumbing and wiring. We put in new bathrooms, remodeled the kitchen, added a new secondary entrance and deck area, and introduced many modern conveniences that simply weren't available when the house was built in 1897.

Almost every decision we made, however, resulted from careful consideration of not only what we wanted and needed but how we could respect the character and quality of the original house. We worked hard to retain what remained of the detailing and overall character of the original home, preserving old elements that survived and restoring lost details. Since we recorded the process on tape for the show, our viewers got to see the transformation of the handsome 1890s Shingle Style home into a comfortable house for the 1990s.

Why is this man smiling? Because he sees great progress being made in the remodeling of his house, of course.
Photo credit: Melissa Marchand

To begin this book, then, I'm going to walk you through that renovation job, just as I did the viewers of my show. We'll look at the challenges posed by fixing up that house and some of the satisfactions it has provided. Whether you're new to the remodeling process or a veteran of large and small home-improvement projects, I think you'll find what follows illuminating.

The best way to get grounded is to examine the house itself. Before we began our renovation, we inspected and investigated the house with great care. What we found—and what you'll find, too, in your house—is that houses are a lot like people. Each one has characteristics that will make you want to be its friend forever but others that will make you wonder how true a friend it will be.

In the case of my 1897 house, our close examination of the exterior produced no great surprises. The stone foundation was sound and attractive. The wood frame that sat on top was intact, but some of the original outer walling (cedar shingles) and all of the more recent roof surface (asphalt shingles) needed replacement. The window sash held mostly old glass with its ripples and waves, and we knew we wanted to save that. The porches and decks needed some reworking. We could see that there was a lot of work to do outside, but the problems concerned mostly the skin, not the structure of the house.

On the interior, the signs and symptoms were harder to read. The major remodeling done in the early 1970s, in keeping with the tastes of the time, had emphasized clean lines at the expense of ornamentation. Many of the moldings had been removed, giving the hall and living room all the character of a bare commercial space. That would have to change.

Some original elements remained, such as a built-in hutch in the dining room. Its glazed doors were missing but the trim around it survived, including fluted flattened columns (pilasters) and its cornice with dentils across the top. The mantels in the living room, dining room, and library survived, as did a lovely staircase in the main hall. The generously proportioned stair was trimmed with a mahogany railing and turned spindles, and it extended all the way to the third floor. All this millwork was thick with a dozen or more layers of paint, but it was original and largely intact.

The last downstairs room was the kitchen. It was a hodgepodge, a mixed-up mess with 1950s walnut grain Formica cabinets and an asymmetrical white teardrop-shaped table from the 1970s. Again, however, some elements survived from the time of the original construction that gave us a flavor of that era. A key survivor was part of a small pantry. Its tall, glazed doors that reached to the ceiling could be the inspiration for new cabinetry. We were also pleased to find that, once it was cleared of unwanted later additions, the raw kitchen space would be a generous 18 by 25 feet—plenty of area to make an open and welcoming multipurpose space for cooking, relaxing, and socializing.

On the second floor, the rooms were small, none of them large enough for the master bedroom we wanted. We knew immediately we'd need to change the floor

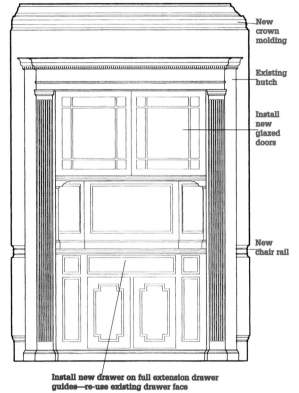

New crown molding

Existing hutch

Install new glazed doors

New chair rail

Install new drawer on full extension drawer guides—re-use existing drawer face

Existing elements are usually worth preserving. In the case of this hutch, the original glazed doors had been lost over the decades but, as you can see from Greg's working drawing and the photograph of the finished product, we re-created them. In its corner of the dining room, this cabinet has proved to be a place both to display and to store china.
Drawing courtesy of Gregory Rochlin, Architect

plan radically. The third floor, which had been used as a rental apartment, was a rabbit warren of small rooms and smaller storage spaces—one closet actually had a closet of its own! But a peek into the attic told us that the roof was sound and that much of the framing of the third floor had come later so, if we wanted to, we could create a tall ceiling there.

A lot of ideas were incubating—the large family kitchen, a master bedroom with his and hers baths, maybe a big room for teenagers on the third floor. But before we could go much farther we needed to learn about the working systems and the structure of the house, which would involve some demolition. But even before we did that, we needed to do some more homework.

Some archival research revealed that the house had been built for a man named W. H. Pickering. An article in the *Cambridge Chronicle* from 1897 identified Pickering as a Harvard professor and described the comfortable house he was building. The house had changed a great deal over the years, but that article helped put us back in time. We recognized the house that we would soon call home.

We learned that the hill where our house is located had been farmland until the 1880s, with a fine view of the nearby Charles River. Then the hill and surrounding acres were subdivided into house lots. Some of those early homes were generously proportioned Victorian houses in the Queen Anne style. Later came homes built in the Georgian Revival, Tudor Revival, and other styles. The empty slots in the streetscape gradually filled over the decades.

Our house was built in the Shingle Style, which had a brief vogue in the last quarter of the nineteenth century. Shingle Style houses were first built in fashionable towns along the coast of the northeastern United States, in particular on Long Island and Cape Cod, and in Maine and that great playground of the Gilded Age, Newport,

Rhode Island. In looking at examples of the style, there are signs of the English-inspired Queen Anne Style, like the wide porches and the overall asymmetry of the design (see also The Queen Anne House, page 100). There are elements that are recognizable as Colonial Revival, another style that developed more or less simultaneously (see page 106).

The Shingle and Colonial Revival Styles were developed by an emerging cadre of imaginative young American architects—among them Charles Follen McKim and Stanford White of McKim, Mead, and White; Henry Hobson Richardson; and even, for a brief period, Frank Lloyd Wright. The Shingle Style was uniquely American. Having celebrated their centennial, Americans suddenly became more conscious of their own history, and in the process rediscovered eighteenth-century homes and adapted colonial shapes and detailing to new uses.

As its name suggests, the Shingle Style used traditional American cladding, the wooden shingle, usually as both the wall and roofing materials. The shingled surface gave the houses an undulating texture that, when swathed around an asymmetrical shape with wide porches, a mixture of windows, and rambling additions, gave these homes an almost sculptural quality.

We learned that our house, along with a number of others nearby, was the work of architects Hartwell and Richardson (not the firm of *the* H. H. Richardson, however, who some years earlier developed both the Romanesque Revival and the Shingle Styles). We were beginning to understand something of the architectural context. As we considered what we wanted to do, we had a deeper perspective as a result of knowing a bit of the house's history.

Thoughts about integrating the new into the old brings us to philosophy. Once you know what you have, you can begin to decide what to do with it. But in the case of a house of a certain age, especially one with some architectural integrity and quality workmanship, it's useful to mull over a little terminology.

The historic preservation movement has become an important force in this country in recent years. Even for the layperson, there is a new consciousness when renovating. It isn't solely a matter of deciding what you want the place to look like—there are aesthetic, historical, and even economic reasons for regarding the intentions of the builders and earlier inhabitants.

If your house has crisp old moldings, wide board floors, and the patina of age, you probably will want to retain those elements. That's *preservation*—conserving what's there. If some or most of the fine details have been removed from your house and you want to put them back, that's *restoration*. (Keep in mind that restoration isn't arbitrary: much detective work must usually be done to determine what originally existed; restoration isn't a matter of adopting details that merely seem appropriate to a given period). *Renovation, remodeling, redesign,* and *rehabilitation* are more general terms for making the house appear the way you want it, with or without particular regard to its history. These distinctions and their ramifications will be discussed at greater length in Chapter 3, but the bottom line is that you may be doing your home and yourself a disservice if you don't view your house from a range of perspectives—personal, practical, financial, *and* historical.

Our philosophy on the Cambridge house? Although a good deal of original fabric was gone, we would preserve many of the surviving original elements. As we went about our renovation, we would try to frame our decisions using what we had learned of the house's past. We were not doing a restoration job, but were remodeling the place. In short, our goal was to use original elements where we could and, even when we couldn't, to use our knowledge of the house itself to inform our thinking.

Let me give you two examples of the kinds of decisions we made. The once crisp profiles on the moldings that remained in the house had lost most of their definition, so initially we resolved to have them stripped. The carpenters then laboriously removed chair rail, door and window casings, and the rest of the moldings. The living room gradually filled with stacks of numbered and coded moldings, all of them coated with a dozen or more layers of paint.

Then the estimates came in. We discovered that having the paint stripped would cost about a dollar and a half per linear foot for the moldings. Milling new ones to the exact profiles of the old moldings would cost an average of about $.85 a foot. We considered the matter. Instinctively, we wanted to use the originals, but financially the difference in cost was significant for some two thousand feet of molding.

What decided the issue was the realization that all the original moldings had been machine-made. If the house had been built a century earlier, the moldings would have been made on site, by joiners working with wooden planes. The flat areas would have had the slight hill-and-valley contour of hand-planed work and the moldings would have had bolder profiles. But our house had always had moldings made by a steam-powered planer in a millwork shop somewhere in Boston. Thus, the

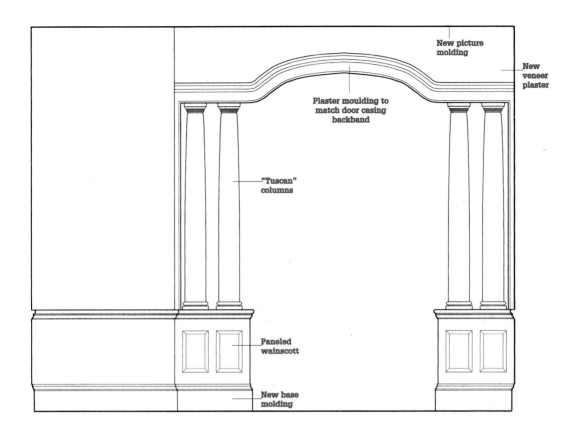

New picture molding

New veneer plaster

Plaster moulding to match door casing backband

"Tuscan" columns

Paneled wainscott

New base molding

Sometimes a small investment in architectural detail at the entrance of a house can help make a statement, as we hoped this elliptical archway in the vestibule of our home would do.
Drawing courtesy of Gregory Rochlin, Architect

purchase order went out to a modern millwork shop for new moldings. We did pre-serve a number of important pieces of original woodwork, like the mantels and a few unique or hand-coped pieces of trim on windows and doors. And the staircase, too, of course. But most of the baseboards, door and window casings, picture rails, and other moldings were restored to their original appearance using new moldings, milled of poplar, of precisely the same profiles as the originals.

Consider, too, the challenge of the front entryway.

It wasn't originally interior space (it had been part of an exposed porch) but had been enclosed decades ago. As a vestibule, the little room suited the shape of the house and was extremely practical, a welcoming space for visitors and Vilas alike. It was very plain, however, with no moldings to embellish its plaster walls. A creative solution was found that served both practicalities and aesthetics.

We decided to add an archway between the entry and the main hall of the house. That broad arch would be supported by two pairs of columns that echoed the columns on the porch immediately outside. Visitors to the house would enter through a combination of exterior and interior spaces that worked together. While we greeted our guests and hung up their coats, they could glimpse the heart of the house, their view framed by the columns and flattened arch.

Actually, the archway was our architect's idea. He was instrumental in thinking through many of the practical and aesthetic decisions.

I'm a firm believer in bringing in design professionals, so Gregory Rochlin was hired early in the process. He's a licensed architect, and he helped us with every step, from the initial inspection through to completion and beyond. Even a year and more after moving in, I continued to call upon him to help with small problems or adjustments as they arose.

As the work was being done, Greg produced plans, elevations, and countless detail drawings. He also supervised every step in the construction. But from the beginning, he brought other skills to bear. One of them was an intimate knowledge of Cambridge in general and its architecture in particular—he's lived here all his life, and he's been paying attention. He knows the ins and outs of its bureaucracy, from the inspectors and the city codes they enforce to the zoning board and the process for applying for variances.

I've always had a feel for the character of Cambridge streetscapes and its housing stock. The history here goes way back to the days of the Puritans. They were not people of means so they built simple houses, like saltboxes and Cape Cod homes. Later came eighteenth-century mansions, built by Tory traders, wealthy from trade with the West Indies. They built great Georgian residences, some of which also survive, providing homes for Cambridge's important universities, Harvard and MIT, their professors, and other professionals. Walking around town, you encounter neoclassical work by Charles Bulfinch, later nineteenth-century works by H. H. Richardson, and twentieth-century designs of note, including buildings by Walter Gropius, Le Corbusier, and an early work by Phillip Johnson.

Another of Greg's talents is that he listens: it's a critical skill in an architect or designer. He walked through the house with us at every stage, looking to read our reactions to every space. He asked us questions, encouraging us to share our wishes, expectations, and needs. He took our architectural pulse about everything.

He studied the house, too, with great care. He took detailed measurements. Only then did he produce drawings—and a great many good ideas.

He put them on paper for us in such a way that we could consider them in context—*and* so we could show them on television. Reading architectural plans takes time and practice, but he used a color code to simplify the process. The portions that were to be demolished were in green, the existing house was in black, and the new work was in red.

In looking at those plans, we could easily see, for example, how he proposed to change the archway to the dining room to align with the window and with the archway across the hall, adding symmetry. I'd asked for shelves in the study for my

Built in 1727, the William Brattle House is very near Harvard Square— on its namesake way, Brattle Street.

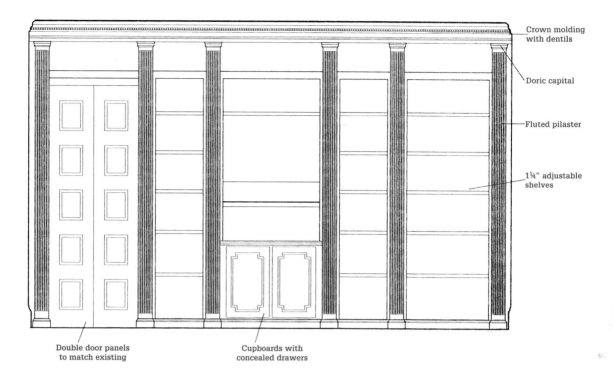

Crown molding
with dentils

Doric capital

Fluted pilaster

1¼" adjustable
shelves

Double door panels
to match existing

Cupboards with
concealed drawers

books, and he recommending picking up architectural details (the fluted pilasters, cornice, and dentil molding) from the surviving hutch in the dining room and adapting them for my bookcases in the study. I suggested a natural finish mahogany stock. The overall approach struck all the right notes: It used the old, yet adapted it to our needs.

Remember that hutch in our dining room? These shelves are its progeny. **Drawing courtesy of Gregory Rochlin, Architect**

The kitchen was a true collaboration. My wife Diana is not tall (just five feet) so that today's standard kitchens tend to be awkward for her. In addition, we all agreed that a new overall logic was required for what had been a rather disorganized set of poorly connected spaces. We rationalized the large space into three parallel zones: an eating area framed by pantry storage; a cooking area; and finally the back-door/larder/home-office area. The cooking area in particular was dimensioned to suit Diana's convenience. The reconfiguration had designated areas for different purposes; yet the overall space would retain a sense of openness.

I felt that we were coming to know this house of ours and, in some dimly lit corner of my mind, an image was emerging of what it would be when finished. We headed toward that goal with all possible speed. We thought we would reach it in about six months.

As the architect drew up plans, preliminary work on the house began. As with any renovation, that meant demolition. The first thing we did was remove the old wall-to-wall carpeting upstairs. The guys brought it to the first floor, turned it bottom-side-up, cut it to fit, and set it down on top of the hardwood floors we wanted to protect. Then the demolition could begin in earnest.

Demolition is actually a three-fold process. First is the demo-and-dumpsters stage. Some materials we knew were destined for the landfill, like the kitchen cabinets and old partitions that were going to be moved. Demolition is dirty and dusty work, involving generations of dirt. It doesn't take a high degree of skill, but attention must be paid in order not to damage what remains.

The removal of trim, doors, and other elements that are to be reused requires a gentle touch. While crude wrecking bars and brute force can be used to rip out landfill fodder, the gentle application of elbow grease is needed to take out hundred-year-old wooden elements that are to be reused. Too much force can result in breakage and dents or scrapes on the pieces to be salvaged. Each piece must be numbered, and often rough sketches are required, keying individual parts to their proper positions. With great care, we removed what survived of the original base-boards, chair rails, door trim, and other moldings. We removed the doors, too, and took off their brass hardware for stripping. We would be reusing window sash, so they went to the strippers.

The third part of the deconstruction process is brains-on as well as hands-on. The idea is to observe and learn from what you find as the layers of the structure come off. Sometimes the discoveries are predictable, like bits of original wallpaper beneath later layers. At times, however, there are genuine surprises. For example, in that 1897 article we'd found about the house, we'd read that "sliding doors will be used between the main rooms." The statement left us confused because we knew of no sliding doors in the house. But it also got us thinking.

Pretty soon our carpenter on *Home Again*, Bob Ryley, figured it out. He noticed that the wall between the main hall and the study was unusually thick. I think I know why, he said to himself. He took a trip to his toolbox. He scored the paint using a small utility knife. With a flat bar, putty knife, and hammer, he carefully separated the stop that was mounted on the surface of the jamb. When he popped the wide board off, his hunch was proven correct: There was indeed a pocket door there. It had been boarded up, intact, within the wall cavity a quarter century earlier.

Another part of the deconstruction task is to identify problems. When we began removing old plaster in the kitchen we discovered that a partition had been removed that had supported the ceiling. Worse yet, we found that the *floor joists* (the parallel series of horizontal members that support the floor and ceiling load) had been chopped and channeled by plumbers running waste pipes while retrofitting bathrooms. Little more than plaster and lath held the structure together, as several joists had been severed and left hanging. It was a miracle that the ceiling and floor above hadn't collapsed into the kitchen. We'd need to address that situation before we could proceed, so we brought in a structural engineer to consult with us.

With the wall and ceiling cavities open, we could also examine the working systems in the house. We confirmed what we already suspected about the plumbing: it would be best to demolish and remove virtually all of it because it was a combination of old brass, which was near the end of its life expectancy, and old iron, which accumulates scale on its inside walls, narrowing the pipes' diameters and reducing water flow. We were also radically rearranging things, especially on the second and third floors, so even if some of the lines could have been reused, it didn't make sense because they were in all the wrong places. We discovered that even the feed from the street would have to be replaced, since it was lead-lined pipe. So out it all came except for one half bath that we left temporarily on the first floor. After all we would have workers in the house for months to come.

The illumination in the house at the time of construction had been gas. Electricity had come during World War I in the form of knob-and-tube wiring. That had been updated, probably in the 1940s or 1950s, so by the time I bought the place it had a 200 amp service. That meant we had a mixture of old, not-so-old, and not-so-safe wiring. The original source of heat had been a hand-fired coal furnace, but subsequently oil-heat and, more recently, gas-heat conversions had been done. The furnace itself was about forty years old and was far from energy efficient. Once again, we realized the best approach would be to remove the old wiring and heating system and to start anew.

Sometimes in the demolition process what you *don't* find is as important as what you do. We removed an unattractive tile floor in the entranceway. That part of the house had originally been a porch but had later been closed in. We pulled up the subfloor beneath the tile and, sure enough, there were the original porch boards beneath, pitched away from the house to shed rainwater. A set of boards called *sleepers* had been added to level the surface and the later subfloor had been nailed to them. The undercarriage was structurally sound but one thing was missing: In the wide bays between the sleepers there was no insulation whatsoever. In fact, as we looked not only in the vestibule but in the attic, the ceilings, and the walls of the house, we found virtually no insulation anywhere.

As the last of the debris went out to the dumpsters, we felt we had reached a sort of architectural ground zero. We now knew about as much as we ever would about the age, character, and structure of the house. We had identified what had been changed, how much of the original remained, and could make educated guesses about what was no longer there.

We had a multitude of decisions to make but, for the first time, we didn't feel as if a surprise awaited behind every finished surface. Frankly, there weren't many untouched areas left. From this point on, day by day, the place would begin gradually to regain the feel and look of a house.

By this juncture we had a team of contractors assembled. Bob Ryley would make a major contribution to the work. But this was a big job requiring a lot of capable workers—I remember one day arriving on the job site to find almost a dozen men scrambling up and down the scaffolding, reshingling the house. Most of them came from Fort Hill, a collaborative construction firm based in Boston.

I cannot overemphasize the importance of hiring the right contractor. Fort Hill was the right one for our job—from rough work to finish work, the right guys were on site doing things well. The homeowner's choice of contractor and his or her ability to interact with the carpenter and other craftspeople determine a great deal about the completed job. You must identify the person with whom you have your conversations about schedule, costs, the quality of the workmanship, and intangibles like attitude, courtesy to the neighbors, and even decorum on the work site. You need to hire a contractor because he or she is the right person for the job, not necessarily because the price is the lowest. But we'll talk about hiring later in Chapter 6, Contractors, Contracts, and Costs.

Once the demolition was completed, we began the structural work. That meant a new beam in the kitchen. And new dormers in the roof, where we had decided to create a generously proportioned entertainment space for my teenage kids to enjoy, with a music system and large-screen television. That meant we had to add more structure, too, to stiffen the roof because of the room's wide span, as well as the added weight of the snow that would accumulate owing to the insulation we would be adding.

On the exterior, the crew went to work removing the deteriorating shingles, especially on the south side where the sun's heat exacerbates the effects of the tough New England climate. That entire south facade had to be stripped and reshingled, although on the rest of the house we had to patch only certain areas. But the work required considerable skill. The shingles flare out at foundation level, a detail that helps shed water as well as give Shingle Style houses their distinctive wavy appearance. It means the shingles at the corners need to be cut carefully—and by hand.

We stripped the asphalt shingles off the roof, too. The top layer was beginning to demineralize (loose its granules) and some of the shingles were curling. Both are sure signs a roof is coming to the end of its useful life and that leaks are imminent. In any case, we had decided to return to the original roofing surface, cedar shingles.

Some of the gutters were badly deteriorated and needed replacement. The design called for a broad wooden gutter and some of it had rotted beyond use. In order to retain the original appearance of the house, we decided not to install an all-new system but to replace the deteriorated part of the old and line it with copper. The gutters were wide, shaped out of solid stock. No one makes that exact profile any longer, but Bob Ryley worked out a way to modify one of today's stock wooden gutters by ripping it down the middle and gluing two additional pieces of stock, one on one side, the other in the middle. It was a good deal of trouble, but less expensive that milling an all-new one-piece gutter.

Why didn't we simply remove the old gutters and retrofit new ones? Those gutters provided more than drainage—they were actually sculptural, a design element essential to the cornice design of the roof overhangs. If they'd been removed

and replaced by a different system, the look would have changed. It would have been as if a man about town took to wearing a baseball cap together with his dress overcoat— sure, the new-fangled gutters and the cap both offer protection from the weather. But they really don't suit the rest of the outfit, do they?

I have a confession to make: even at my house, the work takes longer to complete than it appears to on television. I've had people come up to me in restaurants and complain about that. "Gee, Bob," one guy said to me recently in an airport lounge, "I feel like you set me up. We decided to lay some new tile in the front hall. I figure I can do it in a day, then it takes me twice as long. And my wife says, 'Hey, Bob Vila did that in about five minutes, how come you're so slow?' "

One of the trickiest parts of the reshingling process was to make the skirting flare out at the foundation level.

The truth is we do a certain amount of work to get ready for each segment so we can keep the pace of the show quick and interesting, and so the viewer can see the beginning, middle, and end of a task. But you know what? Sometimes we get fooled ourselves.

One day a few months into the process at my house, I had the following conversation with our construction manager. "Is the project on schedule?"

I knew the answer, of course, and you can probably guess, too.

"No, we're about two weeks behind," he replied. "We've spent a lot of time reframing the second floor because of damage and some errors made in the original building." He was talking about the new beam in the kitchen, the stiffening of the roof, and some other structural work that had to be done before new wall partitions could be built.

Then I heard myself ask, "Are we going to be able to catch up?"

"I think so," I was told, "over the next couple of months."

I believe he did think it was possible, and I wanted to believe it, too. I had to maintain a televison shooting schedule and had to meet the expectations of my fam-

OPPOSITE: **The work progressed quickly and, at this stage in the process, the deteriorated siding had already been replaced and the painters were hard at work.** Photo credit: Melissa Marchand

ily—we wanted to be in residence by the beginning of the next school year, when my younger daughter would be starting at a new school around the corner from the house.

Would we make it? Stay tuned.

When the new partitions and framing repairs were finished, the plumbers, electricians, and heating and ventilation guys began their work. The skeleton of the house began to infill with electrical wires, plumbing pipes, and ducts. Before pouring a new slab floor, we buried waste pipes in the new cellar slab so we'd have a full ceiling height overhead, allowing for a workout room and workshop in the basement. We partitioned a small room for the utilities. We prepared for the installation of a remarkably small new "low-mass" furnace ("low mass" implies a design with a highly efficient but small volume boiler for heating the water), along with air handlers, units that converted the hot water to forced air. We put piping in the floors of the bathrooms for radiant heat (it gets cold in New England, and a warm tile floor on a cold winter day is a wonderful luxury). We decided upon a state-of-the-art water filtration system. Actually, it was *two* systems: One filtered out minerals (the water in Cambridge is "hard," meaning it's laced with minerals) in order to extend the life expectancy of various appliances like washing machines, dishwashers, and even the water heaters. The other, which worked on a reverse osmosis system, purified the drinking water.

We had saved many of the old windows in the house with their wavy glass (I like to call it glimmerglass, as the light seems to shimmer and wave). When the twenty-five sets of old sash came back from the stripper, the layers of paint were gone and the glass had been reset with new glazing compound. But before they could be primed and painted, we needed to retrofit spring-loaded balances.

At the time the house was built, sash weights were standard. The torpedo-shaped counterweights traveled up and down in hidden cavities in the window frame. A rope-and-pulley system connected each sash to a pair of flanking lead weights, making a heavy window easy to open and close. In our energy-conscious age, this approach has a major downside: The shafts where the sash weights travel cannot be insulated without disrupting the function of the counterweights. The consequence is heat loss through those uninsulated areas—taken together, a house with many such uninsulated spaces is the equivalent of an open window all winter long.

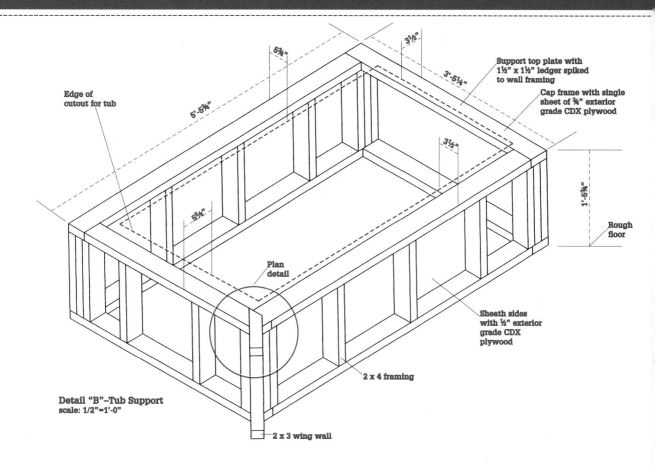

3¼"

5¾"

3'-5¼"

Support top plate with
1½" x 1½" ledger spiked
to wall framing

Cap frame with single
sheet of ¾" exterior
grade CDX plywood

Edge of
cutout for tub

6'-5¾"

3¼"

5⅝"

1'-5⅝"

Rough
floor

Plan
detail

Sheath sides
with ½" exterior
grade CDX
plywood

2 x 4 framing

Detail "B"–Tub Support
scale: 1/2"=1'-0"

2 x 3 wing wall

We decided to replace the old sash weights with a spring-loaded balance system. Housed in aluminum tubes, the springs were set into a groove cut into the side of each sash. This process also gave us the opportunity to reline the side jambs to tighten the fit since, over the life of the house, various refittings had resulted in a good deal of play, amounting to significant gaps on the sides of the windows. The combination of old windows with new fittings proved a good compromise: We got the appearance and character of the original sash yet some of the benefits of a high-performance, energy-efficient window.

Not only did the old windows come back, but some new windows came in, too. Wherever possible we used the old ones, but we changed the *fenestration* (the arrangement of windows and doors) in several places. In the home office at the rear of the kitchen, we added a new double window unit that echoed the configuration

A good
architectural
drawing should
provide the
carpenters with
all the information
they need to put
the pieces in
place.
Drawing courtesy of
Gregory Rochlin,
Architect

19

of the old windows. On the third floor we added two new dormers to help illuminate the family room; the overall shape and configuration of the dormers and of the windows mimicked those of an original dormer. We also added a Palladian window on the south side of that large third floor space. Palladian windows, which are three-part windows with an arched-top central window flanked by matching, flat-topped units on either side, were common to houses of the period.

The doors returned, too. We reused the lock sets, but the stripper had discov-

ered that the hinges were brass plated rather than solid brass. They wouldn't have stripped well, so we went with new hinges.

In the kitchen, the cabinets arrived and in a matter of days the large, deserted space assumed the topography of a real kitchen. At one end was the pantry area, an act of homage to the original butler's pantry, with glass doors on the upper cabinets revealing the bead-board lining within. An island bisected the room, separating the eating space and forming the galley-shaped food preparation area. On the island

I've always admired the geometry of the Palladian window, but in this installation, this Marvin window has the added advantage of letting a lot of light into our generous third-floor family space.

21

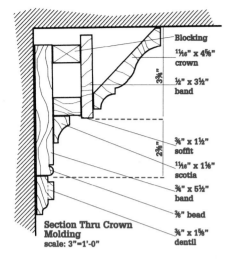

Section Thru Crown Molding
scale: 3"=1'-0"

Blocking
$1\frac{1}{16}$" x $4\frac{5}{8}$" crown
$\frac{1}{2}$" x $3\frac{1}{2}$" band
$3\frac{3}{8}$"
$\frac{3}{4}$" x $1\frac{1}{2}$" soffit
$2\frac{3}{8}$"
$1\frac{1}{16}$" x $1\frac{1}{8}$" scotia
$\frac{3}{4}$" x $5\frac{1}{2}$" band
$\frac{5}{8}$" bead
$\frac{3}{4}$" x $1\frac{5}{8}$" dentil

Elaborate cornices usually look that way because they consist of a surprising number of pieces—in this case, *seven* different pieces of stock.
Drawing courtesy of Gregory Rochlin, Architect

were an oven, trash compactor, sink, and dishwasher, all built in below the level of the counters. From there, the cook could turn 180 degrees and find the cook top with a ventilation hood above. The food preparation area was both spacious and space-saving. A partial partition separated that area from a back entry, secondary sink, the home office, and a generous two-door refrigerator.

Work was going on all over. Plaster was being patched in the library, and a skim coat of plaster was being applied on the attic. The master bedroom was getting a delicious yellow paint job, together with a ragged and textured surface. My home office was getting an oak, herringbone-pattern floor. All in all, the place was beginning to feel like home.

On *Home Again*, I try to integrate a range of segments that take the viewer away from the primary storyline but which bear some direct relationship to the principal job. Thus, we took detours to British Columbia to a cedar shingle plant; to Heritage Cabinets, in New Holland, Pennsylvania, where our kitchen cabinets were being made; and to Country Tile in New York City where we selected tile for our bathrooms.

We also like to tour historic houses. These add diversity and interest to the show and give me, as well the viewer, an opportunity to learn from the curatorial and

Kitchen Island Elevation
scale: $\frac{1}{4}$"=1'-0"

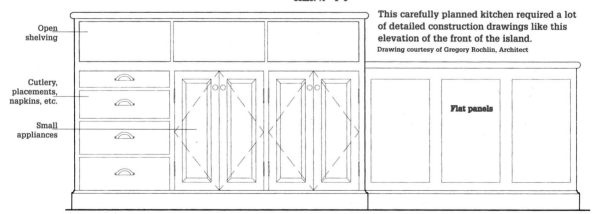

Open shelving

Cutlery, placements, napkins, etc.

Small appliances

Flat panels

This carefully planned kitchen required a lot of detailed construction drawings like this elevation of the front of the island.
Drawing courtesy of Gregory Rochlin, Architect

restoration professionals at the sites. In our attempt to renovate our home in a way that was sympathetic to its original appearance, we visited a number of Shingle Style houses. One of them was right here in Cambridge and had been designed by the same architectural firm responsible for our home, Hartwell and Richardson. Another was in Newport, Rhode Island, and there we got an added bonus.

The house was built in the Shingle Style by a wealthy merchant named Isaac Bell. Major restoration work had just gotten underway, and much of the shingled surface of the house's facade had been removed and temporarily replaced with a skin of building paper or "tar paper" as the asphalt-impregnated material is often known. While you almost had to close your eyes to imagine what the restored exterior would look like, the inside of the Isaac Bell house was largely intact.

It's a giant and glorious house, with grand oriental sculptures and detailing at the entryway. But what stuck me most was the paneling. It seemed like every wall was covered with oak, all of it quarter-sawn, with an intricate pattern of panels between its rails and stiles. The wood surface was all over the place—in the vestibule, on the staircase, in the dining room, around the mantels. It was beautiful.

That paneling got me thinking. In my Shingle Style house, I have a passageway between the front hall and the living room. It's a deep, rectangular opening. A closet is framed into the wall on one side and we were adding a dumbwaiter to the basement on the other to bring up wood for the fireplaces. The walls of that archway were to be flat plastered surfaces. After visiting the Bell house, I decided to panel them.

We picked up the horizontal configuration of the panels on all the doors in the house. We also used the same profile for the applied moldings that frame each pan-

I like to think that the elements you see in this photo *look* like they've been there forever. In fact, the paneling is new, as are the cupboard doors (the lower ones hide a small dumbwaiter for bringing wood from the cellar). The decorative Greek key in fruitwood on the floor is also new, meaning the only original element here is the old cast-iron heating register.

eled opening. We didn't go to the trouble of using oak, since we would be painting it to blend in with the rest of the trim. But the paneled entryway picked up elements of the original house and another house of the period.

Another historic house we visited proved to be the inspiration for the color scheme we adopted for the exterior of the house. We'd examined the paint on our house, using scrapings, a core sample, and microscopic analysis. We found what was originally there, and we painted a small area of the rear of the house with that combination, as well as a couple of minor variations. But we also wanted to consider appropriate options that weren't site specific. We considered dozens of options—greens and blues and beige and even yellow—but the source of the one we decided upon is an 1810 Federal house. It had been remodeled and enlarged in the 1880s by Frederick Law Olmsted, the landscape architect closely associated with New York's Central Park and Boston's string of parks known as the "Emerald Necklace." The house had a wonderful paint job that dated from the renovation. The body color was mulberry, a deep, rich red. The trim was also dark, a strong Essex green. The combination looked great. We test painted another section of the house in that combination and my wife agreed to the choice. We added a couple of twists of our own, too, painting the ceiling of the porch a sky blue and the *muntins* (the wooden elements that divide the individual panes of glass or *lights*) black. Both were traditional techniques in the nineteenth century, which make a porch lighter and the muntins almost invisible.

Not surprisingly, we got some great ideas for our landscape at this house, too.

I had almost as much fun helping to create our small landscape outside the house as I did overseeing the work inside. Again, we hired design professionals—they were named Lamb rather than Olmsted—Rick and Nancy Lamb of Lamb Associates.

When they first arrived at the work site, we toured the existing landscape and talked about what I wanted and what I felt might work. Our conversation was pretty general, but in outlining the task, I did tell them there was one hard-and-fast rule: there was to be no lawn. I didn't want to spend my Saturdays that way. I didn't want the noise, the clippings, any of it. The property isn't large, only a small rectangle squeezed into Cambridge's tight urban grid, so I thought some groundcover, perennials, plants, and bushes would be adequate.

Rick and Nancy immediately reassured me they could meet my demand. In fact, they have such a reassuring air about them that I began to feel as if my property was suddenly larger. They talked about using plant materials to "share and protect"—a flowering bush at a border can be shared with a neighbor, yet offer protection. As we walked around my yard to inspect the existing plantings, they pointed out a couple of big hemlocks, a cusa dogwood with exfoliating bark, and some rhododendrons (a few of which I told them I didn't much like because of their hot pink blooms).

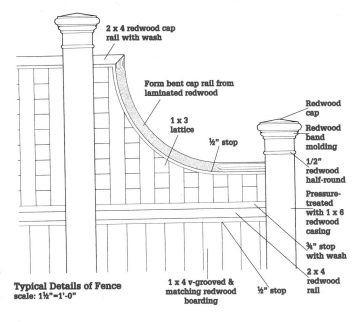

Typical Details of Fence
scale: 1½"=1'-0"

2 x 4 redwood cap rail with wash

Form bent cap rail from laminated redwood

1 x 3 lattice

½" stop

Redwood cap

Redwood band molding

1/2" redwood half-round

Pressure-treated with 1 x 6 redwood casing

¾" stop with wash

2 x 4 redwood rail

1 x 4 v-grooved & matching redwood boarding

½" stop

They told me how certain plant materials could be used to "filter the view." That meant plantings with feathery foliage that would let in light but offer privacy. "Stealing texture" was another concept they explained to me. That means melding in mature plantings on adjacent properties to enhance ours. They identified ways to use new and existing plant material to frame a naturalized alley between nearby houses, enhancing the sense of space.

In addition to plantings, new and old, they created a plan for what they termed the "hardscape." That means the fences, terraces, and retaining walls that form the architecture of the yard. We decided to add a large, open terrace in the back with a surface of a bluestone quarried in New York that has a reddish hue. They suggested a plum tree as a centerpiece with its rich, burgundy leaves to pick up the tone of the stone and of the mulberry-colored house. We came up with a redwood fence design for the boundaries that was equally attractive on both sides. We used a miscellany of azaleas, dogwoods, white and black birch trees, myrtle, spring bulbs, crab apple trees, princess holly, and other plant materials to make the most of different colors and textures at different seasons. And, of course, to avoid having a lawn I didn't want to have to take care of.

As Robert Frost observed, "Good fences make good neighbors." This one acts as a privacy fence (for us *and* our neighbors), as well as being an appealing decorative element surrounding our deck.
Drawing courtesy of Gregory Rochlin, Architect

The balusters were removed during construction, but the treads and risers remained in service throughout.
Photo credit: Melissa Marchand

In the front of the house, Nancy and Rick recommended planting lilac and red-stemmed dogwood along the property line next to the parking area, which would add privacy as well as shield the neighbors from seeing our cars out their windows.

This plan emerged over a period of weeks. But the development gave me a new appreciation of how important it is. Landscaping is often an afterthought, but it most certainly should not be.

We had plenty of setbacks, both in executing the landscape plan and in working on the house. While we were setting the terrace stones, a two-day downpour necessitated a delay of several days to allow the ground to dry. We had to apply to the city of Cambridge for variances to construct one of our fences, the new entrance off the kitchen, and the two new dormers on the third floor. The process was laborious, but we got those changes approved. However, we were not granted permission to move the parking area from a narrow drive on the side of the house to a parking tray in front, meaning the Lambs literally had to go back to their drawing board to devise an alternative landscape design for the streetscape. You win some, you lose some . . . but everything takes time.

The building materials we used came from all around the world. The ceramic tiles alone came from Italy, Spain, Mexico, and Portugal, as well as Oregon and California. The soapstone counters are from Brazil, the mines here having long ago been mined out. The block for the interlocking retaining walls came from Minnesota, the bluestone from New York, the redwood from the West Coast. We used a mix of old and new—in the kitchen, for example, we mixed antique light fixtures with state-of-the-art control systems.

I learned once again how much fun it is to work with pros. You get great finish work from the best workers, yet I appreciate fine craftsmanship almost as much in the prep stuff you don't see. Like the tile surface prep that gets buried. Or the wall-to-wall carpet joints that, when made properly, simply disappear. Or the tricks Ryley used to restore the balustrades when they came back from the stripper. Or the window restoration. The lesson? Hire the best people you can afford and communicate with them as clearly as you can.

Speaking of professionals, don't underestimate what other design pros can contribute. The interior designers we hired from CLC Interiors followed our lead,

using rugs that my wife and I already owned. They used the colors in those rugs as a palette to help select other elements. They integrated pieces of furniture we already owned, but also introduced new wallpapers, fabrics, and paints. They brought a great sensitivity to colors, patterns, and textures that contributes greatly to the finished product. The closer you get to the end of the process, the more important the fine distinctions become.

Perhaps the trickiest job for a carpenter (and for the architect guiding him or her) is the construction of a staircase.
Drawing courtesy of Gregory Rochlin, Architect

It took ten months and, no, we never regained the weeks we lost. In fact, more time just seemed to slip away, so the house wasn't truly finished until just moments before Christmas.

Was the process stressful? Yes, of course, partly because we felt like a family without a country in the months between the projected and real completion dates. Even after we moved in—before the house was finished, a step I could never endorse but one that is often necessary—we shared our space for weeks with plumbers, carpenters, and other tradespeople, as well as my television crew. At one point it became just too much. I was traveling a great deal and my wife and daughter moved in with some close friends who have a large home just a half-mile away. Living in a work-site is never easy, even if all parties are sensitive, courteous, and professional.

Is there a moral to the story? We're very happy in our house. It suits our physical and aesthetic needs.

But was it all worth it? You bet it was.

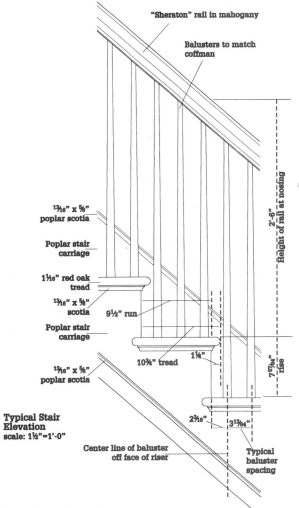

"Sheraton" rail in mahogany

Balusters to match coffman

2'-6" Height of rail at nosing

$\frac{13}{16}$" x $\frac{5}{8}$" poplar scotia

Poplar stair carriage

1$\frac{1}{16}$" red oak tread

$\frac{13}{16}$" x $\frac{5}{8}$" scotia   9$\frac{1}{2}$" run

Poplar stair carriage

$\frac{13}{16}$" x $\frac{5}{8}$" poplar scotia

10$\frac{3}{4}$" tread   1$\frac{1}{4}$"

Typical Stair Elevation
scale: 1$\frac{1}{2}$"=1'-0"

7$\frac{5}{64}$" rise

2$\frac{3}{16}$"   3$\frac{13}{64}$"

Center line of baluster off face of riser

Typical baluster spacing

OPPOSITE: **The restored staircase, with the turnings on the balusters cleaned up and crisp.**

Looking at Your House

Chapter 1

Examining the Existing House

From my house, we move to your house. Together we're going to examine your place in a way you probably never have.

Most people move into a house, arrange the furniture, and get on with the business of living their lives there. Some of those people, upon tiring of the turquoise paint in the breakfast nook or the cramped feel of the living room, decide to embark upon a renovation project. Then they go about getting it done. Perhaps you're about to take that step, too.

To my way of thinking, the process begins not with a call to a contractor or an architect. The first step is to look at and really *see* your house. You may believe you know it intimately, but the typical homeowner recognizes little more than the obvious pleasures of the place and the irritating aspects he or she wants to change.

So you think your home needs a lot of work? Perhaps taking a look at this house will make you feel better about yours. But even this Midwestern row house is rich with possibilities.

Think of it this way. In the early 1970s, pop psychologists introduced the "encounter session." A kind of group therapy, these sessions involved intense but short-term interactions between participants. The point of such sensitivity training was a sort of self-realization or, in the jargon of the time, "self-actualization." That meant that group members were sensitized to feelings about themselves and others.

In a variation on the old know-thyself theme, I want you to "encounter" your house. You need to take an eyes-open, objective look at your home. You need to jar yourself to a new level of consciousness. Before you add new elements, you should know what needs to be renewed. Fixing up the old and adding the new are part of any remodeling job. In order to make the right changes, you need a solid overall feel for the existing qualities, liabilities, and potentials.

Without a thorough working knowledge of your home, you put yourself at risk of rude surprises. There can be excess remodeling costs that could have been anticipated if, for example, you had studied the structure and discovered that certain basic work needed to be done. Other unexpected expenses can be avoided, such as *change orders*, those contractual amendments regarding changes from the original specifications—making changes partway through the process is *always* disproportionately expensive. The worst circumstance of all is the one in which you find your-

THE CLIPBOARD

Keeping careful records is an essential part of any renovation project. As the process takes shape and the paperwork accumulates, you'll want to establish a place for keeping estimates, contracts, invoices, payment records, and the rest.

To start with, all you need is a clipboard. It doesn't have to be a fancy one, just the basic model with a sturdy, sprung clip that most office supply stores sell for a few dollars. Use yours to hold the plot plan, some blank pages for note taking, and any other papers that begin to accumulate, like tear sheets from magazines, sketches, measured drawings, and contractor and architect addresses and phone numbers. In this way, you are organized from the very start.

Remodeling tools consist of more than hammers and saws—clipboards and calculators, phone books, sketches, notebooks, and especially architectural plans are all essential to the process.

self wondering at the time of completion why you didn't do certain things to produce a more satisfactory result—and it's too late to change.

In the following pages we'll walk through the physical structure of the house. We'll look outside first, then visit the interior, moving from bottom (the foundation) and top (the attic) to the living spaces. After describing how to examine your home in order to learn about it in ways you had not before, I'll try to help you put to advantage a sixth sense that you may not even realize you have about your home. It's an instinctive understanding of both your existing space and what you want it to be.

We'll look at your house in a few new ways, from some surprising angles of approach. We'll be looking not only for problems but good work, too, for themes you may want to develop in the renovation. With luck, perhaps you'll also find a little inspiration to help you develop a plan that suits both the house and your needs.

Gardening and landscaping don't have to be elaborate. Even after the blooms have lost their glow, this small dooryard, with its surviving stems, simple fence, and blocks of field stone give this small Cape a timeless feel.

The Surrounding Landscape

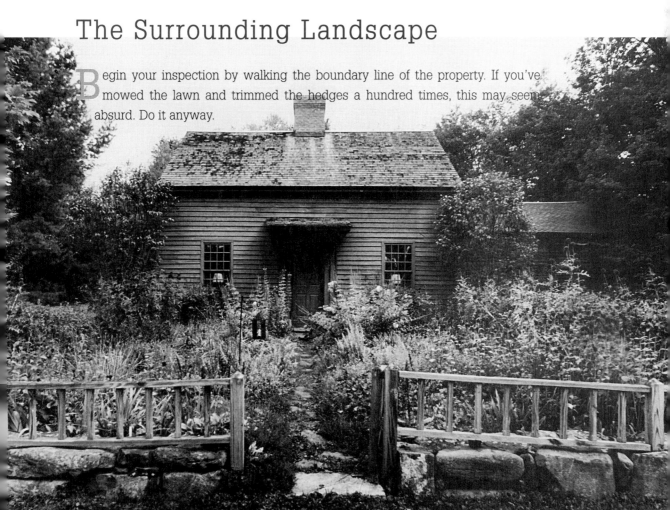

Begin your inspection by walking the boundary line of the property. If you've mowed the lawn and trimmed the hedges a hundred times, this may seem absurd. Do it anyway.

If you have a survey of the property, keep a copy of it at hand. It should indicate, through notations of landmarks and measurements, where your land abuts other properties. Particularly with a small plot where the buildings may be close to the boundary lines, it's important to be sure that your understanding of the outside perimeter coincides with the description on your deed and the survey.

THE LAY OF THE LAND. Look at the topography: Locate yourself with respect to the surroundings. Are you on top of a hill? In a valley? Is the land flat or does it run down a slope? Imagine you're a low-flying bird: shaping a mind picture of a fly-over view may be helpful in thinking about your house and its context.

Look at the nearby houses. In many neighborhoods, more than one house was constructed by the same developer, often in the same or similar styles. We will talk of style at length in the next chapter (see Chapter 2, A Matter of Style), but while casting a glance at your neighborhood, look for houses similar to yours. Notice what they have in common with your home and what's different.

Does a neighboring house have an addition that might inform what you're doing in some way? When differing needs are brought to bear on identical starter houses, strikingly different dwellings evolve. You might also see what you *don't* want to do. That can be valuable, too.

THE PLANTSCAPE. What about plantings? Are there trees or shrubs you want to emphasize? Often a large tree or a glade of smaller ones provides a focus for an overall landscape plan. If you're planning on adding to your house, however, great care must be taken to protect the trees and their root systems from the heavy equipment that is used to excavate, pour concrete, and deliver supplies. A good rule of thumb is that no truck should be allowed within 10 feet of a tree trunk, since the fragile root system at or near the surface can be badly damaged by just one crushing visit of a bulldozer track or even the tires of a heavy truck. A corollary is no trenches should be dug within 20 feet of a middle-sized tree, 30 feet of a large one. Small trees and shrubs can be moved, but only with an adequate amount of soil in a root ball. And preferably by experts.

Look at the neighbors' properties, too. Are there mature plantings along your property line or trees that you could use as a backdrop for your yard?

While there may be plantings you want to preserve, chances are that some will have to go. Overgrown shrubs may need only to be pruned; dead trees or bushes will have to be removed. Branches that overhang the roof are hazards, as are tree roots that are heaving up areas of your drive or walkways.

Note, too, a strictly practical consideration. Does the grade around the home slope away from the house at the rate of an inch per foot for 10 feet or more? While the precise pitch isn't important, a noticeable slope away from the house is essential to keep water away. Are there any low spots in your yard that stay wet much of the year? What is the pattern of runoff after a heavy rain or as the snow melts? Water is the chief enemy of any house, whether the structure is stone, wood frame, or brick. An efficient system of gutters, down spouts, grading, and other drainage will prove valuable in any but the most arid climate. If the drainage isn't adequate at your house, this is the time to correct the problem.

It's a bird's-eye view, but a careful landscape plan can help you envision how your property can look.

THE HARDSCAPE. Examine your stone walls, retaining walls, terraces, decks, fences, driveway, or concrete constructions. Consider their condition: Do they need immediate maintenance? Are the walls intact or in need of resetting? Is the patio cracked? Is the deck sound or is the railing so rotted it's ready to give way? Are the walkways level or do they have high spots or potholes that are insurance claims just waiting to happen? Will any of these elements interfere with your renovation? Fixing and

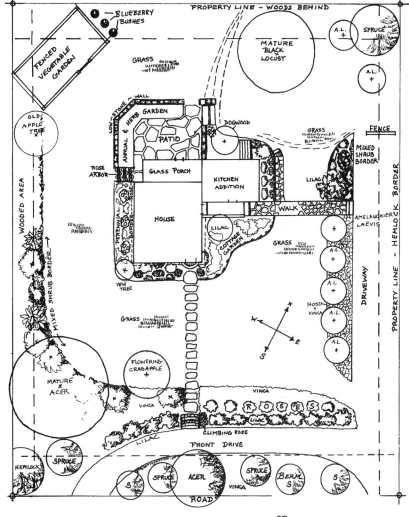

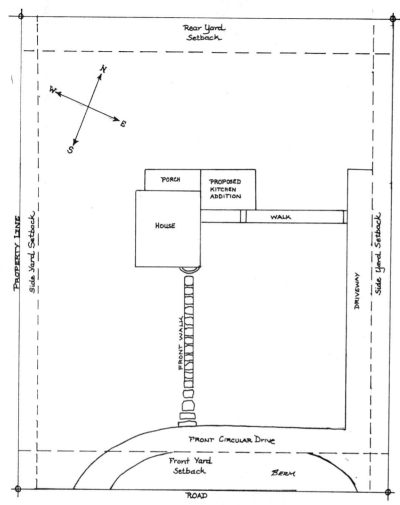

Rear Yard Setback

N
W
E
S

PORCH

PROPOSED KITCHEN ADDITION

HOUSE

WALK

PROPERTY LINE

Side Yard Setback

FRONT WALK

DRIVEWAY

Side Yard Setback

FRONT Circular Drive

Front Yard Setback

BERM

ROAD

Though much simpler than the landscape plan, a *site plan* conveys much about the basic geometry of your property.

moving existing elements costs money so, if such work will be required, you should have a landscape preparation and repair line item in your budget.

THE PLOT PLAN. As you go about your examination of the property, update your plot plan (or sketch one if none exists). Incorporate substantial elements that aren't represented: the garage, garden shed, or other ôutbuildings; the driveway and walkways; large trees; established shrubs, gardens, and other major plantings. Don't forget to indicate the house on the survey. Sketch its outline. Pace off distances and dimensions and try to keep these elements roughly in scale. You may be surprised how putting what you know on paper helps you see it anew.

EASEMENTS. Not everything about your lot can be seen with the naked eye. *Easements* are rights of access that utility companies and the owners of adjacent properties may have to some portion of your property. If, for example, there's an underground electrical service beneath the site of your proposed addition, you're probably going to have to shift sites.

Are there any restrictions on your deed? Is there, for example, a right-of-way through the property? In one instance in a small Massachusetts town west of

Boston, a friend of mine was horrified one day to receive legal notification that a road was about to be cut across his property, right through his vegetable garden. A previous owner had agreed to a right-of-way in the deed and, years later, a local developer took advantage of the option to construct an access road in order to build a subdivision behind my friend's house.

ZONING. Some communities have *zoning*, local ordinances regarding land use restrictions. Zoning ordinances typically specify what can and cannot be done in designated areas, mapping out residential, commercial, industrial, or agricultural zones. In general, there are fewer limitations as you move down the scale from residential to agricultural. Take a trip to city hall and learn what restrictions, if any, apply in your neighborhood.

Zoning requirements can protect you from undesirable construction or development in your neighborhood, so you won't wake up one morning to discover a dump site next door, or a factory, store, or trailer park under construction. But zoning can also prevent you from doing certain things. In a residential area zoned for single-family dwellings, for example, you probably wouldn't be allowed to rent a "mother-in-law" apartment over the garage to a tenant without first obtaining the permission of the city's planning board or zoning officer. Zoning or municipal regulations often specify *setbacks*, requirements that houses be a minimum distance from the street and property lines.

Learning what your limitations are can save you headaches now and money later. Many communities have established restrictions on building height. There may also be a limit on maximum allowable lot coverage, meaning you'll have to build up rather than out to comply with the regulations. As we discovered in Cambridge, there are rules here about parking and even on changing the roof line of a house. Find out what restrictions apply to you.

BUILDING PERMITS. While you are at city hall learning about local zoning, inquire about the procedure for filing for a building permit. In order to put new cabinets in your kitchen you probably won't have to obtain a permit, but if your job will involve rewiring, new foundation work, or major structural alterations, a permit will be required. Find out what paperwork you will need to submit. Many municipalities require plans that have been prepared (or, at least, reviewed and stamped) by a

---

THE WISH LIST

As you look around the yard, are there fond desires or minor irritations that you would like to address in your renovation? Maybe you need more light on the driveway or the terrace. Perhaps you've always wanted a raspberry hedgerow or a pair of crab apple trees. How about a parking space beside the garage? Do you need to think about handicapped access for that elderly parent in a wheelchair?

Keep a wish list, and add to it as you look at the outside of the house (*That old deck has really got to go!*) and the inside, too (*Please, can we add a couple of closets?*). You'll find there's a great deal to remember as you get into the remodeling process, and your written notes will be helpful in trying to convey your needs to the design and construction people you hire to help.

---

licenced architect or engineer, as well as detailed specifications and a budget. Ask about the fee schedule, too.

DESIGN REVIEW. In some communities there are established design standards to be met. Many developments and historic districts require that construction or remodeling plans be approved by a design review board. This may mean nothing more than that you must fill out one more form when you get your building permit, but the approval process is rigorous in some towns or neighborhoods. You may find your plans subjected to a detailed critique, and the review board may require design changes. Some communities even specify color choices, thereby limiting your palette to a few designated choices.

COVENANTS. Restrictive covenants are also found in the deeds to homes in many recent suburban developments. Some are binding rules, others voluntary, but often there are restrictions on the kinds of alterations that can be made to homes within the boundaries of the development. Additions almost always fall within the purview of such covenants, but the construction of pools, tennis courts, and even the manner in which you label your house with your name and street number may be prescribed. Again, find out what the rules are.

The Exterior of the House

Even if your proposed renovation concerns only interior spaces—say, a new kitchen, or converting an old closet to a second bath—a thorough examination of the exterior is still essential.

AT A DISTANCE. Begin by taking the long view. Look at each elevation of your house from 100 feet or more away. It may help you to squint slightly as you try to see the house as a whole and not be distracted by individual elements or colors. The idea is to see the forest for the trees.

Try to look and think in three dimensions: Do you see one uniform symmetrical volume? Are there apparent parts to the house, such as the main block with one or more smaller elements stepping down on one or both sides? Does a simple shed addition stand out distinctly as a later alteration to an otherwise symmetrical house? How about a boxy protrusion along the length of the building (a wing) or an addition that extends at a right angle from the main building (an ell) from the rear?

Keep in mind that only a generation or two ago, most new houses were typically more modest in size than new homes today. Children shared bedrooms and the whole family shared a bath. There were fewer single-purpose spaces (laundry rooms were a corner in the cellar, home offices rare, family rooms retrofitted into basements). As needs changed over the decades, what were once small starter houses

Houses evolve over time as needs, means, and times change. Sheds, garages, ells, barns, and even outbuildings get added, though usually the volume of the original house can still be discerned amid the later additions.

At first, this house may appear to have been built all at once. On closer examination, however, it is apparent that this circa 1800 house started out as a symmetrical Colonial home, its end walls defined by two tall chimneys. Then the remodelers, working early in the nineteenth century, put a large addition on one end. It all works . . . but it's not all original.

ca. 1820

ca. 1800

were remodeled. On narrow in-town lots, additions were often extended off the back. Dormers may have been punched through the roof, offering light to living spaces on the top level of the house. A recent trend has been to remove the original roof altogether, to strengthen the old ceiling joists, and to add a whole new story and roof above the old main floor.

Most builders in the past tended to keep a uniform roof shape, so if the roof line and pitch change dramatically from one section to another, they may indicate where changes were made. Are there dormers on the roof? They, too, could be the result of renovations, especially if the placement is eccentric. Houses built before 1850 tended to be symmetrical, and Victorian houses built in the next half-century often were L- or T-shaped. If your house was built before 1900 yet isn't recognizable as a box, an L, or a T, try to determine why. Later, as we examine the foundation more closely, you may observe clues, such as variations in materials (stone in one area, perhaps, cement block in another) that indicate different dates of construction. On the inside of the foundation, a cellar that is not of uniform height and appearance can be another clue. An old, low-ceilinged crawlspace with a rubble stone foundation adjoining a full cellar of neatly laid up cement block is a dead giveaway: *there's* the old section, *here's* the addition.

GET A LITTLE CLOSER. To get a fresh vantage on the dwelling you see every day, try examining your house with binoculars. Look at the place from both near and far. With the binoculars shaping your view, you may see details and compositions that

All right, it's a wreck, but what possibilities! The building looks square and sound and that gingerbread could easily be repaired and reproduced. Opportunities like this one are all too rare these days.

43

This late Federal Style doorway—note the two pairs of pilasters and the eight-panel door—certainly needs some work. But when restored, it'll be a showpiece and a centerpiece.

Behind that peculiar aluminum covering, a triple-curved Victorian headpiece reveals itself. Lots of prep and paint are required, but the pieces are all there. Once restored, the window will be a good deal more pleasing to the eye than when it was obscured by its aluminum skin for two decades or more.

surprise you. It's rather like seeing snapshots of people you know well—sometimes they just don't look like themselves, largely because you detect features you hadn't noticed before.

Next, focus on the front door. Often the main entrance is the single best exterior clue to the floor plan of a building. If it's located at the center of the house, that may indicate a balanced arrangement of rooms on either side of a central hall. Is there a discernable pattern of windows? Do the details on each window frame match the others? How about the sash: does each have the same number of lights (panes of glass)? One or several that are trimmed differently, contain different-size sash, or are out of alignment with the others may indicate an addition or remodeling. Is the trim at the corners and the roof line consistent from one portion of the house to another?

Now think about the house in two dimensions. In a traditional home, you should see a series of perpendicular lines on each plane. Is the roof line straight or does it dip in the middle? When you see wavy or undulating lines of siding or a wall surface that bulges, that may indicate a structural problem. If it is apparent to your eye that supposedly horizontal surfaces are not *level* and vertical ones are not *plumb*, you and probably a contractor should find out why. In an eighteenth-century colonial, elements that are out-of-square may be regarded as part of its character and the house perfectly sound. In newer construction, however, such signs may represent something to worry about.

While you are standing at a distance, can you detect any curling or missing shingles or other signs of roof deterioration? How about the chimney: Does it stand straight and tall, or are the mortar joints deteriorated so that it's angling to one side?

Moving closer to the house, continue your examination on the south or southwestern side. These exposures are subject to more weathering, as the warming and drying of the sun exaggerates the effects of wind and rain.

What is the external wall covering? Wood is the most common siding in North America, with roughly 90 percent of houses clad in wood. Is it clapboard, shingle, board-and-batten (consisting of wide vertical boards, with the joints covered with narrower boards)? How soon will a paint job or more serious scraping, patching, and painting be necessary? If the walls are of brick or stone, is the surface in good condition? What about the mortar joints—do you need to *repoint* (replace the deteriorated mortar joints)? With stucco houses, look for cracks and bulges. If the siding material is aluminum or vinyl, check for dents, missing pieces, and discoloration. In an older home, these artificial sidings may have been added on top of the original clapboards or shingles which may be intact beneath and well worth restoring. Later in the process, you may want a contractor to help you investigate this option. If so, make a note on your wish list.

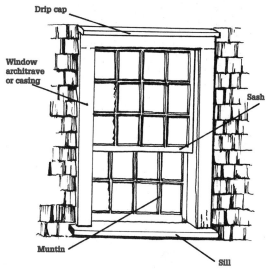

Look closely at the windows. Is there peeling paint? Where the vertical frame members abut the sill, are there signs of decay like softened and discolored wood, mold, and blistering paint? Is there missing or cracked putty where the panes of glass join the frame and muntins (the elements between the panes in a divided-light sash)?

Look at the foundation. Is it of uniform material and finish? Do the walls appear plumb, solid, and the mortar joints sound? How close are wooden elements to the ground? If any siding or other wood is closer than six inches to the soil, that's a problem that needs to be addressed. The excess soil should be excavated to prevent decay.

Walk around the perimeter of the house and look carefully for problem areas. If there is a porch, examine it with particular care. Porches are exposed to the elements, so posts, floorboards, and railings are subject to decay. Have you noticed soft spots on the porch floor? How about railings that tend to give a little? Look with care at the joining of the house and the porch. If there is decay, that may indicate that water has been moving from the porch into the structure of the house.

Before proceeding inside, try to think about the exterior of the house as a unified whole. What do you like (or dislike) about it? If your house consists of several

Window trouble—the result of water entering where it should not—must be corrected in order to prevent more expensive damage. If the flashing fails over the drip cap, water will enter at the top of the window; cracked or missing putty will lead to decaying muntins; when the paint on any part of the window breaks down, water can enter the grain of the wooden elements and lead to rot.

47

This is why
untreated wood
should never be
set close to the
ground, at least in
damp climates.
The decay and
deterioration in
the *sills* of this
nicely finished
garage threatens
the health of the
entire structure.

sections that were constructed at different times, do they work together nicely—or maybe the last addition seems somehow wrong and you'd like to devise a way to make it look more of-a-piece with the rest of the house. Perhaps you think the front of the home looks dull: many a plain ranch in recent years has been given a more stately appearance with the addition of an imposing entranceway. Perhaps there's a design detail that you especially like—a decorative window, a band of molding, a porch post, an unusual building material like glass block, or some other element that you might like to revisit in your proposed renovation.

Muse a little on what you see. Dream a little about what you'd like to see.

This siding needs more than a coat of paint. It needs to be scraped, primed, then carefully painted. And *maybe* a bit of water has gotten inside the wall, too, so a careful inspection must be made of the roof above.

The Cellar and the Attic

Before we progress to the living spaces in the house, an examination of the out-of-sight, out-of-mind spaces may be useful. If you're thinking about converting an unfinished basement or attic area, this part of the inspection tour is especially important. In general, the least expensive way to add living space is by finishing unused areas—but to do so, those areas must be dry, adequately ventilated, and spacious enough to be usable. Even if you have no intention of converting any of your cellar or attic to living space, this step in the inspection process can still be valuable for the insights it can offer into the structure and working systems of your home.

When inspecting the cellar or attic, wear old clothes. A long-sleeved shirt and trousers are best, along with sneakers or work shoes. Basements and attics tend to be dirty and damp, and have awkward spaces that may require getting down on all fours. A couple of simple tools will be useful, too: a tape measure, a hammer, jackknife, maybe a screwdriver, definitely a flashlight. Grab your clipboard and you're ready.

THE FOUNDATION. In areas where the ground freezes in winter, the foundation must reach below the frost line. That means the base of the house is buried below grade to a depth so that the freezing and thawing cycle won't cause it to move. The cellar may be tall enough to stand up in (a *full cellar*); it may be a half-cellar called a *crawl space*; there may be no cellar at all if the place was built on a simple slab of concrete. In all cases, the principle remains the same.

When inspecting your cellar (if there is one), you're looking for bad news first. Investigate the perimeter of the foundation. There are three categories of trouble common to basements: *uneven settlement; dampness and decay,* and *insect infestation.* You're seeking signs of all three.

Uneven settlement means that certain portions of the foundation have settled more than others or that the action of the frozen ground has heaved some sections upward. Cracks in the wall are the classic sign of uneven settlement. When the walls are made of block, settlement cracking may resemble a staircase, climbing from one block to the next. Don't panic if you find hairline cracking, but cracks of more than an eighth of an inch should be noted prominently on your list of issues to discuss later with your designer/contractor team.

What is the floor? If it's just dirt, then water problems are likely, as the dampness can rise up every time there's a heavy rain. Except in very arid climates, however, some basement dampness is normal. Cellars are cooler than the rest of the house, and the humidity in the air will condense on the walls and floor during warm weather. However, puddles or serious water stains on the wall can indicate the presence of too much water.

Keep an eye out for any signs of insect damage or structural decay in the wooden members. Despite the name, wood that has always been dry will never develop "dry rot." *Dry rot* is a misnomer: "wet rot" or "damp rot" would be more precise names. Such decay occurs when wood is alternately dry and wet. Thus, a wooden pier that is consistently submerged in water won't rot, but a fence post that is alternately wet and dry will. You can test for decay using your screwdriver to probe for softness. In some unobtrusive location, jab the tool into the wood—the force required is more than a tap but less than a punch. If the driver penetrates the wood easily and deeply, serious rot is present. Make a note of it.

Insect damage is most likely in damp, dark environments. If in probing any wooden structural members you find channels in the wood ("galleries"), you probably have a termite or carpenter ant infestation. Note whether there are tiny pellets or gray residue (that's insect excrement). Wood dust on top of foundation walls or on the floor far from any recent saw work can also indicate the presence of carpenter ants or powder-post beetles. If you see lots of tiny, round holes in wooden members, those are exit holes for beetles. Cobwebs with a dusting of what looks like sawdust is another sign. If the wood dust is a bright yellowish brown, it's recent; if it's gray, it's been there a good while. Again, if you find insect signs, add that to your list of items requiring further investigation.

Typically cellars are crisscrossed with a network of pipes, wires, and perhaps ducts. While detailed evaluations of the working systems in the house are best left to the experts who will come later, take a commonsense look at the HVAC, electrical, and plumbing equipment. Is it a hodgepodge of new and old? Is the installation neat and orderly? Would you guess that each system was installed at one time or piecemeal, over many years, by a variety of installers and repairpeople of varying skills? If you detect leaks, rust, open electrical boxes, or any other signs of potential trouble, note them, too.

Do you have any plans for using the basement? If you're thinking of converting part of the basement to a playroom or other living space, you need to have adequate ceiling height, dry conditions, and safe access (cellar stairs that are steep, narrow, or that lack a proper railing are an accident just waiting to happen).

THE ATTIC. For the moment, bypass the inhabited portions of the house and visit the attic. Even if the area is too small to be converted to living space, take a look there anyway.

There are three basic kinds of attics. In the *unfinished attic*, the walls and roof are open to reveal the structure. In the *crawl attic*, the structures are revealed, but there's no place to stand meaning that, as with the crawl space foundation, you have to get down on all fours to move about. In the *finished attic*, the walls, floors, and ceilings are already finished and, therefore, "livable."

Access varies greatly from one kind of attic to another. In many imposing Victorian houses, a full stairway leads up to a generously proportioned attic. With crawl attics, there's often a ladder-stairway that pulls down from a hatch in the ceiling of an upstairs hallway. More than a few crawl attics have nothing more than a trap door that requires climbing a ladder to reach it.

Once you're up there, you're looking to assess the health of this portion of the house: Is the attic dry, well ventilated, and structurally sound? Can you detect any signs of leaking? Look around the chimney for water stains on the masonry. How about on the insulation and along the length of the rafters? Are there water stains or fungus on the underside of the roof? Is there ventilation up there, such as windows, an attic fan, or louvers?

Are there streaks of *creosote*, a sticky brownish by-product of burning wood, on the chimney? Creosote is also flammable and means, at the very least, that the chimney needs to be cleaned. It may also mean that the flue liner isn't doing its job.

Now, record what you've learned and let's go back to the living quarters.

The Living Quarters

Again, the biggest challenge in inspecting your own house is to be able to see it as if for the first time. As you're about to go into the living spaces, let me suggest one mind-set you might adopt that may help detach you from your day-to-day life. Try thinking like an archaeologist.

You don't have to wear a pith helmet to do it; this is an architectural kind of archaeology. Your job is to go back in time and try to identify layers of change in the house. You're seeking signs of alterations made in the past. Unless your house is very new, some changes were made, even if they were only cosmetic. Most older homes have seen a lot of change: remodeled kitchens, added baths, dropped ceilings, partitions added or removed, paint jobs, floor or carpet changes, updated lighting fixtures, and on and on.

Unless you just bought the place yesterday, you've probably made some changes yourself *and* encountered evidence of other people's changes. Is there cheap paneling on the walls? How about a ceiling with dusty old acoustical tile? Such surfaces are probably evidence of 1960s remodeling work. In a house that's more than thirty years old, you are likely to find wood floors beneath wall-to-wall carpeting while such carpeting in more recent homes typically was laid directly on a plywood subfloor. Narrow strip flooring in a house you know was built before the Civil War was probably applied in the twentieth century directly on top of earlier wide-board floors. Beneath a surface layer of wallpaper may be more layers of paper, as well as wall board or perhaps plaster and lath.

If you are lucky in your archeological investigations, somewhere beneath the layers you'll find much evidence of the original house. If you're not so lucky, someone gutted the place and off to the dump went much original *fabric* (that's preservationist jargon for the physical material of the building, the implication being the original component materials were interwoven).

The changes made in remodeling usually go more than skin deep. Often the floor plan gets transformed, too, with new walls added, old ones removed, new doorways introduced or old ones closed up. A small bedroom or pantry may have become a bath. Perhaps two original rooms, such as the kitchen and dining room, were opened into one another to create one larger, multipurpose space.

If you have already detected changes made to spaces in the house, how was the floor plan changed? Look for evidence of new partitions. If you noted any apparent additions while examining the exterior, follow up those clues inside. Closets may have been added. How about the bathrooms? Patch marks or long straight cracks in a plaster wall are often indicators of change.

When you were examining the exterior, did you detect certain windows that differed in form, style, or detailing from the rest? Look carefully at the window trim on the inside. Follow the baseboard, cornice, and other moldings from room to room. Does the trim remain the same throughout?

Often in older homes, there are fancy areas with more elaborate moldings (the parlor, the entry hall, the dining room) and private areas with fewer and simpler profiles (the bedrooms upstairs). Even when such differences are evident, however, the moldings usually relate to one another and are consistent within a given room or area. But when the same room has two different window treatments, the chances are that you are looking at two different generations of construction work. In a house that has been renovated over the years, it's not surprising when different molding profiles have been used—tastes change, and the local millwork supplier will sell different molding profiles from one generation to the next. So look for things that are different: When there are two or three interior doors that are different from the rest or if the floorboards vary only in one area, those are clues that something changed.

TRIM AND WALL AND CEILING SURFACES. Examine every surface. You're looking for cracks, stains, and peeling paint. Look at the corners in particular: they're structural points where problems often reveal themselves. Are there water stains anywhere? Look with especial care at ceilings and walls beneath upstairs bathrooms. Showers and bathtub enclosures are notorious for leaking. Is there peeling

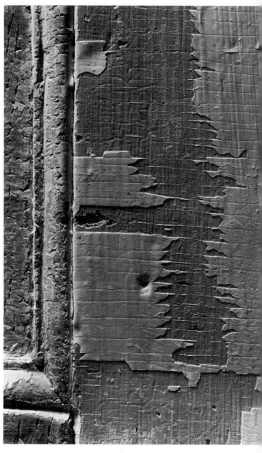

When you encounter "alligatored" paint such as on this old door, chances are the flakes of paint contain lead, a grave danger to the health of children. Talk to your local board of health for help.

VENTILATION AND INSULATION

Ventilation is to insulation as Stan Laurel was to Oliver Hardy: very different indeed, but thinking about one is virtually impossible without reference to the other.

The purpose of insulation is twofold: the fluffy fiberglass batts, loose fill, or rigid panels insulate you from the cold outside and seal in the heat your heating system generates. An appropriate insulation barrier conserves energy since lost heat (or cool, in the case of air-conditioning) translates into additional fuel that must be used to make up for the loss.

R-value is a key concept. The R-value is a measure of insulation capacity. In a cold locale like, say, Minneapolis, you want high R-values, perhaps R-38 in the ceilings and R-19 in the walls and floors. With fiberglass insulation, that would represent layers of roughly ten and five inches, respectively. In designing a house with thick layers of insulation, the designer will specify wall and ceiling thicknesses that are adequate to accommodate the thicker insulating layers. That's why much new construction in northern climes has walls that are framed with two-by-sixes rather than two-by-fours, providing an additional two inches of space for rigid insulation and added R-value.

But what about that insulation-ventilation connection? Where there's a lot of insulation, there also needs to be adequate ventilation. The insulation needs to "breathe" to do its job, so there must be a flow of air to the outside surfaces of the insulation. Paradoxically, insulation also needs to be sealed off on the inside surfaces. Walls or ceilings must be lined with a *vapor barrier*, a layer of a watertight material. Until recently, this was typically polyethylene plaster sheeting, but there are also new proprietary products that are designed specifically for use as vapor barriers.

The vapor barrier is intended to limit the movement of moisture. When the airborne water molecules normally found inside the home are allowed to commute through the insulation, they will condense when they meet up with cooler air in the wall. The condensation will then accumulate, and the insulation will become damp. This has two consequences: First, wet insulation is a very inefficient insulator; second, moisture within the walls or ceilings of a house can lead to peeling paint outside or inside and even decay and rot in the wooden structures.

If you add insulation to an attic, you almost certainly will have to add ventilation, too. The options include vents in the soffits (the underside of the roof overhangs outside), roof, or walls of the house. These vents will also help keep the house cool in the summer. The rule of thumb is 1 square foot of ventilation for every 500 square feet of insulated surface.

Another word often uttered in the same breath as insulation is *infiltration*. Infiltration refers to the flow of air that enters the house through gaps around windows, doors, electrical boxes, and other exterior openings. A properly installed vapor barrier closes off much infiltration and the exterior of a new home typically is wrapped in an envelope of house wrap, a fabriclike covering that has superceded the tar-impregnated building paper that for many years was standard. Newer house wraps bear proprietary names like Typar and Tyvek. These products serve the dual purpose of simultaneously limiting air infiltration while allowing moisture to escape.

OPPOSITE: Blowing in cellulose insulation is a messy job but somebody's gotta do it.

paint? In an old house, this can actually be a health hazard, especially for children, since lead paint was once commonplace.

THE FLOORS. Perhaps the most common floor covering is wood, whether it's hardwood like oak or maple or a softwood like pine or fir. Wood has a literal and visual warmth that can enhance the comfort of a room. A quality wood floor, when well maintained, can be beautiful and durable. Do you have wall-to-wall carpeting? If you're going to change it, you need to see what's beneath. If there are tile floors, are there loose tiles? Have the grout joints deteriorated?

WINDOWS AND DOORS. Are the windows loose in their frames? Are the window sash suspended on sash cords and pulleys like mine were? Again, in a cool climate that means the cavities in which the weights are hung are energy eaters, allowing heat to escape. Do any of the doors stick? Is there a thick buildup of paint on the edges of the doors or on the jambs (the inside surfaces of the door frame)?

Examine all the details of the house. Make notes of problems—and any desires you might have to change things.

LAYOUT. There's a common philosophy behind most appealing and practical domestic interiors. Fundamental to that philosophy is an organizing principle: The home is to be divided into three main areas.

The first includes the private areas of the house, principally the bedrooms. The second is where work of the house gets done, including the kitchen and, in some cases, a utility room and a secondary entry area, where boots and raincoats are removed and stowed. Area three is for relaxation, and may include a living room, dining room, and a family room. In some houses there may be subdivisions within these three major divisions, as in instances when the relaxation areas consist of both public spaces where the family entertains visitors (such as a formal living room and dining room) and private relaxation areas that are generally reserved for family use, such as a teenage party space or a study.

In a well-laid out house, these areas are separated physically as well as philosophically. Bedrooms are often best located at the opposite extreme of the house from the entertainment areas in order that sleepers won't routinely be disturbed by the laughter and energy of the night owls in the house. Work areas may also be discrete from public spaces so that guests don't have to see piles of laundry on their way to the dinner table. In smaller houses, the sleeping, working, and relaxation areas of the home are more likely to overlap.

Consider your home in this context: Does its layout separate the life of the house into areas? As you contemplate changes you would like to make, will they respect this division of work, play, and sleeping areas? Do you have special criteria that should influence your thinking, such as a teen's enthusiasm for head-banging rock or a dad's love for string quartets?

THE KITCHEN. The busiest room by far in most houses is the kitchen. Even in houses where cooking isn't a top priority, the kitchen is usually a gathering place for after-school snacks and snatches of conversation. Guests at parties seem often to gravitate to the kitchen, whether for the drinks and hors d'oeuvres or to enjoy the warmth of the household. Yet there is no one model for a kitchen space that suits all needs.

Lifestyles are changing so a more fluid arrangement of kitchen and attendant spaces may suit your needs. For example, food preparation has become something of a social activity in many homes. That has meant that casual entertaining is done and much of the life of the home is lived in the same area as the cooking. In addition to appliances and counterspace, kitchens now often feature islands with tall stools, televisions, and even couches. If your social rituals have changed but the old-fashioned separation between work and relaxation areas remain, your remodeling plans may involve incorporating social spaces into the kitchen in order that the cook need not be isolated while cooking. Later in this book, we'll talk further about options for you to consider (see *Chapter 3, Looking at Buildings,* page 115), but for the moment think about the mix of spaces and how they work (or don't work) for you and your family.

In the food preparation area, the *kitchen triangle* is the usual standard. It's actually an arithmetic formula: *The sum of the distances from sink to stove to refrigerator and back again should not be less than 12 feet nor more than 22 feet.* Furthermore, the kitchen triangle rule specifies, *no one side of the triangle should be less than 4 feet nor more than 9 feet.*

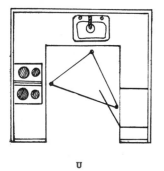
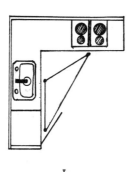
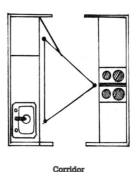
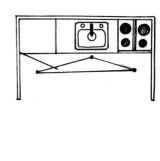

U   L   Corridor   One-wall

The Kitchen Commandment? Thou shalt put thy sink, refrigerator, and stove in a triangular arrangement. But such an arrangement can take many shapes, including U-shaped, L-shaped, in a gallery or corridor configuration, or along one wall.

When I first came across the kitchen triangle rule, I wondered to myself, *If only good design sense could always be reduced to a simple formula . . . or perhaps it can be?* Over the years, I've seen a lot of wonderful kitchens and, in most of them, the triangle rule has been obeyed. But there are exceptions, such as tiny galley kitchens and giant professional ones where there's to be a division of labor. But if you're planning a kitchen renovation, you can use the triangle rule to your advantage. It saves footsteps and helps ensure that you won't create a kitchen in which it's difficult to work.

More basic concerns? Is there enough counterspace? You need some on both sides of the sink. The distance from front to back splash is typically two feet; for a good-size kitchen, a total of at least 20 linear feet of countertop is desirable. Do you have sufficient cupboard and shelf space? Is the lighting bright enough, especially near the sink, cutting board, and stove top? Do any of the doors to the appliances block one another so that, for example, the oven door can't be opened when you're loading the dishwasher? Are there enough electrical outlets, at least one for every 3 linear feet of counter space? Is there a service exit from the kitchen to make it easier to bring in groceries and carry out the garbage?

Look over your head, too. The kitchen ceiling is the one in the house most likely to need resurfacing. Is it discolored from years of smoke and moisture?

What is the floor surface? Is it attractive? Is it in good condition? If the flooring changes from the kitchen to adjacent rooms, look closely at the transition point: Many old kitchens have several layers of sheet flooring or other materials on top of one another, so the level may be raised above that of adjacent rooms. If you're planning a kitchen remodeling, you will need to determine the condition, utility, and character of what's beneath. You might find early hand-planed boards.

Are there indications of water problems in the kitchen? Look around the sink (both from above and below). Inspect carefully where the counter surface joins the back splash and the floors inside of and in front of the sink cabinet. Also check the joint of the wall and floor at the perimeter of the room. This is a wet-mop space and the water can produce mold, decay, or peeling paint when it gets into the structure of the walls and floors.

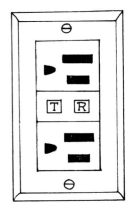

A ground-fault-interrupter receptacle.

THE BATHROOMS. One of the most common home renovations is the addition of a bathroom. Most older houses were built with no more than one bath; in today's world, there's almost no such thing as too many baths. In new construction, the rule of thumb is at least one bath for the master bedroom, one bath for every two additional bedrooms, and a half-bath (toilet and sink) near the relaxation area of the house. If you have fewer baths, that may be why you're reading this book.

You know whether your bathroom facilities are adequate or not. But there are other questions you need to ask yourself as you continue your inspection tour. Is there an electrical outlet in the bathroom and, if so, is it a ground-fault interrupter (GFI) receptacle? This is a safety device that functions as a second fuse and will, in the event of a fault in the ground, shut off power to the outlet and prevent electrical shock. They're recognizable by their small, rectangular reset buttons located between the plug receptacles.

Is the water pressure adequate? Run the cold water in the tub or shower and then flush the toilet: If the volume of running water diminishes noticeably, the pressure is low. Do you need a second sink? Is there enough ventilation, or does the bathroom fill with steam and remain damp for hours after every shower? Is the tile around the bath or shower tight or are there signs of deterioration at the corners or at the junction between the tile and the tub or shower base? Use the heel of your hand to exert some gentle pressure on the tile walls at the point where they join the tub or shower pan. Is there any give? Springy tile may indicate the wall has gotten damp and deteriorated over the years. The absence of a grout line and the presence of mold are signs that water may be seeping into the wall cavities.

Are the porcelain fixtures in good condition or is there cracking or pitting? Are any of the fixtures of a certain age? Older fixtures, even if they have age lines, can add character. Pedestal sinks, claw-foot tubs, and pull-chain toilets are cherished by some home renovators.

Well, at least the space is large. That much at least bodes well for this kitchen's future.

Examine the floors around the toilet: Irregularities in the floor (dips, discoloration, softness) may indicate leakage that has caused decay in the subfloor or even the structure around the toilet. That will need to be repaired. Examine the floors around the perimeter of the room, too. Like kitchens, bathroom floors require wet mopping and if the joint where the floor abuts the walls isn't watertight, moisture can be wicked by the walls and produce peeling paint or wallpaper and, over the long term, deterioration of the wall itself.

SAFETY CONCERNS. Does each staircase, inside and outside, have a handrail? Are the railings solid? Is there adequate lighting? In an older house, an occasional creaky tread is not unusual—but if virtually every step complains when you walk up the stairs or there's a noticeable give, it's time to check that out.

Are there smoke detectors on each floor and, in particular, is there one near the bedrooms?

Is there a window in each bedroom that opens enough to serve as a fire exit?

Don't leave out the fireplace: Is the chimney lined? Is there adequate hearth in front of the fire box? (According to most building codes, it should project at least 16 inches and extend at least a foot on either side of the firebox opening). Has the chimney been cleaned recently? Is there a damper? The damper—which closes off the chimney flue when not in use—is key to conserving energy in the house. Without one, the chimney flue continually draws warm heated air out of the house.

In order to restore, preserve, or simply renovate your home, you need to examine the place in detail as you think through your needs and desires. You know your house and what aspects of it make you unhappy. Make notes not only during your walk through, but as you go about your daily activities. Are there rooms that are too hot or cool? Are there too few electrical outlets? Not enough of this, too much of that . . . keep a running list.

Experiencing Your House Anew

After you have taken a careful, objective look at your home, I'd like you to try a softer approach.

Some evening when the house is quiet, after sunset and after the dishes are done, shut off all the lights. Electric light is the rule in virtually all homes today. Steady, bright, safe, and reliable, electric light illuminates our lives. Ironically, though, its very clarity can blind us to seeing what's around us.

To jar your perceptions a little, try looking at your house using another source of light.

Light a candle. Or use a flashlight. Or both. You may occasionally dine by candlelight, so you know how flattering the light can be: the soft, yellowish glow seems somehow relaxing. But in other rooms, you truly will see things in a new and different light. Shadows appear and colors soften. Shapes can become more dramatic, exaggerated, and fluid thanks to the alternative source of light.

This exercise will not reveal to you a totally different and unfamiliar place. But it may give you an alternate way of looking. Moldings stand out more in shadowy light: electric light makes them seem almost two-dimensional. The nature of candlelight is such that you focus on smaller areas: a candle on a table illuminates it and perhaps the chairs immediately around it. The rest of the room is at best a dim presence at the perimeter. Candlelight can help you see spaces within a space. Have a glass of wine or even have a conversation while you're going about your candlelight tour of your house. Does anything surprise you about the scale, shape, or relationship of the rooms? Do any objects look different and suddenly out of place—too large and clumsy, so delicate they disappear? Even if you have no immediate revelation, I suspect your perception of your home's spaces will be subtly altered.

Here's another exercise that may also be useful. Use a low stool or even an upside-down pail. Plant yourself in places where you would never otherwise be seated: in a corner, at the center of a hall, at the foot of a staircase. Again, as you look around you, perhaps as other people in the house go about their business, you'll see the place in a new way.

These may seem like bizarre exercises. The goal is to break away from the fixed pictures you have in your mind of your home. Looking at the same old space in

Sometimes the past seems able to speak. This wall is ready to be wallpapered, just as it was after it was first plastered almost sixty years earlier and a proud workman signed his work. Perhaps today's craftsman should leave his mark here, too, once again to be preserved for later rediscovery.

the relative darkness or from the perspective of a five-year-old or a person in a wheelchair may help you think anew about solutions. But envisioning changes in a space one knows very well requires getting out of yourself, thinking like someone else in a new place.

At the same time, however, don't underestimate what the experience of living in a house can offer. Over time you've learned the house and established patterns of movement. You've positioned furniture in such a way as to minimize traffic lanes through living areas, to take advantage of light at certain times of day, or of cool or warm spots. Think about those changes, too, and about other things you'd like to change.

The process of discovering your house takes time. Weeks or even months may be required for you to see through both the layers of changes made to the house and your own patterns of use. But with a little patience, you will develop a deeper understanding of the place. After months of wondering at some peculiarity of your home, you may realize all in a moment why things look as they do. Give yourself the opportunity to absorb what your examination has revealed to you. When combined with a basic understanding of architectural style (to be discussed in the next chapter), your examination and your intuition will eventually reveal your house to you.

Chapter 2

A Matter
of Style

"S tyle," like "love" and "intelligence," is something that everyone wants

to have. Yet it can't be calibrated and there are no objective means of

distinguishing the stylish from the *outré*. Style is an abstract

concept—but somehow most of us think we know great style when we see it.

In aesthetic terms, the subject of style may seem intimidating, the sort of

thing for which people earn Ph.D.s in art history or spend their lives developing

expertise. In fact, this is an area where a little knowledge can actually be very

helpful when thinking about your remodeling. You really don't have to be an

architectural historian to locate your house within the time line of architectural

history, and failing to do so might result in making your house *less* attractive and

perhaps *less* valuable.

Not all stylish buildings have columns, but, as this ionic capital suggests, a well-built classical building usually has style. These wooden details were common during the Greek Revival, from roughly 1830 to 1850.

Here's an untold story. The basic shape of the home is that of a mid–nineteenth century vernacular Greek Revival house, with a gable front on the left and, set back and extending to the right, a tall ell. But there's a much later turret surging like a missile from the roof. Yet the place has its own eccentric appeal, doesn't it?

If you have ever read *The Old House Journal*, you know what I'm talking about. One ever-popular feature is the "Remuddling" page. Each month the editors select one house and recount a bit of its history in a few words and, typically, two pictures that are worth a few thousand words more. One shows the appearance of the house early in its history; the other shows how it was "remuddled." As readers of the magazine can attest, it's endlessly surprising what people do to their homes. Some of the changes are obvious insults to the integrity of the house—bad additions that bear no relation to the original structure are a classic example. Another is a large picture window that's been punched into an otherwise symmetrical facade. But the variations on the remuddling theme are endless, and include roof lines that look worse than cheap toupees, residing jobs where the original trim was crudely chopped off, ugly porch conversions, and the replacement of columns or piers with spindly pressure-treated posts. The examples of witless disregard for the existing

THE ELEMENTS OF STYLE

The word *style* came from the Latin word *stilus*. To the ancient Romans, a *stilus* was a writing instrument, a tool used for incising letters or symbols on waxed tablets. In Middle English, the word *stile* came to be used to describe the manner of composition. As Jonathan Swift put it years later, "Proper words in proper places, make the true definition of a style."

Over the centuries, the word continued to evolve new and broader meanings. From its purely literary applications, it came to be used with reference to other arts, including works of music, literature, painting, and sculpture. Thus, the *stilus* started out as a tool used in writing; thereafter it became the *style* in which a work was written; eventually the word came to be used to describe the manner and materials of one or several arts, as in the Romantic *Style* or the Classical *Style*. Describing something as having a certain style usually carried the added implication that the work was skillfully executed.

The evolution seems pretty logical. But in an architectural context, etymologists have identified another possible source for the word. The alternative explanation is this: In Greek, the word *stylos* means column. In classical architecture, the column was perhaps the most essential decorative element. Greek builders constructed what were really just post-and-beam buildings, and they made them more attractive by supporting the horizontal beams with handsome vertical posts—that is, with columns. The notion appeals to me that a designer, working with a *stilus* would design a building decorated with columns or *stylos*.

Whatever its true origins, style, when used in reference to a work of architecture, implies the conscious use of recognizable elements in a distinctive way.

Photo credit: Hugh Howard

character of houses are numerous, but the effect is invariably the same: The houses are robbed of original charm.

In order to help you make better remodeling decisions, we will now move from the specifics of your house (and mine) to a more general consideration of American architectural style. This chapter is divided into three main sections. The first, The Handmade House, discusses homes that were built largely by laborers working with hand tools. The second, The Victorian House, describes houses built after the

Industrial Revolution. That cultural sea change transformed house building along with most everything else, since millwork, hardware, lumber, and other elements began to be produced by machines and factories. The third section, The Twentieth-Century House, describes homes built after 1900. Most them would have been recognizable to us even when new because they had indoor plumbing and electricity.

Within each of these sections are numerous subsections that describe individual architectural styles. Thus, within The Handmade House you will find The Basic House, The Georgian House, and The Federal House. In the discussion of Victorian homes, you'll find Greek Revival, Italianate, Shingle, and other styles. In the twentieth century, you'll encounter bungalows, modern Cape Cod homes, and ranch houses.

You may wish to read this chapter in its entirety; I'd recommend that you read start-to-finish at least the section devoted to the era of your house (for me, since I live in a Shingle Style house, there's much that is relevant to my home in the other styles described in The Victorian House). So let's learn a little something about architectural style.

The Handmade House

In architectural history, there is one major dividing line that separates the handmade house from all those that came later. It is, of course, the arrival of the machine.

In America, the effects of the Industrial Revolution trickled down to almost every stratum of the building business by 1830. The advent of the circular saw—which came into general use about that time—made wood cutting more efficient and economical. Machine planers were patented as early as 1828, meaning that for the first time boards arrived at building sites having already been planed smooth. Machine-made nails superceded handmade nails shortly after 1800. And all these materials began arriving from considerable distances, pulled by the newfangled Iron Horse. Thus, circa 1830 can be seen as the boundary between the Victorian House and the earlier Handmade House.

Handmade houses gradually became a thing of the past, but their very obsolescence is essential to what has made them so cherished. Before the railroad system developed, builders had to rely almost exclusively upon local materials (typically, the exceptions were hardware and glass, which continued to be imported from England into the Victorian era). The frame of an early house was made of wood felled on the owner's property. On the house site itself, trees would be hewn (squared off, using a hewing axe or adze) into beams and posts for the structure. In the seventeenth and early eighteenth century the smaller lumber, too, would be cut on site, though by the time of the American Revolution, felled trees would usually be delivered to the town sawmill to be cut into boards. In fact, the standard pattern of development in the northeast was for a mill to be established on a natural watercourse—and a community to develop nearby. The process of building was very localized.

Boards cut at a sawmill had a rough surface, scarred by the up-and-down cutting motion of the reciprocating saw blade. Smoothing them for use as finished surfaces involved an investment of time and skilled labor by the builder himself. In a two-step process, the rough-cut board had to be planed by hand. A large plane called a *jack plane* flattened out the roughest spots and eliminated the evidence of saw cuts. Next a *smoothing plane* was used to give the boards a smooth appearance.

Notice the verbal distinction: the boards were made smooth to the *eye* rather than to the *touch*. In fact, a slight arc on the blade of the smoothing plane meant that hand-planed stock was not perfectly flat like those produced later by machine planers. If you run your fingers across the grain of a hand-planed board, you can feel its contours. This is an invaluable trick for identifying early planed paneling, floorboards, door panels, and other wooden elements, and you can master it in a matter of seconds. Find an old dresser that you think dates from the mid-nineteenth century or earlier. Open a drawer and slide your fingers across the grain of the underside of the drawer bottom. If it's smooth and flat, it's probably a later dresser made with machine-planed boards or even plywood. But if you feel a perceptible hill-and-valley texture, that's a hand-planed surface. A flashlight held at an acute angle to the board will make the rippling texture visible to the eye.

The appeal of a handmade house always comes down to one thing: The hand of the workman. In a way that later houses do not, homes built before 1830 are the product of a craftsman who truly shaped the elements of the house. There are virtues to be admired in houses from all periods—the typical Victorian house will be larger and more elaborately decorated, the twentieth-century house will contain more creature comforts—but craftsmen are a living presence in an early house. Before the turn of the eighteenth century, the nails were made by a blacksmith, the moldings

MOLDINGS

By definition, a molding is simply a strip of wood (or, occasionally, of plaster or other material) that is used for finish or decorative purposes. It has regular channels or projections, and it may be flat, curved, or both.

Moldings are used as transitions from one surface to another. They can cover, for example, the joint between the wall and ceiling (these are termed *cornice* moldings); or the joining of the floor and wall (the *baseboard* or, in Britain, the *skirting board*). Since World War II, moldings have tended to be small, plain, and purely functional, but these decorative elements can represent much more.

In the past moldings were an opportunity for the builder, designer, or homeowner to make a statement. In a way that building big houses today conveys a sense of the owner's wealth and standing, moldings were once the means of sending a message about the importance of a place.

Moldings can be an invaluable decorative element, so it's useful to understand some of the terminology involved. The first distinction concerns a molding's *position*. In addition to the cornice and baseboard, the terms *picture rail* and *chair rail* refer to where certain moldings are located on a wall. The picture rail is attached beneath the cornice and is used, as its name suggests, to suspend pictures, while the chair rail travels around the perimeter of the room at the height of a typical chair back to protect the plaster. The terms *architrave* and *casing* are used interchangeably to describe the trim around a window or doorway.

The shape or *profile* of a molding is another identifying characteristic. The trained eye can read profiles—the shapes and curves of moldings signify much about the age, origin, and character of a handmade house. Moldings in the great Georgian houses of the eighteenth century (see The Georgian House, page 76) were big and bold with gracious curves. During the early years of the American republic, builders in the Federal Style (see page 82) used fewer moldings but when they did, the profiles were smaller, more subtle, and featured elliptical curves. During the Victorian era, there was an eclectic variety of profiles and sizes—it was a time when people freely interpreted an ever-larger variety of historical sources, from classical Greece, Medieval England, Renaissance Italy, seventeenth-century France, and ancient Egypt. In the early twentieth century, natural finishes on oak and other woods were common in Craftsman-Style houses and bungalows. Design came full circle with the Colonial Revival styles, including the Georgian, Spanish, and Dutch Revival houses that reprise the detailing of the eighteenth century. Recognizing which moldings in your home are original, which reflect later changes, and where some have disappeared can be very helpful in planning your renovation.

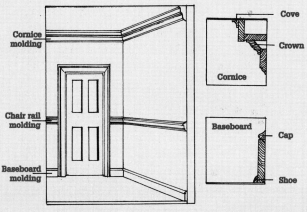

shaped by the builder, the bricks individually molded in wooden forms then fired in a nearby brick kiln, and the windows and doors were made by joiners with planes and chisels. All of the wooden pieces were fitted together individually by the carpenter, one painstaking joint at a time.

While handmade houses have much in common, they are still a diverse lot. Much of their individuality results from the building traditions within which the builders worked. Most carpenter-joiners were English, but Dutch and Spanish traditions also left their marks on American housing stock. And later, the American Federal Style assumed an important place. In the pages that follow, we'll look at each of those.

The Basic House

The generic, early American house is known by many names, among them the English Medieval House, the Cape Cod, the saltbox, and the double-pen log cabin. While each of these differs in detail from one another, they are simple, rather plain houses that collectively represent America's most enduring house designs.

In most of its many incarnations, the Basic House shares with this home a gable roof, a single-story design, a center entrance, and a certain elemental charm.
Photo credit: John A. Eberle, Red Rock Historical Society

Seventeenth-century settlers arriving from England adapted the Medieval cottages they had known at home to conditions in America. The earliest houses consisted of one room with a hole in the ceiling to allow the smoke from the fire to escape. A chimney was soon added on an end wall; the addition of a second room came next. This new configuration was called the "hall-and-parlor house" because the two principal rooms were a "hall" for cooking, eating, and working and a more formal "parlor" used as a master bedroom. Later, larger versions often had a narrow kitchen to the rear of the two front rooms, a one-and-a-half room deep configuration we know as the Cape Cod house. Early log cabins typically followed a similar evolution, with a single unit or "pen" followed by chimney construction and the addition of a second pen.

Building the Basic House was (and is) quite simple, with a shoebox-shaped first floor and a plain gable roof rising from the front and back. As originally laid out, these houses consisted of living areas downstairs and unfinished sleeping or storage spaces above in the tall attic. While these boxy houses have never gone out of favor, the range of variations on the original theme multiplied with the passing decades.

Because of the harsh climate on this side of the Atlantic, the Basic House in New England typically had a central chimney stack that contained two or more fireplaces. This functional design provided a masonry mass that absorbed the heat from the open fireboxes and radiated warmth to the entire house. In Virginia and other southern states, a variation evolved with chimneys in the end walls, in order to dissipate unwanted heat in the warmer southern climate.

Over the centuries, the Basic House assumed still more guises. The earliest Basic House probably wasn't symmetrical—that is, the entrance was not at the center of the front of the house and the number of windows flanking the door on either side often differed. By the early eighteenth century, however, symmetry had become standard. These houses were originally found in rural settings surrounded by farm buildings. In New England, the barn and the house over time came to be connected by shed buildings, producing a progression of linked structures off the back of the main house.

The roof pitch of the Basic House flattened and, by the late nineteenth century, dormers often poked through, adding light and space to what had become upstairs bedrooms. Another common variation was a shed addition to the rear. Second stories appeared as well. A Basic House with both a second story *and* a shed addition at the rear became another familiar form of the Basic House, the Saltbox.

REMODELER'S NOTES. In remodeling a Basic House, it's important, first of all, to be sure that your house isn't actually a Georgian House, a more refined and decorated style common in the eighteenth century (see page 76). The configuration I like to refer to as the Classic Colonial, for example, is a two-story, two-room deep house with a center entrance and five sets of openings across the front. The Classic Colonial is, however, a descendent of the Georgian House rather than being a Basic House. Some Victorian styles, too, apply different detailing to the same volumes as the Basic House (see The Victorian House, page 85).

In thinking about your house, don't forget whence the inspiration came: Primarily English settlers arrived in America in need of simple, economical shelter. I visited a house a few years ago on Cape Cod. Its owner told me it had started life as a ship captain's house in the eighteenth century. I don't know about the ship captain, but the handmade nails, the hewn frame, and other details told me the house had been built about the time of the American Revolution. The rooms in the original house were small but comfortable, which made the addition its owner had built all the more shocking. It was essentially one great room, with a handsome coffered ceiling, bold cornice moldings, and tall windows. It was a lovely room—but it didn't relate in any way to the original house. It was as incongruous as a Wall Street investment banker would be if he wore sneakers with his gray flannel.

Basic Houses consist of four walls and a pitched roof to shed the rain and snow. Their builders may have added paneling, moldings, or other trim to decorate the house but the enduring appeal of these houses comes not from the way they echo other styles and cultures. These are elemental houses whose simplicity and practicality are to be respected.

The Georgian House

If the ups and downs of architectural history were to be represented by a line graph, there'd be a tall spike at the time the Georgian House came into existence. It didn't happen all at once, of course, but the emergence of the Georgian House was a watershed moment in the history of American domestic architecture.

The floor plan of the Georgian House is actually two hall-and-parlor houses turned sideways and connected by a central hall. The result is a two-room wide, two-room deep (*double pile*) house, with two chimneys, one on either side of the house. The Georgian House is also a full two stories tall, an imposing presence on any streetscape with its broad facade that is also five openings (five *bays*) wide. With this design, American builders transcended the humble Medieval origins of the Basic House and went upscale. The name Georgian comes from the kings who held the English throne for more than a century starting in 1714. Georgian Houses are com-

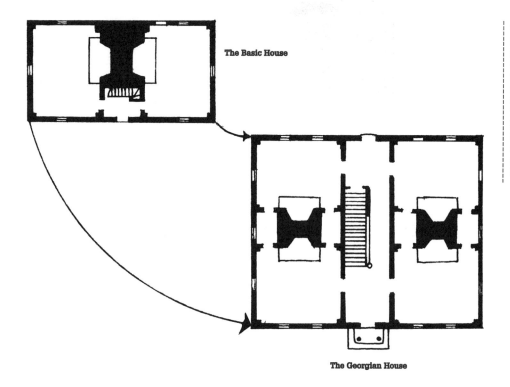

The Basic House

The Georgian House

The Basic House, consisting of two rooms flanking a chimney, proved to be an adaptable plan, *and* a highly adaptable module. The later Georgian House merely doubled the two-room plan, adding a center hall and stair in between.

monly found in old trading towns along the eastern seaboard, early inland villages, and on southern plantations.

Once again, the inspiration came from Europe. But this time the line of transmission reaches back to classical antiquity. The front door assumed new prominence, sometimes with a front portico supported by columns. Flattened columns or *pilasters* became standard on each side of the front door and on the corners of the building. The projecting cornice line of the roof was elaborated with moldings. The sources for such detailing were the monuments of ancient Rome and Renaissance architects like Andrea Palladio, the great sixteenth-century Italian designer who had established the appropriateness of using elements from the temples of antiquity on domestic architecture. His Palladian window often appears in Georgian Houses, with its arched central opening flanked by two flat-topped windows.

If plainness was the most obvious characteristic of the Cape and other early houses, in the Georgian House the keynote became stylishness. Most of the early settlers in America had been poor and all of them had been concerned with shelter first and style later. Only after they could be assured of surviving in the North American wilderness did they shift their attention to elegance and decorative detail. In that sense, the Georgian House was an expression of the advance of American civilization.

The open central hallway meant there was space for a generous staircase which quickly became a design statement, an opportunity for the householder to proclaim his wealth and status. The ceilings in Georgian houses are taller, the rooms decorated with bolder moldings. Window technology had advanced, and the double-hung sash window became standard in the Georgian house. Georgian houses were symmetrical to a fault—many of the great surviving Georgian houses have false interior doors to maintain the illusion that each room was carefully balanced.

REMODELER'S NOTES. One key precept to follow is *Respect the symmetry of the house.* That's especially true on the facade where even a small change can scar the appearance of the house.

Cherish and, if necessary, restore the front entrance. Carpenter books of the time referred to the doorway as the "frontispiece" of the house and indeed it is. All of the details are important: the pilasters, the decorative cornice, a fan sash over the door if there is one, and even the door itself. Entrance ways are the hallmarks of the Georgian House.

As with any house of a certain age, a key guideline is to save the good old work. In a Georgian House, this may include six-panel doors, multipaned windows (12/12s in the north were usual, 9/9s in the south), raised paneling, the staircase, early flooring, and other details.

The Dutch Colonial House

Most houses that survive from the Colonial era—such as early Capes, Saltboxes, and Georgians—are descendants of English styles. But in some regions of the country, settlers originating in other lands put to use the building traditions they knew to create distinctly different homes.

Consider the Dutch Colonial House. This house is a variation on the theme of the Basic House (see page 73), but there are important differences. The Dutch were known as the Old World's best masons, so not surprisingly many Dutch houses built in America between the seventeenth and early nineteenth century were constructed of brick or readily available local stone. The Dutch colonized much of New York's Hudson Valley, as well as portions of New Jersey and Pennsylvania, so it is in those areas that the majority of early Dutch houses survive.

When you think of a "Dutch Colonial house," perhaps the image that comes to mind is of a gambrel roof, in which the plane of the roof on both sides of the cen-

Another variation on the theme of the Basic House, the Dutch Colonial House often had a sprung roof that curved up and out at the roof overhang.

tral ridge is broken roughly halfway down, with the lower half of each side falling at a steeper pitch toward the eave. In fact, gambrel roofs aren't uniquely Dutch, though when the style reemerged in the suburbs of twentieth-century America, the gambrel roof had become standard in the Dutch Revival House (see page 112). In contrast, the prototypical Dutch house in early America was one-and-a-half stories tall with a steep gable roof that flared toward the eaves. Such "sprung roofs" provided deep overhangs, often covering open porches.

REMODELER'S NOTES. Another construction detail that distinguishes the early Dutch house from the Cape and other English-inspired homes of the era is the design of its wooden skeleton. All these houses have a timber frame, but in Dutch houses there are more beams traversing the ceilings downstairs. Typically, these ceiling beams are spaced about four feet apart and they have been planed smooth. Unlike the unplaned structural timbers in English houses, the ceiling beams in Dutch houses were intended to be left exposed. In Dutch houses where the ceilings beams were covered in later renovations with boards or lath and plaster, your renovation might reveal those early beams, both to restore the original appearance and to add character to the space.

The Spanish Colonial house often had a low-pitched tile roof. The multiple doors of this house telegraphs another important and typical characteristic: The interior rooms are not connecting, but are accessible only from the exterior.

The Spanish Colonial House

Homes from early Spanish settlements are found in St. Augustine, Florida; San Antonio, Texas; Sante Fe, New Mexico; Tucson, Arizona; and along the California coast. Relatively few survive, in part because of their construction.

Though some were built of stone, most have *adobe* walls, which consist of bricks of sun-dried clay. Adobe walls, which are often three feet or more thick at the base, are covered with a wash of clay or gypsum to give them a uniform appearance. Adobe walls require continued maintenance to survive the elements, as rainwater entering an unprotected wall will simply wash it away. Countless examples have been lost over the centuries to abandonment and the onslaught of wind and rain.

While Spanish Colonial Houses in various regions of the country differ from one another, most share certain elements. Most are one-story buildings. Their roofs are flat or low-pitched, and extend over covered porches. At the time of original construction, most adobes were single-room structures, with additional rooms added over time. Typically the rooms do not open into one another, but onto the porch or, in larger examples, onto a common courtyard surrounded by the house and attendant buildings. The rear of many Spanish Colonial Houses opens onto a patio or garden.

The roof frame often consists of *vigas*, horizontal logs laid across the top of the adobe walls. Layers of sticks and branches crisscross the vigas and, in turn, are covered with a thick coating of clay. In some regions, baked clay tiles were used as the roof surface.

Spanish Colonial Homes tended to be very utilitarian structures: missions built for the church and governmental buildings were more likely to be ornamented with Baroque detailing, giving them a more stylish appearance.

REMODELER'S NOTES. These houses are rare indeed since only a few years of neglect can reduce them to unrestorable piles of mud. The remodeler with a true Spanish Colonial House should attempt to conserve as much of the original building material as possible, in particular the adobe and the vigas.

The Federal House

After the Revolution, Americans wanted cultural as well as political independence, and they began to change the style of their buildings to reflect their change of allegiance. While the houses were not radically different—and still drew upon British sources—the high-style buildings of the new era bore a new and American name.

The Federalist party which, ironically, tended to favor British interests in foreign affairs, was the party of the merchants and landowners. These were the people with the means to build important houses—houses that came to be known as having been built in the *Federal Style*. Like "Georgian," the name "Federal" has more to do with who was giving orders than with who was designing the buildings, but somehow the name has stayed with us. It's a catch-all for buildings that date from the close of the Revolution (1783) until the first great machine-age style, the Greek Revival, became popular in the 1820s and 1830s. Other terms used for buildings of the Federal decades are *Adamesque* and *Neo-Classical*.

A trio of Scots brothers named Adam developed a distinct decorative style that became widely popular in England. In particular, Robert Adam brought to British architecture a first-hand knowledge of antiquity. He had visited the recently discovered ruins at Pompeii and Herculaneum, and he shifted the emphasis from columns and other echoes of classical elements to applied decorations, like urns and swags. The exteriors of his buildings tended to be less decorated than earlier Georgian Houses but his interiors were practically encrusted with neoclassical details. The Federal House looks much less like a temple than the Georgian designs that came before or the Greek houses that were to follow. None of the Adamses ever worked in America, but through their publications and other authors' builders' books, their style reached the United States.

In Massachusetts, two architects named Charles Bulfinch and Asher Benjamin took the Adamesque style and helped make it more American. Bulfinch's fame is tied to his important Boston buildings, in particular the Massachusetts State House. But Benjamin is best remembered for his pattern books. He adapted the Federal Style to the predominantly wooden American house. Since he was working with boards rather than blocks of stone, his details tended to be thinner and more attenuated than his British antecedents'. Benjamin also believed that there should be a trickle-down of the neoclassical style of fine houses to rural farmhouses and more modest urban buildings, too. If the Georgian Style was primarily an aristocratic style, then the Federal had democratic aspirations appropriate to the politics of the new country.

The typical Federal house shared the same basic configuration as the Georgian House, the form real estate agents today are fond of calling "colonial"—again, the Classic Colonial is a double-pile structure (that is, two rooms deep, front to back), with a street facade on the long side that features a center entrance in the third of the five bays. The Classic Colonial is two stories tall, and in its Federal form typically had at least two and often four chimneys arranged symmetrically on either side of the house. Hip or gable roofs were usual, though with a pitch that was typically flatter than on the Georgian House. The first floor plan of the Georgian House, with four rooms, two on either side of the main hall, remained the norm, but often the rooms themselves assumed a greater variety of shapes and sizes.

In the northeast, most Federal Houses were wood; in the south, brick was more common. The exteriors generally had fewer moldings though many examples took their cue from the Adams and featured carved decorations, like urns, swags, elliptical motifs called *patera*, and other elements borrowed from ancient Roman buildings. The windows were taller and narrower than in the Georgian House, the sticking between the individual panes of glass much thinner. Sidelights appeared on either side of the front door. The tradition of the fan sash over the entrance continued from the Georgian Style but with an important difference: In the Federal House, the fan sash is elliptical, rather than circular. While the corners of a Federal house are less likely to have pilasters than their Georgian predecessors (or the Greek Revival homes that would succeed them), the front doorways typically had flattened columns, usually in pairs on either side of the entry. The tradition of the entrance as statement, as "frontispiece," continued. Inside, classical details adorned window and door architraves, mantels, cornices, and ceilings. Plaster and wood ornamentation tended to be graceful and delicate.

REMODELER'S NOTES. The interior details of a Federal house are important attributes to be conserved. Ceiling medallions came into vogue at this time, many of them of plaster. Mantels had elaborate moldings, pilasters, and characteristic carving work and sometimes applied decorations. The front door and the staircase were two other elements of the house where the builder was likely to lavish much energy and skill. A good rule to follow in your Federal house is to respect the original symmetry of the house and, as always, be on the lookout for original work.

The Victorian House

The name comes from the English queen who assumed the throne in 1837 and remained in power until 1901. Victoria wasn't a designer. As with her four immediate predecessors, the kings named George, her name came to be applied to the houses of her time out of chronological convenience rather than any true aesthetic connection between the monarch and the buildings of her age.

In fact, her long reign saw more architectural styles rise to popularity than had developed during the years of all the other British monarchs put together. If it weren't for the far-flung influence of the British Empire in all parts of the world and in all manner of trade, art, culture, and industry, another name might well have evolved to describe the diverse building styles of the nineteenth century. Perhaps "The Eclectic Age" would have conveyed more precisely the fluidity and variety of domestic architecture in her time, but the name that has come to be applied is "Victorian."

85

If Victoria cannot be credited with instigating the fruitful architectural experiments of the time, the advent of the machine must be given some of the credit. Steam- and water-driven machinery made it possible for more people than ever before to afford well-made basic house parts like windows and doors, as well as decorative details like moldings and trim. Eventually stoves, plumbing fixtures, all kinds of millwork, and other goods were delivered via a growing network of canals and railroad tracks. Raw materials were also shipped inexpensively and new markets were opened up. In the forty years preceding the Civil War, America's population tripled. All of which resulted in the greatest construction boom the world has ever seen.

The world was changing at an unprecedented pace. Not surprisingly, people's tastes changed, too, and not once but again and again. The first great style of the Victorian age in America was the Greek Revival. In the eighteenth century, the new science of archeology had revealed that ancient Greek and Roman buildings were not indistinguishable but dated from different eras altogether. Archaeologists found that Greek architecture had come first and that Grecian building was a key source for all subsequent European architecture. In America, the Greek Revival found fertile ground and grew into the dominant style for some three decades (see The Greek Revival House, page 87).

The Gothic Revival developed at about the same time. Its popularity and affordability was in part the result of advancing technology, as new power saws could shape the decorative woodwork (*gingerbread*) characteristic of the style (see The Gothic Revival House, page 89). A wonderful Victorian eccentric named Orson Fowler dreamt up the octagonal house (he also was a practitioner of phrenology, a "science" that claimed to be able to assess character and mental abilities on the basis of the patterns of bumps on peoples' skulls; see The Octagon House, page 94). The Italianate House was broadly popular before the Civil War (page 92); the French-inspired Second Empire Style reached its peak after the Civil War (page 96). Primarily German sources and the proliferation of inexpensive building materials produced the Stick Style (page 99), and students of early eighteenth-century English architecture developed the Queen Anne style (page 100). The Shingle Style was the last great style of the century (see page 102). There were styles to suit almost any taste.

The Greek Revival House

The Greek Revival captured the American spirit as no other style had done. To visit an unspoiled town that prospered in the years between 1820 and 1860 is to see democracy at work. There are grand Grecian houses with freestanding columns that frame gracious front porches (some people think of such places, in a small simplification of architectural history, as "Gone-with-the-Wind" houses). But there are also simpler dwellings for workers. Take one of these plain structures, strip it of its Greek Revival details, and what would emerge would be the Basic House, perhaps a Cape Cod in disguise, that highly adaptable eighteenth-century design (see page 73). And these Greek-inspired buildings were found all over the nation, moving from the East Coast in the 1820s westward where, as late as the 1860s, Californians were still building Greek Revival houses.

The same writer-carpenter, Asher Benjamin, who helped get the word out about the Federal House, lived long enough to play a role with the Grecian style, too. His later pattern books reached builders who would never travel to American cultural centers like Boston, Philadelphia, or New York and see the major Greek Revival buildings in those cities, much less go abroad to visit the Parthenon. They didn't have to, thanks to Benjamin's careful prescription for Grecian proportions, window

Here's a double-take for you: It's a stately Greek Revival house, though the doorway and other first-floor details can no longer be seen. As reworked as it is, this building still reads "Greek"—note the pediment, the bold cornice across the front, and the pilasters at the corners. They're the ingredients of the "temple front"— even though this house has become a temple to convenience stores rather than domestic tranquility.

detailing, staircase construction, and much else. The Grecian mode had patriotism going for it, too. Just as the Greek Revival Style was gaining popularity in the United States in the 1820s, the Greeks themselves were fighting for independence. Perhaps that parallel to their own revolutionary history was part of the appeal to Americans of Greek architecture.

For a lot of reasons, the Grecian style appeared on streetscapes from Connecticut to California. The single most apparent characteristic of the Greek Revival House is its exterior trim work. A generation earlier, wide expanses of trim would have required much hand planing, but new planing machinery produced wide smooth boards at reasonable cost. Suddenly even people of modest means could afford homes that replicated the appearance of a Greek temple. There were pilasters or wide corner boards defining the corners of the structure. Above, a broad horizontal frieze board with molded trim separated the wall of the Grecian house from the overhanging cornice of the roof. Bold moldings added shadows and scale. The effect was to create a style that was at once uniquely American yet proudly linked to a great historical tradition.

The classic Greek Revival House has a main facade with a gable that faces the street. On top of a boxy base sits the triangular roof, supported either by columns or pilasters. The roof isn't steeply sloped. Greek trimmings were also applied to houses of many different shapes and sizes, including the compact, single-story Basic House and the larger Classic Colonial with its two stories.

While its designer might have wanted to allude to the ancient Greek ideals of democracy, the Grecian style house had a distinctly practical bent. Symmetry was quickly abandoned—an ever-popular configuration of gable-front Greek has the entrance not in the central bay but on one side. Known by the rather misleading name of "side-hall colonial" (the colonies having long since won their independence and become a republic), this proved an enduring formula. Often Greek Revival houses had an ell that extended from one side, fronted by a porch.

Porches were new in this era, but the tradition of the front door being a bold statement remained, and doorways on Greek Revival homes generally have heavy pilasters or columns, as well as rectangular sidelights and transoms. The scale of the moldings in general may seem to a student of Federal design very heavy and even clumsy, but in a sense they were a celebration of the lumberman's new ability to produce wide, machine-planed boards.

REMODELER'S NOTES. Where there were farms in the nineteenth century, you'll probably find Grecian farmhouses. Most are sturdy, practical homes. The details aren't fussy, and these houses are easily restored and repaired. Greek Revival houses often have been added on to over the years, and adding on again is easier than with earlier symmetrical houses. If you plan to add on, try to replicate the moldings, frieze, corner boards, and other trim to unify the whole. The Greek Revival House has less of the handmade charm of earlier homes, but these are practical, sturdy houses that speak honestly for their time.

The Gothic Revival House

The Gothic Revival began in England and it, too, was the result of new investigations of antique buildings. The Gothic had been overshadowed for more than two

This happens to be a half-scale child's playhouse, but its size actually makes the detailing easier to appreciate. Note the gingerbread vergeboard, the ornamental cresting and finials on the rooflines, and the board-and-batten siding.

centuries by Renaissance and classical styles, but in Britain countless spectacular Gothic buildings survived. Westminster Abbey was among them, yet even a national monument like the Abbey remained a mystery, with little hard knowledge about the evolution of the Gothic style or what portions of the building had been built when.

Decades were required for researchers to sort it all out and, in the meantime, a not-so-scholarly but highly popular variation on the Gothic theme came into vogue. A writer named Horace Walpole published one of the first Gothic romances and proceeded to Gothicize his country house, Strawberry Hill. The domestic style he and his advisers pioneered became an overnight sensation in England but, initially, it didn't travel to the United States. When it did, it was thanks to an architect named Alexander Jackson Davis and a landscape designer named Andrew Jackson Downing.

When it comes to popular taste, timing is everything and the arrival of the Gothic is no exception. The Gothic was primarily a rural style, as is suggested by the titles of Davis's 1837 book *Rural Residences* and Downing's immensely popular *Cottage Residences* (1842) and *The Architecture of Country Houses* (1850). These books illustrated not only parts of houses, as Asher Benjamin's had done, but added floor plans and even atmospheric perspective drawings of the houses set amid verdant settings. These books were popular among homeowners as well as builders, and led to the appearance of Gothic "cottages" from Maine to California.

Technology played an important role in the emergence of American Gothic, as the decade of the 1830s was a time when the steam-powered scroll saw was developed. Early versions of this saw look like a large sewing machine, though the device had a reciprocating blade rather than a needle. It was this tool that made the Gothic Revival possible in the United States and gave it a character different from its English forebear.

While most English Gothic homes had been built of stone, in America the material of choice, as usual, was wood. The scroll saw made it possible to cut elaborate wooden trim into curved patterns that echoed the tracery work on Medieval Gothic windows. The *bargeboards* or *vergeboards* that decorated the rooflines, along with the porch, window, and doorway trim, came to be known as gingerbread. Downing didn't like the term because, as he put it, "gingerbread" made the decorations sound as if they were "flimsy and meager decorations which have a pasteboard effect." Despite his objections, however, the name stuck and, though this and other

Victorian decorations were for many years dismissed as grotesque and even ugly, more recently homeowners have come to admire the elaborate detailing that often decorates the roof line of the Gothic Revival House.

Earlier house designs tend to sit solidly on their sites, as if a low center of gravity was basic to their design. In contrast, the Gothic house seems to reach for the sky. *Verticality* is the word architecture critics like to use to describe the effect of buildings that direct the eye upward. The spires of Medieval Gothic cathedrals convey this sense very directly, but there is a similar effect in American Gothic houses. The steep inverted-V of the gable ends are frequently topped by finials. Window trim and even the windows themselves may have the characteristic pointed top of the Gothic arch. American Gothic buildings aren't especially tall, however, usually one and a half or two stories in height.

Another innovation found in the American Gothic house is an asymmetrical floor plan. Like many of the Greek Revival houses built in the same era—these styles overlapped in the United States—the Gothic Revival house often had an L-shaped floor plan.

REMODELER'S NOTES. Gingerbread is back—more than a few new developments across the country have reintroduced Victorian styling and put elaborately sawn trim to effective use. Conserve the original gingerbread where possible, replicate it where necessary, and use its shape to unify new additions to older structures.

Symmetry is no longer a watchword: In fact, Downing himself characterized the ideal rural residence as having ". . . a style marked by irregularity of form and outlines, a variety of effect and boldness of composition."

In earlier houses, clapboards were the rule, but the American Gothic house popularized *board-and-batten* siding. This siding method used vertical boards, nailed to the frame of the house, with narrow boards (called battens) applied over the joints between the boards. One good strategy is to use the detailing of the original house when remodeling.

The bargeboard lining this roof makes clear why one class of Gothic Revival houses came to be called "Carpenter Gothic." These are simple materials, but used to very dramatic effect. The walling of the house itself is board-and-batten.

91

The Italianate House

Alexander Jackson Davis and Andrew Jackson Downing, the men who helped launch the Gothic Revival, also did their bit in developing the Italianate House. Beginning in the 1850s and extending into the 1870s, this style was used in all sorts of buildings across America. The Gothic Revival never quite rivaled its contemporary, the Grecian Style, in popularity. But the Italianate House succeeded the Greek as the most popular style of its day.

Houses described as Italianate are actually a diverse mix of shapes and sizes. Most were tall, typically two or three stories (one-story examples are rare). As with the Gothic Revival and later Victorian styles, there's more of a sense of upward thrust about Italianate houses. Yet there's also an attempt to emphasize a solid, massive quality consistent with the houses that inspired them, those being stone-and-stucco villas back in the Old World countryside, especially in the Italian province of Tuscany. In wood examples, the walls were sometimes painted or scored to resemble masonry; brownstone came to be commonplace on Italianate houses built on cityscapes. Stucco was also used to give the feel and character of stone.

An alternative and perhaps more immediately descriptive name for the several varieties of Italianate house is "American Bracket." This designation derives from one of the key architectural elements typical of the American Italianate

House, the brackets that decorate the eaves. Deep overhangs distinguish all Italianate houses, and the supports for those eaves are brackets that came in a wide variety of shapes and sizes. The brackets are consistently found in the Italianate house, though the overall shapes of different Italianate houses vary considerably.

The type usually called "Italianate Villas" have octagonal or square towers attached to them. Other Italianates, essentially cubes with cupolas protruding from the centers of their roofs, are usually referred to as simply "Italianate." But American Bracket houses are found in other configurations, too, with their brackets applied to the familiar volumes of the Basic House and the Classic Colonial (again, the Classic Colonial is two-rooms deep, two-stories tall, with the main facade on the long side and a center entrance in the third of the five bays).

A gentle roof pitch is typical of the Italianate House. Tall, narrow windows with only two panes of glass per sash (2/2s) are usual. Arch-topped windows are also common, typically with molded crowns. The entrance ceased to be the dominant element and often was recessed slightly into the volume of the house. But it was still

Although this is a secondary building to a larger house, its builders lavished plenty of care and Victorian decorations on it. Note especially the brackets and the decorative truss on the center gable.

93

decorated with handsome trim and often featured a double door. For the first time, some of the doors had panes of glass in them. Many Italianate houses were asymmetrical, featuring towers, ells, bay windows, balconies with balustrades, and verandas. Virtually all Italianate houses were built with porches.

REMODELER'S NOTES. As Downing himself wrote, the Italian style ". . . has the very great merit of allowing additions to be made in almost any direction, without injuring the effect of the original structure; indeed such is the variety of sizes and forms, which the different parts of the Italian villa may take, in perfect accordance with architectural propriety, that the original edifice frequently gains in beauty by additions of this description." That's a good rule of thumb, though in the case of Italianates that are basic symmetrical boxes, a bow to symmetry is still in order.

The tall windows and high ceilings of Italianate houses make them gracious homes, though in northern areas they are more expensive to heat than their lower-slung predecessors. That's one reason dropped ceilings were once commonly inserted into Italianates. But that was a bad idea, and is best undone. Added insulation, tightening up the windows, and other energy efficiencies can help compensate without sacrificing the style and grace of the taller room spaces.

These houses often have fine old woodwork: handsome staircases of imported woods like mahogany or native cherry and walnut. Moldings tend to be large and bold, and heavy plaster cornices are common. These are elements to be valued and preserved.

The Octagon House

Octagons are not the most common Victorian style, although following the publication of *A House for All* in 1848, as many as several thousand were built over the next ten years. These unique houses are a pleasant surprise when spotted on an older streetscape. Their appearance and the philosophy of the man who wrote the book distinguish them from other homes of the era.

For once, no European style figures into the inspiration for these homes. The author of *A House for All*, Orson Squire Fowler, believed that the circle was nature's most perfect building form. He pointed out that the circle encloses the greatest amount of interior space with the least exterior wall. This apparent efficiency also presented a problem, however, because the building materials of the

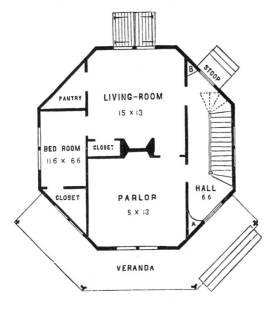

day tended to be straight rather than curved. But Fowler thought the problem through and devised a flat-sided shape that remained essentially circular but that could be built with rectilinear materials. The Octagon House, with its eight flat sides, was born.

The Victorians had a great confidence in progress and a belief in America's Manifest Destiny. Fowler argued that his circular form of building was the most healthy and efficient, that it enhanced airflow and natural lighting. His thinking suited the optimism of the time and many

Taken directly from the pages of Orson Fowler's book, here is a prototypical eight-sided house of his design. The floor plan suggests how tricky the geometry can be in an Octagonal house.

communities that prospered at the middle of the last century have at least one octagonal house to attest to the persuasiveness of Fowler's argument.

The shape of the house makes it unmistakable, with its eight equal sides. Typically two stories tall, many examples also have cupolas on top and one or more porches. Fowler was more interested in theory than in alluding to architectural history, so he did not dictate stylistic details. As a result, those found on octagonal houses vary greatly. Some octagons are decorated with the classical pilasters and frieze boards of the Greek Revival House (see page 87), others with the brackets usually found on Italianate Houses (see page 92). Still others have details more characteristic of the Gothic Revival House (page 89).

REMODELER'S NOTES. The Octagonal House had a brief vogue, and "Fowler's Folly" (as his own house was also known) fell out of favor by the beginning of the Civil War. However, there was a second brief octagonal fad in the 1970s: If you live in an octagon, open-plan interiors with few partitions and modern methods of construction (two-by-four framing, plasterboard walls, and other contemporary materials) will immediately distinguish a twentieth-century octagon from those of Fowler's era.

In the Octagon Houses, some rooms will have triangular shapes, with corners at acute or oblique angles. This can make furniture placement difficult, although most layouts tended to divide the floor plan into rectangular major spaces, leaving oddly shaped secondary rooms like pantries and closets built into the acute angles.

Putting an addition onto the Octagon House is usually difficult. From the start, Fowler envisioned his design as being regular in shape with eight equal sides. Adding a boxy wing that would jut out from one or more of those sides is in conflict with that conception. One solution to space limitations that was adopted on the seventies revival was pairing two octagons, but that in most cases is neither practical nor a visually satisfying solution. A low wing off the rear of the house, however, can be an effective answer, particularly if it shares the detailing of the main house.

The Second Empire House

A single characteristic distinguishes the Second Empire House: its dual-pitched hipped roof. From the eaves, the roof rises steeply, then becomes almost flat (and invisible from below) as it extends to the center of the building. The steeper pitch of

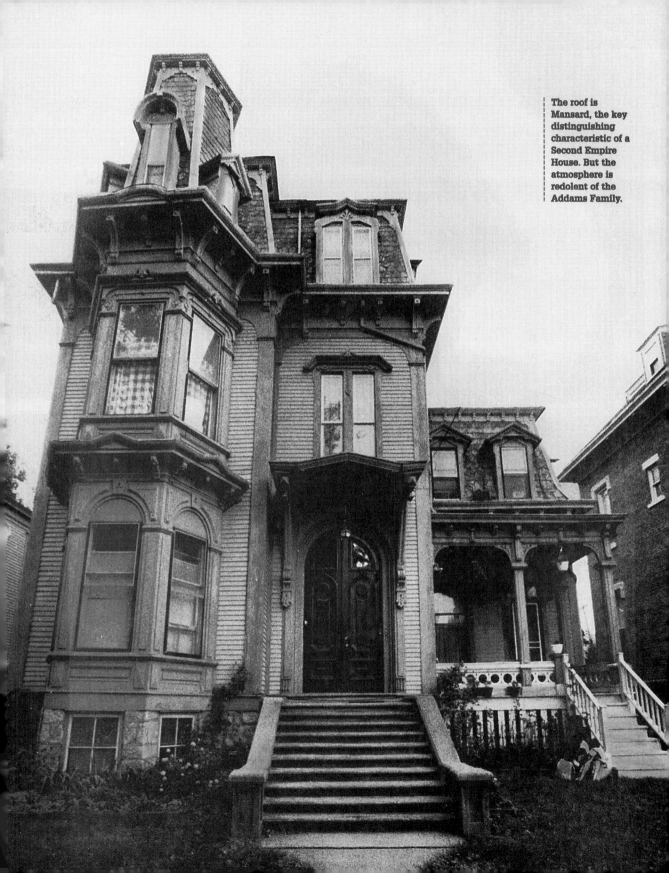

The roof is
Mansard, the key
distinguishing
characteristic of a
Second Empire
House. But the
atmosphere is
redolent of the
Addams Family.

the roof typically has multiple dormers so that the attic of the house is essentially a third floor.

This configuration is known as a Mansard roof, getting its name from the seventeenth-century French designer François Mansard. Its nineteenth-century popularity, however, owes its occurrence to the Mansard-roofed wings added to the Louvre in the 1850s when Napoleon III was Emperor of France. That brings us back to where we started, as his reign was known as the Second Empire. In America, the design, although based on earlier prototypes, was regarded as a very contemporary echo of a modern Parisian style, rather than an allusion to an earlier one.

The Mansard roof is most often found on two-story houses. The footprint is usually square or rectangular, although some examples are L-shaped and others have a tower at center front. Brackets typically support the eave overhangs and other details resemble those of the Italianate House. The entrance usually features a double door and the windows are tall and narrow, typically two-over-twos (2/2s).

The Second Empire House became particularly popular in towns and cities. The two main floors plus a tall attic floor produced a surprising amount of living space for the size of the footprint, an efficient design that made the style well suited to narrow in-town lots with limited light and space. These houses were popular in emerging manufacturing cities in the decades after the Civil War. In fact, for some years these houses were referred to as having been built in the "General Grant Style" because of their popularity during U. S. Grant's presidency, when many administrative buildings in Washington, D.C., were built in the Second Empire style.

REMODELER'S NOTES. The typical Second Empire House is large and comfortable, reflecting the growing wealth of the American nation in the years after the Civil War.

The roof of a Second Empire House distinguishes it, but that same roof is often an expensive challenge to its owner. Frequently the roofs were originally covered with multicolored slates or tin plates, both of which are expensive to maintain or replace. Any roof work on a Second Empire House is likely to be expensive because staging is required. Yet maintaining the original character is important—replacement of an original polychrome roof with asphalt shingles does not do justice to the building, especially if the steeper slope of the roof flares or curves as many Mansard roofs do.

At the height of the popularity of the Second Empire House in the 1860s and

1870s, Mansard roofs were also a popular choice for renovating earlier houses. The spaces beneath the tall roof line provided useful living space, so framing a new Mansard roof atop an existing home could add considerable living space to the home. In examining your house, perhaps you have noticed stylistic inconsistencies, like an earlier timber frame, a mix of earlier and later windows, or other elements that might indicate the Mansard roof was a later addition.

The Stick Style House

The origins of the Stick Style are European Gothic, but an American architect named Richard Morris Hunt actually developed the style in America. Hunt had studied in France at a time when a revival of half-timbered architecture began, inspired by the restoration of Medieval German towns. The exterior walls of those houses consisted of an exposed frame of horizontal and vertical timbers, with an in-fill of stucco or masonry in between. The Stick Style House didn't replicate the Medieval half-timbered house (the later Tudor Style came closer), but reinvented the decorative geometry and adapted it to commonplace American materials.

In three dimensions, the shape of the Stick Style House is relatively uncomplicated, with plain gable roofs, perhaps with a second cross gable, and occasionally with a tower. In keeping with Gothic precedents, the roof pitch tended to be steep. Yet it is the two-dimensional wall surface that truly distinguishes the Stick Style House.

The exterior walls of these houses were an opportunity for their builders to display both their skills and their excitement at the proliferation of building materials. A variety of economically priced factory-made materials was suddenly put on display all at once—the growing network of railroads, which delivered precut architectural details all across the country, deserves some of the credit for making this highly decorated style possible.

The inverted-V of the gable typically has a decorative truss. The walls are crisscrossed with patterns of wooden bands (the "sticks" from which the name of the style is derived) that divided the wall surfaces into separate areas.

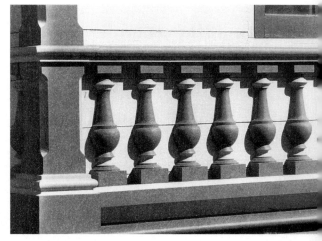

Machine-made goods made high-style decorations like these half balusters affordable to middle-class Victorians.

These are in-filled with clapboards and shingling, which were often painted in a range of colors to draw attention to the display of materials. When the materials changed, often the colors did, too. Porches had decorated galleries and posts; windows were tall; double doors at the entrance were the rule.

The Stick Style House is an exuberant expression of building energy. San Francisco's "Painted Ladies" are perhaps the most famous examples of the Stick Style and of the related Queen Anne style that was to follow (see below).

REMODELER'S NOTES. These durable wood-frame houses look their best when polychrome paint jobs draw attention to the variety of elements. Painting in multiple colors can be prohibitively expensive when contractors do the work, but the energetic homeowner who brings a little painting skill and a lot of enthusiasm can greatly enhance the look of one of these houses.

The Queen Anne House

Many Octagon, Second Empire, and Stick Style houses survive, but it was the Queen Anne House that inherited the mantle of Most Popular House Style from the Italianate House in the 1880s.

Again, we have to reach back in time for the origins of the style. Anne ruled England between 1703 and 1714, and there was a revival in England during the nineteenth century of the architecture popular in Queen Anne's time. Following the 1876 Centennial Exhibition in Philadelphia, at which half-timbered designs of Englishman Richard Norman Shaw were displayed, the American variant of the Queen Anne style began its run, which lasted until the turn of the century. Queen Anne and her contemporaries, however, probably wouldn't have recognized the houses that bore her name.

All pretense of symmetry has been abandoned by the builder of the Queen Anne House. The steeply pitched roofs are irregular, typically a complex fusion of hipped and gable roofs, chimneys, dormers, and turrets. Seemingly at random, bay windows protrude from the side walls. Porches add to the asymmetrical effect but the main facade of the typical Queen Anne House usually features a gable that dominates the elevation, giving it a single center.

The details of the house are a complex mix of shapes, textures, and colors. Like the Stick Style House, there are miscellaneous walling textures, often including

varied clapboard treatments, shingle patterns, and moldings. Combinations of spindles, brackets, finials, and columns are also common. Paint schemes add to the busy effect, as bold, rich, bright colors gave the Queen Anne visual impact.

In the same Queen Anne House, a number of different window designs are often found. Most would be double-hung sash windows (2/2s, sometimes 6/6s or 6/1s,), but round-headed windows and round (oculus) windows are also common. Windows with colored panes of glass ("picture windows" they were called at the

A handsome Queen Anne House displaying various wall textures, a mix of roof shapes, a tower, and of course a porch, which helps draw the differing pieces together.

101

time) were also an element of many Queen Anne homes. The Palladian window also made a big comeback in the Queen Anne House, with its central arched window flanked by two shorter, flat-topped windows.

REMODELER'S NOTES. The Queen Anne House was widely popular—so popular, in fact, that many earlier houses were updated at the end of the nineteenth century, and had turrets, bay windows, or porches added to make them appear to be Queen Anne Style homes. In inspecting your house, be alert for inconsistencies in the house that suggest a Victorian renovation that might have transformed the place, such as a timber frame or the traditional geometric shape of a Basic House or Classic Colonial to which later Queen Anne elements have been added.

The Queen Anne House is typically large so additions may not be what you require; more often, interior renovations can address changing needs without affecting the exterior. On the other hand, these houses tend to have such a variety of features that thoughtful additions can actually add to the character of the house without calling attention to themselves.

The Shingle Style

As an owner of a Shingle Style House, I obviously have a great affection for the style. While they never attained the popularity of their contemporary, the Queen Anne House, these shingle-clad and usually coastal (though sometimes suburban) homes occupy a pivotal place in the time line of American architecture.

Earlier styles in the United States tended to echo European idioms. They were variations of well known themes, adapted to American materials, sites, and tastes. The Shingle Style is a bit different: it, too, alludes to the past but to an *American* past.

In the two decades before 1900, several of America's greatest architects, including H. H. Richardson, Frank Lloyd Wright, and the New York firm of McKim, Mead, and White designed buildings in the Shingle Style. They referred back to early American houses in their designs. They emphasized grace and simplicity; they used what seems like acres of plain, unpainted shingles to clad these large houses in a way that was a stark contrast to the ornate busy-ness of the prevailing Queen Anne Style. Men like Stanford White and Charles Follen McKim had visited the Colonial coastal towns of Salem, Massachusetts, and Portsmouth, New Hampshire. In their partner Mead's words, "[A]ll of us had a great interest in Colonial architecture, and . . . [w]e made sketches and measured drawings of many of the important Colonial houses."

They produced a truly American style that came from here and, for that matter, never went anywhere else. It didn't travel abroad, but it worked on the seascapes of the East Coast and even on the streetscapes of New England and, surprisingly, the Middle West.

These houses were typically two or three stories high with tall gabled roofs. Porches and dormers were usual. As in the Early House, the windows tended to be of modest size with numerous small lights but, unlike earlier precedents, multiple window units were grouped together into horizontal bands. Palladian and bay windows were also incorporated into some Shingle Style Houses. The shingle cladding of these houses allowed for rounded contours and for a continuous, flowing look. The Shingle Style house has a simple, graceful, organic feel.

Inside the Shingle Style house, another leap of the imagination took place. The open plan was being developed, in which interior spaces, previously neatly separated by doors and partitions, were open to one another. In the same way, the bands of windows and French doors tended to connect the wide verandas to the house, mingling the indoors and out. The result is a less compartmentalized feel to the living spaces of many of these gracious homes.

REMODELER'S NOTES. The average Shingle Style House was constructed with wooden shingles on the roof as well as on the walls. Over the years, the original roofs were often replaced with less expensive asphalt or other materials. If you're restoring or renovating a Shingle Style, consider returning the roof surface to wood shingles. The texture and color of the wooden surface will add to the character of the house.

The Foursquare was truly a national house, found in Colorado and California, in Maryland and Missouri, and all the other states in the then forty-eight-state Union. Its boxy practicality was rarely the work of architects, but these sturdy houses worked as well as rural farms as on suburban streets.

The Twentieth-Century House

Looking back a hundred years, we can see the magnitude of the changes that occurred in the opening decades of the twentieth century. In 1900, few houses had electricity; twenty-five years later, nearly two-thirds of all homes were illuminated by electric light. The horseless carriage was merely a rumor to most people in 1900; by the mid-1920s, Henry Ford had sold fifteen million Model Ts. With the growth of the industrial economy, Americans had more money and became increasingly concentrated in urban centers—by the 1920s, the majority of Americans lived in cities for the first time.

Given the rate of change, it's hardly surprising that so many Americans embraced an eclectic variety of homes that shared a common theme: They indulged in a bit of nostalgia, looking backward to the pre–machine age.

The Arts and Crafts movement actually began in England, initiated by the likes of John Ruskin and William Morris as a reaction to an increasingly mechanized world. In the building arts, the traditional joiner-builder no longer had to shape or make anything on site—he assembled parts that had come off the end of a production line. And much of that was surface ornament, such as gingerbread, brackets, and other decorations that had no structural purpose. They were, in a favored term of the day, "dishonest."

In contrast, the Arts and Crafts movement put the emphasis on goods that were simple, inexpensive, comfortable, and produced by hand. Two gifted California builders, the brothers Charles Sumner Greene and Henry Mather Greene, were present at the creation of the Craftsman-style house, building beautifully detailed bungalows of large scale in and around Pasadena. The movement in America was also led by Gustav Stickley, a furniture maker who published an influential magazine called *The Craftsman*. In its pages, he promoted his philosophy of using natural materials, like unpainted wood, ceramic tile, and wrought iron. He himself made furniture, much of it oak, that today is highly prized. But *The Craftsman* also featured simple houses like the Bungalow that reflected his philosophy.

In talking about the Shingle Style House, I invoked the name Stanford White. White also helped initiate another historicist movement that has ever since played an important role in American house design. White and some of his colleagues examined a number of important early American houses along the New England coast. Some of the flavor of those dwellings informed the Shingle Style, but there was a larger cultural phenomenon that resulted from the work at McKim, Mead, and White and a confluence of other events. Called the Colonial Revival, this movement reinvigorated the taste for things colonial. The Centennial celebration in Philadelphia helped build interest; the growing economic health and power of the country gave Americans the luxury to look back into the country's past. Furniture, household goods, clothing, and houses in early American styles became broadly popular in the early decades of the twentieth century.

Consider the Cape Cod house—it's a Basic House of the sort we talked about earlier but during the Colonial Revival it was reborn. The same is true with the Classic Colonial: In its original guise it was Georgian, later Federal, and still later was decorated with a range of Victorian details, but it, too, had a new incarnation during the Colonial Revival. While the Cape and the Classic Colonial have remained popular ever since, two other revivals, the Spanish Colonial and the Dutch Revival Styles, found a briefer popularity at the turn of the twentieth century and after; all are manifestations of the Colonial Revival. Still more revival styles, like the Tudor Revival of the twenties with its English precedents and half-timbered exterior, had important periods of popularity, too.

Not all new houses in our century looked backward. Thanks in part to Frank Lloyd Wright, a style evolved in the Midwest called the Prairie School. The lines of these houses paralleled the prairie itself, sitting long and low with broad roof overhangs and horizontal bands of windows. Wright, like Stickley, decried the dehumanizing effects of the machine age, but he recognized its inevitable importance.

The Prairie Style house is truly American and truly original. Yet perhaps the most popular house design to emerge from drafting boards of the Prairie Style designers was the Foursquare. Unlike many of Wright's inimitable Prairie School houses, this was hardly a revolutionary house. It's a cube with wide eaves and dormers that peer out of a pyramidal roof. But it's a very efficient design whose simplicity, honesty, and practicality helped it make its way into the pages of Stickley's magazine, *The Craftsman*. But let's get specific and look at some popular twentieth-century styles.

The Georgian Revival House

Some Georgian Revival Houses can, at least from afar, be confused with eighteenth-century precedents; others resemble later Federal Houses, but most are a mix of elements that allude to the past but are actually quite modern, comfortable homes.

The Georgian Revival often has the Classic Colonial shape. Typically two or three stories tall, these designs are symmetrical with hipped, gable, or gambrel roofs. Elaborate doorways are usual, with pilasters, sidelights, and even porticos. In a departure

This may, at first, look like a two-hundred-year-old house. But look again: Those three-part windows are common to the much later Colonial Revival Style. This is a sturdy, even stately, twentieth-century home.

from true colonial houses, there are combination windows in some Georgian Revival Houses, with two or even three separate units installed as one. The sash may have multiple lights or a single pane of glass, as 12/1, 6/6, or 1/1 configurations are all common.

Inside the typical Georgian Revival house, the symmetry is maintained with the entrance and stair hall at the center of the home. However, the rooms on either side rarely mirror one another. These are houses where the emphasis has changed from a stubborn insistence on balance to practical considerations like squeezing purpose-specific spaces such as the kitchen, dining room, and living room into an efficient floor plan.

REMODELER'S NOTES. The typical Georgian Revival House built before the Depression is thought by some architectural historians to be the best ever built in America. That isn't to diminish the finest of houses from a range of other times and in many other styles, but taken as a group, Georgian Revival houses are well built with an eye to the quality materials and craftsmanship that later houses often lack. In addition, they are modern houses, with kitchen spaces, bathrooms, and floor plans that suit today's needs without requiring wholesale gutting to reengineer the floor plan.

The Cape Cod House

The word *snug* comes to mind when I think of the Cape Cod House. These are efficient and economical houses, putting the one-story Basic House back in business. The main living spaces are on the first floor, laid out in most instances around a center entrance. Most Capes are symmetrical, with two windows on either side of the front door. Upstairs there may be dormers to add light to rooms built in what is essentially converted attic space.

REMODELER'S NOTES. The Cape is a perfect starter house. In fact, many Capes built immediately after World War II were sold initially with their upper stories left unfinished. That strategy meant the house was more affordable to a larger audience, and as the buyer's family grew and more space was required, the rooms upstairs could be finished to suit specific needs.

It was an intelligent marketing strategy, but it also meant that in your Cape Cod House, you may find the level of finish upstairs is of a lesser quality than the work downstairs. Many homeowners did the work themselves and their inexperi-

ence may be apparent. As you consider making changes in your Cape Cod House, look for indications that the house was finished over time. You may wish to remove and remodel work that came later and was done less well. You may be able to rethink the upstairs spaces, too, since the partitions are probably not structural, giving you the freedom to remove or reposition them to enlarge one or more rooms or entirely reconfigure the floor plan.

It's really just a one-story house with a gable roof steep enough to allow for living space on a second level. This Cape Cod was probably built in the 1950s.

109

A California Bungalow, as pictured in a circa 1920 catalog.

The Bungalow

The name is Indian, adapted by the British in India to describe a one-story house with a porch. The bungalow may have begun as an unpretentious house for travelers in India, but in America it swept across the suburban landscape, reaching from California to the New England seacoast with a Prairie-style variation found in between.

The basic Bungalow is a one-story house with a broad, gently sloping hip or gable roof, often with rafter tails at the eave that are left exposed and decorated. Dormers are common. Typically there's a porch at the front or back supported by square posts that taper to the top. The walling may be clapboard, shingles, brick, or stucco.

Casements are common, but so are double-hung windows. Decorative windows with stained glass lights are often found in earlier examples; doorways typically have small openings for glass.

Entering the home, the open floor plan is usually evident the moment you step in the front door. It looks directly into the living room in most Bungalows. The main design element is a fireplace, typically of rough brick or stone, or even cobblestone. Unpainted wood trim was the rule at time of construction, though many Bungalows have had their trim painted in the intervening years.

The Bungalow has proved to be a rugged, adaptable, and economical design. Many early twentieth-century suburbs, from Washington to Los Angeles, from Chicago to Florida, derive much of their character from these houses, which settle nicely into narrow suburban lots.

In California, there's an upscale variation of this house, with the somewhat misleading name of "Western Stick." Typically it presents a pair of gables to the street, one offset to one side and to the rear of the first, which usually has a porch across the front gable. In other regional variations, the Bungalow is found with Colonial, Swiss Chalet, or Tudor detailing while retaining its basic shape. The earliest Bungalows were built before the turn of the century, and the years before World War I were the heyday for the style. It went out of vogue during the years of the Depression.

REMODELER'S NOTES. Like the Cape Cod House, many Bungalows were constructed with unfinished attic spaces. These were typically low-ceiling spaces wedged into the eaves and lit by a dormer or gable windows. They may (or may not) have been finished as well as the spaces on the main floor. Renovation possibilities often offer themselves there, especially with the addition of more dormers (shed dormers being an especially practical approach to add space and light).

Many homeowners have found it rewarding to invest their own time in stripping and restoring the original unpainted surfaces of interior woodwork, but precautions should be taken to ensure that any lead paint is properly handled. Your local health department can provide guidance for testing and disposal procedures.

Recognize this one? It's a Dutch Revival Colonial, typified most by its gambrel-style roof.

The Dutch Revival House

You may be one of the many who believe Dutch houses have gambrel roofs (a variation on the gable roof in which the plane on each side of the ridge is broken roughly halfway down, and the lower half falls steeply to the eave). In fact, some Dutch houses in the colonies did have gambrel roofs, but so did some Basic Houses built by English builders. It was only in the early twentieth century that the gambrel came to be regarded as essential to the Dutch *Revival* House.

To many, the Dutch Revival House is the perfect middle-class suburban home. It's an efficient design, with two stories of living space neatly packaged into a modified one-story house. It's more modest than the Georgian Revival House, but the second floor is more spacious than that of the Bungalow or the Cape Cod House. These houses were popular across the country, especially in the years between the two world wars.

A Visual Essay on Architectural Style

Houses—including your home and mine—are all related to one another. When new, each one assumes its own identifiable place on the historical time line; any later remodelings also have chronological importance. Somehow, the wide range of American houses fit together like a great puzzle, a diverse display of times, styles, and domesticity.

In the images on the pages that follow, we'll look at some of the important moments in the evolution of American building. You'll see characteristics that distinguish certain architectural styles, building techniques, and materials. You'll see elements that look familiar; you'll see others you might want to adopt as your own.

I hope you enjoy this little journey through several centuries of American buildings.

First, there came the Basic House. It wasn't always symmetrical, and it sure wasn't fancy. A simple gable roof, one story plus an attic space, and a chimney for warmth complete the composition. Houses like this one at Old Sturbridge Village in Massachusetts, with variations large or small, have been built as long as European settlers have been in North America.

RIGHT: One common variation on the Basic House theme is the Cape Cod. Rather than relying upon decorations, the beauty of this house results from its simplicity of line and symmetry.

BELOW: The Saltbox house—the name is derived from the shape of salt containers in early America—is the Cape grown two-stories tall and with a shed extension at the rear. But it shares the same humble grace.

ABOVE: As Americans grew prosperous, their houses became decorated. This grand Georgian House boasts a bold pavilion front, pilasters across its facade, and a decorative balustrade to top it off.   BELOW: Though more understated, this brick Georgian House has a classically decorated center entrance together with a lovely Palladian window above.

ABOVE: When the colonists sought political independence, architectural freedom shortly followed. This Federal House is simpler than its Georgian predecessors, though it shares the same basic design.   BELOW: Some Federal Style houses were highly decorated. This Adamesque Federal reveals its builder's debt to the English Adam brothers and to the buildings that inspired them, the works of Renaissance architect Andrea Palladio and the ruins of Classical Rome.

ABOVE: This Federal Style house is distinguished by its delicate roof balustrade and swag decorations as well as the pastel paint job. BELOW: Look closely and you'll see a Federal Style house peers out from beneath the Gothic decorations. This is the famous Kennebunkport, Maine, "Wedding Cake" house. PHOTO CREDIT: HUGH HOWARD

The houses on this and the two following pages are the same yet very different. Each of them is a "classic colonial," a configuration that, along with the Cape Cod Style, has proved to be an American perennial. Each of these houses is five bays wide, with a center entrance on the first floor flanked by pairs of windows. The houses are two rooms deep (double pile) and (with one exception) two stories tall. These examples all date from the handmade age, but countless later versions have been built ever since in the nineteenth and twentieth centuries.

ABOVE: This New York State brick Federal has many elements that speak for its vintage, but a key one is the delicate tracery in the central window and doorway.   BELOW: This eighteenth-century house is truly a "colonial," complete with its Connecticut River valley doorway with split pediment.

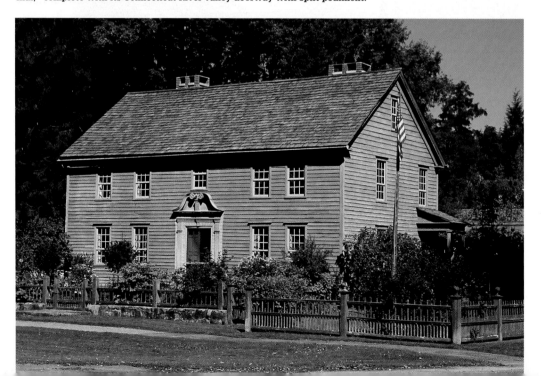

Examples like this three-story house were once common on the cityscapes of early nineteenth-century cities. This home, with its later Greek Revival Portico, is on the grounds of Strawbery Banke in Portsmouth, New Hampshire.
PHOTO CREDIT: HUGH HOWARD

ABOVE: This imposing Greek Revival home certainly makes a statement. The ionic columns and bold temple front identify this as a high–style example.   BELOW: The Gothic Revival is most easily identified by highly decorated gingerbread as on this stone example *(right)*, but the revival of Gothic tastes also allowed for the use of such Medieval elements as the crenellated tower *(left)*.

Not all Greek Revival homes had temple fronts. These two farmhouses have Greek detailing, but their masses are obviously those of the Classic Colonial and the Cape Cod House.

ABOVE: Although inspired by Italian villas, this house has brackets supporting its roof overhangs that are distinctly American. Whether you call this an American Bracket or an Italianate, the view from the cupola of this handsome farmhouse is breathtaking.　　BELOW: The Second Empire Style was perhaps the most popular of its day, at least among city dwellers after the Civil War. There's a great deal of living space inside this stolid house, thanks in part to the generous windows that stand out from the Mansard roof.

Characteristics of the Stick Style are apparent in this house thanks to its polychrome paint job. Those horizontal and vertical bands (sticks) that divide up the walling are typical of the style and tell you something about the joy the builders and designer took in the sudden range of affordable, machine-made materials available to them.

ABOVE: The Queen Anne House often had enough roof shapes for several houses, and this example is no exception. Note, too, the decorative work on the porch.   BELOW: Typical of the Shingle Style, this house has its obligatory cladding of shingles. But there's a grand porch, a tower that blends into the walling of the house, and an overall sense of irregularity.

The streetscapes of many cities—in this case the Upper West Side of Manhattan—still reflect the architectural tastes of another time. Here the dominant flavor is Victorian, the material the famous brownstone from which a whole class of buildings got their name. PHOTO CREDIT: HUGH HOWARD

ABOVE: *Now this is a test.* With your growing expertise in looking at historic houses, examine this house. What stylistic elements distinguish it? No, really, look closely before you read the rest of this caption. You should see the Classic Colonial shape and a Palladian window, both of which would suggest this house dates from the turn of the nineteenth century or before. Yet what about that tower and the decorative porch over the front door? Those are more Victorian, aren't they?

If you saw all that then you get a gold sticker. This is Lindenwald, home to Martin Van Buren, our eighth president. When he retired to this house in Kinderhook, New York, upon leaving office in 1841, he remodeled an earlier home, transforming it into a fashionable Italian villa. You see, this remodeling thing isn't exactly new.

This may be the perfect suburban design. The Bungalow seems somehow settled and relaxed amid the grassy lawns and tree-lined streetscapes of so many early twentieth-century residential neighborhoods.

This revival Spanish Colonial house, remodeled and adapted for life in the 1990s, is a rich reprise of traditional detailing with its red tile roofing, the oculus window on its facade, and other details. It's perfectly suited to this palm-lined Florida street.

ANDREA CLARK BROWN, A.I.A.

If you wait long enough, most any style will get revived. This new home echoes a mix of early nineteenth-century styles—it's a side hall colonial but features both Federal and Greek Revival detailing.

Another new home, this one in South Bend, Indiana, is an act of homage to Andrea Palladio. It bears the richly allusive name "Villa Indiana."

DUNCAN G. STROIK, ARCHITECT;
PHOTO CREDIT: L.K. DUNN

That's right, it's the Classic Colonial again. This time, though, it's brand new—the paint is barely dry on this reproduction house.

KATE JOHNS, A.I.A.; PHOTO CREDIT: D. CRAIG JOHNS

REMODELER'S NOTES. The roof line of this house is its single most distinctive design element: If you're adding on, take pains to respect and perhaps reflect its shape in complimentary fashion.

More Styles for Modern Times

After World War II, other new styles evolved that were adapted to the desires of people moving from the streets of the city who wanted to live in homes on lots of their own. The Ranch House quickly proved its popularity. The split level came next, offering its inhabitants more interior space atop the same footprint as the Ranch. In the 1960s and 1970s, the A-Frame and Buckminster Fuller's brainstorm, the Geodesic Dome, each saw bursts of popularity. In the last quarter century, French Chateau, Tudor, and even Mansard-roofed buildings reappeared in suburban developments. More recently, Victorian styling of the sort that helped inspire the reaction that became the Arts and Crafts Movement back at the beginning of the century has had a renaissance, with the brackets, spindles, and other machine-made surface decorations. There's a classical revival occurring, too, and in the 1990s there has even been a trend to build new homes integrating house parts salvaged from antique homes. The mining of the past for styles and ideas has become a literal borrowing of doorways, windows, mantels, and other elements that date from the handmade age.

Which leaves us back on your doorstep, as you seek to make your house better suit your needs.

Chapter 3

Looking at Buildings

We're talking about change. You've got mental snapshots of your existing house stored in your memory. In some other corner of your mind, you may also have a few blurry images of what you think the place *might* look like after you've remodeled. But this being real life rather than science fiction, no one can instantaneously beam you into another time and place where, miraculously, your renovation is already complete.

In Chapter 1, we looked at the structure of your house, and in Chapter 2 our subject was the full spectrum of American architectural style. Now, like an alchemist trying to convert the common into the precious, you need to combine what you've learned with what you want, and do so in a way that respects your home's existing virtues yet serves your needs. That's a big assignment.

Here's a house with an idea for everyone. It has porches, turrets, bays, pediments, posts, and gables, yet manages, somehow, to make all the pieces fit neatly together.

You need to put your imagination to work. I'm not suggesting you act as your own architect. On the contrary, I'm a big believer in hiring professionals and, in Chapter 4, Thinking Through the Design, the topics covered will include how to establish a working relationship with a designer (see page 143). But I'm not proposing you put anybody on the payroll quite yet.

We're still thinking things through.

In this chapter, I will try to convey what I've learned about *seeing buildings*. Not looking at, mind you, but *seeing*. This is about taking the house that your eye perceives and allowing your brain to process that visual image in such a way that you better understand the relationships among its parts, its environment, and you. Further, you'll begin to think about changing what you see and transforming its shapes, details, and interrelationships. The idea is to combine the mental snapshots you're carrying of the present with those blurry images of the imagined future, in order to synthesize something new.

It's easier, you'll find, than it sounds. Let's get started.

The Language of Design

We'll begin by considering a handful of words that are especially useful when the talk turns to buildings.

SYMMETRY. In the last chapter, the word *symmetry* seemed unavoidable. The Georgian House was strictly symmetrical; later, the Gothic Revival House was consistently asymmetrical. But let's go back to basics.

The dictionary tells us that the word *symmetry* describes a "correspondence in size, form and the arrangement of parts on opposite sides of a line or plane." In practice, that means that if you draw a horizontal line and then a vertical one that intersects the first at its center point, you will have a *symmetrical* figure, with one side that balances the other. In the same way, if you begin with a rectangle and bisect it, it too is *symmetrical*. Let's add some openings to a four-sided box—windows on either side of the central axis, perhaps a door at the center. All in a rush, a house begins to emerge. All we need to do is add a roof, and a

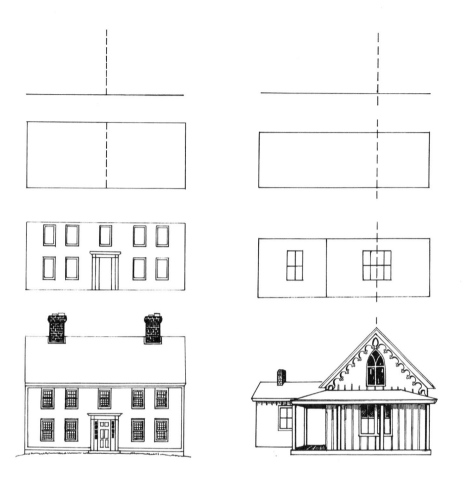

couple of chimneys and we have a two-dimensional representation, an *elevation* they call it in drafting class, of a recognizable Georgian House (or the Classic Colonial, as this configuration can also be described). Needless to say, the place is *symmetrical*.

ASYMMETRY. Again, we start with a line, but this time we consciously divide it into two *asymmetrical* (uneven) parts. We make it a box, add a couple of openings, then put on a gable end (centered on our perpendicular). After adding a few details, we have a Gothic Revival Cottage. The place looks great, doesn't it?

117

A flattened *elevation* view can assume the appearance of three dimensions as an *isometric* drawing. With the addition of a chimney, entrance door, and windows in a recognizable pattern, a Cape Cod House appears.

MASS. This talk of symmetry may seem to imply that houses exist only in two dimensions and that, by looking at an elevation drawing of a structure, we can understand it. In fact, thinking how the facade of a house appears on a piece of paper is helpful, but other angles of approach are essential, too.

Instead of a piece of paper, think about a small waxed cardboard milk or juice carton, the kind that holds a ½-pint of liquid. It's a three-dimensional object, meaning it has width, height, *and* depth. It takes up space, just as people, books, and bricks do. And, for that matter, just like buildings.

Unless you stand very far away and align yourself precisely with the center of a building (or a milk carton), you will see it as a three-dimensional object. From an angled view, represented here by an *isometric sketch*, a simple, shoebox shape is recognizable as a three-dimensional *mass* and, in short order, it becomes a house.

A *one-and-a-half story house* has a full ceiling on the first level and enough height on the upper floor that portions of it can be used as living space. Lower the pitch of the roof and you have a ranch house, a one-story home, in which living areas are found only on one level. The Cape Cod is a popular compromise because living quarters on the upper floor are to be had for virtually no additional expense over the cost of a one-story house. To some, however, the built-in limitations on ventilation, light, and head room make it less of a bargain than at first it seems. For them, perhaps the two-story house is the answer. In this configuration, the roof stands a story higher, atop a full second story.

118

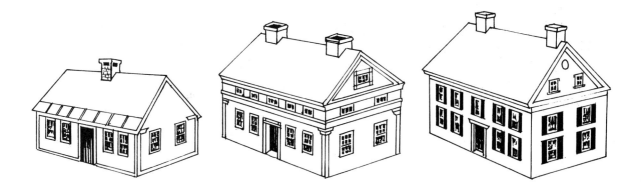

Thus, the same footprint can accommodate houses of radically different *mass*. In order to have a ranch house with an equivalent amount of interior space to a two-story house, however, the ranch will need to have a footprint twice as large as the two-story house. That makes the ranch best suited to larger lots, while two-story homes are well adapted to in-town plots or small suburban settings.

On much the same footprint, one story, one-and-a-half story, and two-story houses offer very different amounts of living space.

SHAPE. Thus far, we've talked about houses in the *shape* of a box. Some are taller or wider or deeper than others, but they're basic boxes with four sides and a top and a bottom. In the past, consolidating the living space around a chimney and within such a regular form made good sense. But changing needs, advances in heating technology, and evolving tastes led to what architectural historians often call "breaking the box."

The devolution of the box took time. Early houses often had ells added off their rear elevations, resulting in T-shaped plans. As asymmetry became acceptable with the Greek and Gothic Revival Styles, wings appeared on the sides of new houses, resulting in L-shaped homes. In some instances two or more secondary structures were grafted on. Many houses had bay windows, towers, turrets, porches, or other elements that broke the planes of the box. When a number of different *masses* are combined (think about the way some great Victorian houses seem to ramble), the term *massing* is applied to describe the assemblage of the various three-dimensional elements.

For a moment, though, let's return again to the box house. After all this talk

The different masses of a house can often be deconstructed to reveal its construction history, one stage at a time.

about T-shapes and L-shapes and the rest, you may be surprised to find what a difference a simple change in roof design can make.

Certain roof shapes—the Mansard being the best example—telegraph the style of the house (a Mansard roof means the dwelling is a Second Empire House, see page 96). Some roofs are tall in order to maximize the living areas beneath them (like the gambrel or the Mansard), while others are lower and enclose little more than storage space. Some are simple, others require complex carpentry full of compound angles. The roof of a house may seem like little more than necessary weather protection, but it also communicates much about the design of a house.

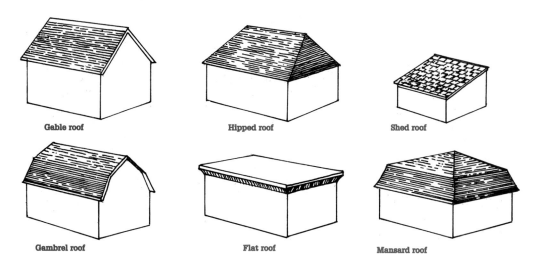

Gable roof   Hipped roof   Shed roof

Gambrel roof   Flat roof   Mansard roof

120

VISUAL BALANCE

Some buildings are symmetrical, others asymmetrical. But good houses, regardless of their symmetricality, usually share one thing: They are *balanced*.

All right, you say, *I know how symmetrical houses balance. But how can an asymmetrical house balance?*

Look at the two houses illustrated. They have in common identical gables with first-story bay windows, but their ells are different. One is too sparse: It looks light enough that, were the house to be set upon a seesaw, the gable would tilt the building heavily to its side. The second house—with its small cross gable on the V and the added windows—is *visually balanced*. The design still isn't symmetrical, but it doesn't look conspicuously out of balance.

Balance is a concept that designers grapple with to make buildings more satisfying, but one that you, too, can recognize as adding (or detracting) from the appeal of a house.

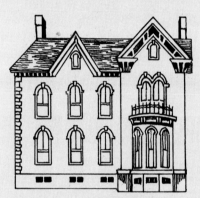

Unbalanced . . .   . . . and balanced.

The overall shape and mass of a house convey a great deal about the place. Consider the contrast between two different houses that date from the same era. A Foursquare has a boxy, two-story mass with a tall roof; the Prairie Style home is low-slung, consisting of only one story with a flattened roof and broad overhangs. While the Foursquare and the Prairie Style House share similar origins, one is essentially vertical, the other horizontal. One seems to have been wiped across the landscape, the other to have grown out of it. One sits atop the landscape, hunched as if to confront the challenges of Mother Nature; the other rests more easily, going with the flow of the terrain. In the examples here, however, they contain the same amount of living space.

121

Both the Foursquare (left) and this Prairie Style home are early twentieth-century houses inspired by the work of Frank Lloyd Wright, but the resemblance would seem to end there. But look again: despite their very different footprints, these houses contain the same number of square feet of living space.

All right, let's take a short break from talking about shapes and masses, symmetrical or otherwise. Remember that the shape of every house—whether it resembles a single milk carton or a dozen cartons that collided—tells a story of whence it came. Understanding the geometry of your house, even in such broad strokes as these, can help you think about changing it.

Combining the Old with the New

Restoration. Preservation. Renovation. Rehabilitation. Remodeling. I touched on these terms in the introduction, so you know they don't all mean the same thing. But let's consider some formal definitions, according to the Standards of the Secretary of the Interior, under whose auspices are the National Park Service, the Preservation Assistance Division, and the Historic American Buildings Survey:

PRESERVATION. "The act or process of applying measures to sustain the existing form, integrity, and material of a building or structure, and the existing form and vegetative cover of a site. It may include stabilization work, where necessary, as well as ongoing maintenance of the historic building material." Loosely translated? The task is to save—to *preserve*—the existing bits and pieces (fabric) that survive from earlier eras.

RESTORATION. "The act or process of accurately recovering the form and details of a property and its setting as it appeared at a particular period of time by means of the removal of later work or by the replacement of missing earlier work." In other words, the restorer turns back the clock and attempts to replicate what was originally in place but subsequently removed or destroyed.

REHABILITATION. "The act or process of returning a property to a state of utility through repair or alteration which makes possible an efficient contemporary use while preserving those portions or features of the property which are significant to its historical, architectural and cultural values." Translation, please? The rehaber renovates a place the way he or she chooses without going to great lengths to preserve or restore elements exactly as they were. Rehabilitation is used more or less interchangeably with remodeling and renovation.

Curators of historic houses rarely rehabilitate—they might adapt an old dependency or basement space for a contemporary use, but they're more likely to be concerned with *preserving* what survives and, in some instances, restoring what doesn't. Living History museums have traditionally identified a single point in the past that becomes the target date, and then *restored* the buildings on the grounds consistent with that historical moment (which often implies removing later work that would appear anachronistic, out of sync with the established moment when the calendar is said to have stopped). Increasingly, however, there is a trend among amateurs and professionals alike to save good old work, whatever its era.

How do you, as a homeowner, translate these various approaches into action? I recommend you begin by establishing what you *won't* be changing. The following should probably be on your preservation list.

THE FLOOR PLAN. In older houses, the flow between the principal living spaces is usually quite logical. The interrelationship between the main entrance, the parlor, the kitchen, and the secondary entrance typically is practical and workable. In some homes, later additions changed the patterns of use (often confusing rather than clarifying things). If possible, retain the floor plan at least in the original portion of the house.

Note the entrances in this traditional floor plan, dating from the early twentieth century. It's all symmetry and balance at the front, with center entrance and hall. At the rear, it's more pragmatic, with a convenient entrance to the kitchen.

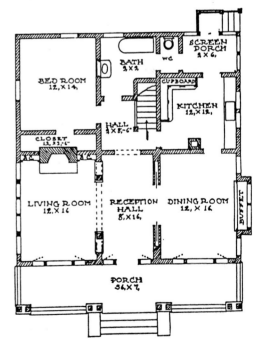

In some cases, that may even mean restoring elements removed by previous remodelers. In just the last twenty-five years, I've seen the trend for opening up spaces arrive and then go. In the early seventies, no one wanted a dining room, so the trend was to open them up to adjoining food preparation areas in order to create "country kitchens" or other multiple-use spaces in an open plan. Today the dining room is back—relaxing with friends, food, and wine is high on my list of activities. In general, the trend seems to be to more purpose-specific spaces (offices, children's play spaces, breakfast rooms) and fewer open, multiple-use areas.

The paint and plaster need repair, but *this* masterpiece is a stairway worth saving.

Perhaps you're thinking about enlarging the kitchen or adding a downstairs bathroom. At first, an older floor plan may not seem flexible enough to allow for such renovations and a wholesale rearrangement may seem necessary. Try looking again.

Think about the traffic flow and how the spaces are used: Can you keep the main arteries the same but add peripheral circulation? At our house, for example, we changed the kitchen radically, but kept its relationship to the other rooms the same. Often existing subsidiary spaces can be opened up, since many Victorian houses have maid's rooms or butler's pantries and even modest houses until quite recently often had storage pantries. Bathrooms, especially half-baths, can be secreted in surprisingly small places, such as converted closets, back halls, and beneath stairs. Again, start by thinking how *little* you can change the floor plan rather than how much. You'll save money as well as respect the integrity of the original design.

STAIRCASES. As the cost of quality craftsmanship has soared, the quality and character of the typical staircase have plummeted. If your stairway(s) have original balusters, rails, and newel posts, restore them. Strip them if they're of hardwoods or so coated with paint that turnings, panels, or other details are no longer crisp. Find ways to stabilize them (if necessary) that don't detract from their appearance. Badly worn treads can usually be replaced without too much difficulty, but be sure the details are restored, too, such as the nosing returns (that's where the rounded edge continues around the open end of the tread). New balusters to replace broken or missing ones can be milled surprisingly inexpensively if you shop around. Staircases are key design elements in a house, and well worth extra dollars to conserve and restore them.

WOODWORK. Up until the years after World War II, moldings remained important design elements even in unassuming

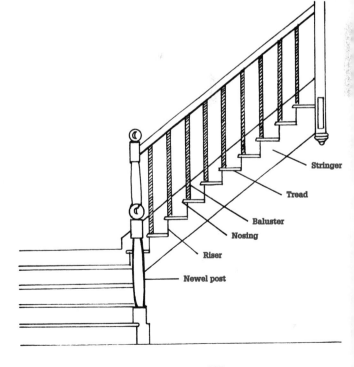

Stringer

Tread

Baluster

Nosing

Riser

Newel post

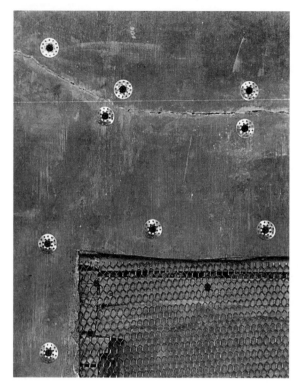

Saving old plaster can require a variety of techniques. In this case, plaster washers have been used to refasten loosened plaster to its original wood lath. In addition, fresh plaster will be applied to the expanded metal lath to cover a larger area of broken plaster.

houses. Baseboards and casings around the windows and doors were made of wide stock, often with applied moldings to add shadow lines and a bolder, three-dimensional effect. Particularly in the late nineteenth century, cornices were heavy and dramatic. Save all that you can of the original woodwork, including any early paneling, built-in casework, spindle work, and other decorative wood treatments.

Think of such wooden elements as worthy of restoration, but also as a source of inspiration. If your plan involves new elements such as windows, doors, or cabinets, try to replicate existing details. Using existing quality work as a source for new detailing will help give the new space a feeling that it is of-a-piece with the existing house.

PLASTER SURFACES. Save original plaster where possible. New drywall lacks the strength, durability, soundproofing, and character of traditional plaster. Many techniques have been developed to preserve old plaster walls and ceilings, including special plaster washers that can reattach and stabilize loose and cracking plaster. When an existing partition is to remain in place, try to retain its plaster surface.

FLOORS. The history of change in a house is often to be read most easily in its floors. One with wide, hand-planed pine boards upstairs and machine-planed oak strip flooring down has been visited by remodelers, probably in the last few decades. A series of joints that form a line across the floor in the middle of a room for no apparent reason can indicate the shifting of a partition or the removal of a chimney. Unless your floors are both uniform and consistent with the style and vintage of your home, they probably can tell you something about the house.

When you select flooring for new work, whether it's to be an addition to the house or a remodeling of existing space, consider how the new surfaces will suit surviving older flooring. Should you consider trying to find salvaged materials that will make the transition from the old to the new seamless? Do you wish to resurface much of the old flooring to match the new? Is there something in an original wood floor you can echo without copying its every detail—perhaps a border design, the board width, or the species and color of the wood? Or do you want to use an entirely different surface, like wall-to-wall carpeting in a new family room or tile in the new kitchen that coordinates with the old while not copying it? There's no one answer but ask yourself the question: *Will the new suit the old?*

WINDOWS. In houses with wavy old glass, windows seem to offer a view of the past. From the exterior, multiple small lights provide texture, adding to the timelessness of a period house. From the interior looking out, the muntins divide and frame the view.

There are many window configurations, including *awning* and *casement* windows, both of which break the plane of the wall. *Awnings* swing open from hinges at their tops, *casements* from hinged sides. Less usual are fixed windows, while by far the most common is the *double-hung sash* window. These are the traditional sliding variety that, within the plane of the wall, travel up and down in their frames.

Double-hung windows also come in many varieties. These are distinguished not only by their overall size but by the number of panes of glass or lights. In the eighteenth century, windows with twelve lights in each sash (called twelve-over-twelves or 12/12s) were common, as were 12/8, 9/9, and 9/6 windows. In the first half of the nineteenth century, 6/6 windows were the rule, before 2/2 windows took over.

There are four basic window configurations. Double-hung windows are the most common, followed in no particular order by sliding, casement, and awning windows. Most of the windows in a typical house will be of the same type, though other designs may be used in certain applications such as bathrooms, porches, or other spaces.

Double-hung

Sliding

Casement

Awning

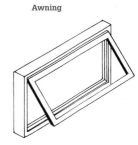

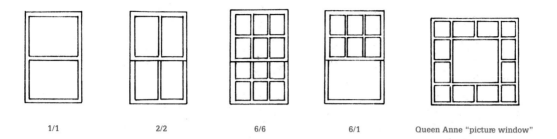

1/1   2/2   6/6   6/1   Queen Anne "picture window"

After about 1880, 1/1 windows became the norm until various revival styles made all 6/6, 6/1, and other multi-light sash common once again.

Wavy glass with bubbles and other imperfections was all that was available until about 1880 when large, optically perfect, factory-made sheets of glass became generally available. At about the same time, panes of colored glass became affordable. Thus was born what was then known as the "picture window." In the late nineteenth century, the term identified a window with panes of colored glass. Only after World War II did the term "picture window" come to refer to enormous, single-pane windows.

Today, talk of windows usually focuses first on *R-factor*, a measure of the insulating capability of the windows. A single-glazed window has an R-factor of about one; double-glazed windows have an R-factor of roughly two. Storm windows and other innovations like argon gas sealed in the insulating cushion of air between the layers of glass in a thermal pane window can bring the R-factor up still higher.

If your home is a century or more old and its windows are original, the best approach almost always is to conserve rather than replace them. New weatherstripping can be added quite inexpensively, as can storms (sometimes on the *inside,* especially on historic houses). Old glazing compound can be repaired and even rotted elements can be replaced or the wood stabilized with epoxy or other consolidants. On newer houses, good copies of the original windows may well be available inexpensively.

Whether you choose to replace or restore, do try to retain the original configuration. A homeowner who replaces the original multilight windows with single-pane sash (substituting, say, 1/1s for 6/6s) will change the appearance of a house, rather in the way that a pencil drawing is transformed when someone erases some of the shading. It's probably a bad idea.

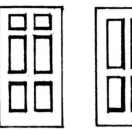

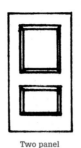
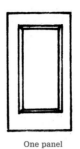
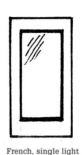
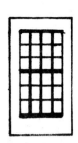

| Six panel | Four panel | Two panel | One panel | French, single light | French, multilight |

DOORS. In the eighteenth century, doors typically had six panels; early in the nineteenth century, four-panel doors became the rule. One-panel doors, hollow-core veneer doors, and reproduction doors are common to our time. Batten doors—which are made of vertical boards fastened together with horizontal boards nailed across them—are commonly used as secondary doors in homes and in outbuildings.

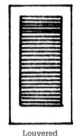

Louvered

Rail-and-stile or *panel* doors have long been popular. They consist of vertical boards (the stiles) and horizontal boards (the rails) with panels inset between them. These doors are traditionally held together with mortise-and-tenon joints, in which tongue-shaped projections slide into cavities cut into the sides of the stiles and then are fastened with wooden pins.

Batten

As with windows and other details, try to save original doors. Doors removed in one part of the house can be recycled elsewhere. Find similar style doors at architectural salvage—they don't have to be identical, but if they resemble the originals, they won't seem out of place.

Flush

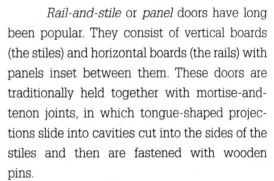

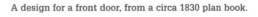

A design for a front door, from a circa 1830 plan book.

129

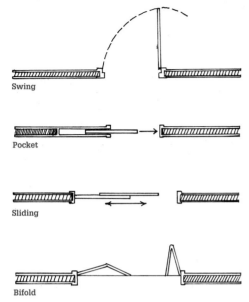

Swing

Pocket

Sliding

Bifold

Doors can also be installed in a variety of ways. Some operate within the plane of the wall, others swing outward.

The hold-on-to-the-original notion applies to exterior doors, too. Replacing a paneled front door that shows the wear and tear of many years may seem like just the right thing to do to save energy and tighten up the house. Yet many replacement doors today—sometimes of steel, often with faux graining stamped into the sheet metal—look like the architectural equivalent of a black eye. Think first about restoring the original door or, at least, finding a replacement in the same spirit as the original.

HARDWARE. Most vintage houses have been altered over the years and, typically, hardware is among the first elements to be changed. Hardware can wear out or break. Changing tastes may make a different style of doorknob desirable. Added security may call for updated locks. As a result, many houses have a range of hardware.

Past remodelers may also have skimped on hardware. In new construction, most contractors specify inexpensive hinges and lock sets—and they look cheap, too, as the plating scrapes off. Often the quality of hardware changes from the public sections of the house to the private—expensive mortise locks in a high-style Victorian house often give way to simple latches in upstairs bedrooms.

Know what your house has for hardware. Make sure you recognize the evolution of locks, latches, hinges, door knockers and bells, hooks, and the rest. Hardware is too often overlooked, both as a source of style ideas and for the clues it can offer about how the house was changed over time. A simple latch from an upstairs cupboard can prove to be the inspiration for the closure on the cabinets in your new kitchen or, when removed from a door, may reveal unpainted wood beneath, indicating it is original.

An early nineteenth-century surface-mounted locking mechanism called a carpenter's lock.

130

OTHER ORIGINAL ELEMENTS. The skeleton of the house—its wooden frame, usually visible in the cellar and attic—may also give you some ideas. Solid old beams have been revealed in many old houses, though they often look like what they are: rough structural elements that the builders never for a moment intended visitors to see.

Old masonry is to be regarded with the same wary eye: always conserve what you can, but don't be tempted to reveal surfaces if you believe that was never the mason's intention. Sloppy, untooled mortar joints and broken brick pieces that are just packed at random into openings are signs of masonry work that was to be covered up, perhaps by plaster or other surfaces.

Rehabilitating a house requires more than satisfying your own desires. The best remodeling work on old houses almost invariably involves preserving some original elements, restoring others, and identifying how the new work can augment the old.

The Sensitive Addition

There's been a lot of talk invested in the last few years in trying to define what is an historically sensitive addition. The National Park Service has published guidelines, which, in short, recommend preserving historic features and materials in order to preserve a building's historic character. That's the goal.

The Park Service also suggests, in a general way, a means of accomplishing that. The recommendation is that any addition to an historic structure be designed in such a way that it look enough different from the original structure that a *visual distinction* be apparent to the casual observer. In short, respect the old building but don't try to fool anyone that what you've added is old.

There have been a number of strategies devised over the years that aim to accomplish this, and I'll discuss those shortly. But first there's a question to be considered: Although the visual distinction notion has been widely accepted, is it always appropriate? In a word, *no*. I agree it's a good first assumption but in some cases an architectural solution will emerge that closely mimics the original and looks just right. It's probably a good first position to assume that a visual distinction is desirable, but working on older houses requires nothing if not flexibility.

The possibility of not obeying the Park Service dictum raises another important philosophical issue: Is it somehow dishonest to add a new-old structure that isn't distinguishable as being different from the original? Is that playing fast and loose with history?

Some would say, *Yes, absolutely.* I'd say, *Maybe, it depends.*

For me, it's case-by-case. It comes down to whether or not we identify a given dwelling as an historic house. No, I would never recommend that their caretakers put an addition on Monticello, Mount Vernon, or any major architectural monument. On the other hand, the definition of historic house has broadened greatly in recent years. You ask Foursquare and Bungalow owners whether their old houses are historic, and lots of them will tell you from the bottom of their hearts that, surely, yes indeed they live in historic houses. And I'm not going to tell an enthusiastic wave of volunteer preservationists they're wrong.

So let's look at some strategies.

REDUCED SIZE AND SCALE. One good way to think about an addition is that it should be smaller in scale and overall size than the original house. If your house is a Classic Colonial, with a facade that's two stories high and 40 feet wide, the wing you add to one side might be a story and a half and 30 feet wide.

RECESS THE ADDITION. Another common recommendation is that the front plane of the addition be noticeably recessed back from the original structure, a visual acknowledgment of its secondary status. A variation on the same theme is to separate the addition from the house with an even smaller hyphen or connecting structure that further distances the original house from what you've added. Another proven strategy is to make the addition invisible from the front—for centuries, here and around the world, important building facades have been left unchanged when necessary additions were attached to the back rather than to the front of a building.

TO MATCH OR NOT TO MATCH THE EXTERIOR FINISH. Not everybody agrees here: One camp argues that the siding, window trim, and other detailing should be consistent with the original; another group advises subtle changes are essential, such as simplifying the trim or using shingles to contrast the original clapboards. Both approaches are, in my opinion, perfectly correct under the right circum-

stances, but the nature of an individual structure must be factored into deciding what to do.

RESPECT THE ROOFLINES. Different rooflines will probably draw immediate attention to the addition. A radically different roof shape (a flat roof abutting a gable roof, for example) is likely to look wrong. Adding dormers, a cupola, or other elements not on the original may also look peculiar. While you don't have to copy the cornice, eave overhang, pitch, or even the overall roof shape, a complementary configuration that echoes the original is probably the best strategy.

I recommend you take all of this reasonable advice and mull it over. Take what fits and feels right—and be forewarned that you won't please everyone. The truth is that working on an old house requires a series of judgments. You need to think like an architectural historian, a builder, a curator, *and* a homeowner.

Remember, too, that you're just passing through. The odds are that the house will be there generations from today . . . so treat it with respect.

This house has considerable charm—even though the mass of its addition strongly contrasts with the original Cape Cod house. While creating a complementary addition is never easy, seemingly incongruous approaches like this one can be made to work, in part as a result of the reuse of basic details like the clapboard siding and the consistent scale of the openings.

More Design Language

We've talked about visualizing your house in geometric terms, to consider its *shapes*, *massing*, and *symmetry*. These characteristics can be considered from afar but, as you get closer, finer distinctions become more important. Among them are *scale*, *proportion*, *texture*, and *pattern*.

SCALE. I'm a man of average height. However, a couple of the members of my television crew are quite tall. I can go into a room of modest scale and feel right at home, but they have to duck their heads going through the door and then the ceiling seems to be encroaching on their headroom. It's all a matter of *scale*: what's in scale for a 5-foot-something person isn't for someone who's a foot taller.

Scale is about relative heights, widths, and sizes. In house design, windows and doors, room dimensions, furniture, and other elements are usually of recognizably *human scale*. Buildings adjacent to one another on the same streetscape generally look better if they have the same scale—were the Empire State Building adjacent to a picturesque Cape Cod House, the juxtaposition would be odd indeed. In contrast, a row of Victorian brownstones with neatly aligned cornices looks very much of a piece. Buildings don't have to be the same size but they should relate to one another.

PROPORTION. Scale and proportion work together. Proportion refers to the relationship of elements to one another. Thus, a giant window that dominates the facade of a small house with other smaller windows looks disproportionately large. A gracious room with a vaulted ceiling 20 feet tall may look wonderful and feel very grand indeed. As an individual space, it may be very satisfying, but if it's been shoe-horned into a small house, it may also be asking the question, *Why am I here?*

As you plan your remodeling project, consider how the various new elements relate to the old. Do they share the same scale? Are they in proportion to one another? Sometimes a surprising contrast in scale or proportion is very effective, but make sure you think it through. More often disproportionate elements that are out of scale just look as if somebody wasn't really thinking.

PATTERN. When you look at any symmetrical house, the *pattern* of its basic elements probably calls out to you. Most obvious are the openings, the windows and doors. Are they evenly spaced across the facade or is there a dot-dash-dot quality to their positioning? Notice whether the openings on the house are aligned. Or do they have a zigzag quality with some higher than others? The way the openings are set into the elevation gives it its own *rhythm*. Often subtle variations in spacing add visual appeal.

The siding also adds to the patterning of a house. Clapboards give a house a horizontal feeling; board-and-batten siding adds verticality. Shingles add shading, while brick has its own unique patterning.

Trim can add to the pattern, as in the case of houses where trim boards frame and accentuate the clapboarded areas. Trim around windows also adds emphasis, enlarging the wall area devoted to the windows, which can affect the proportion and rhythm. Mixing different patterns can be very effective (see The Stick Style House, page 99), adding texture and interest to the surface of a house. But different elements on the same house must be handled with great care.

Here's a chance to practice using those new words. This complex of barn buildings certainly embodies multiple masses; its step-down sequence of rooflines conveys an organic sense of pattern as does the string of windows. The silo and the other small structures offer a sense of balance to what is certainly an asymmetrical structure. Yet, I must admit, none of those words quite manage to convey what makes this such a satisfying building.

A common strategy these days is to use shingles for an addition to a clapboard house as a kind of acknowledgment, an honest statement that yes, this section is indeed new. It can work very well. But in general using more patterns requires more design skill if you want to avoid a too-busy look.

SOLAR ORIENTATION. Another consideration from outside your house is its relationship to the sun. Unless you're planning on moving your house, its solar orientation isn't going to change. The sun rises in the east and sets in the west and, depending upon the season, brightens certain rooms at certain times of day. But if you are planning an addition, its location can have an impact on existing spaces (creating new openings or closing off old ones). And where you put the addition will also determine how much sunlight it gets. A kitchen/breakfast room addition is best located on the east side of the house to gather morning light, a new dining room probably belongs on the west side to take advantage of late afternoon and early evening light.

VOLUME. That's a fancy word, *volume*. In an architectural context volume describes space, specifically interior space. While the exterior of a structure appears to be a solid *mass*, it actually encloses a three-dimensional *space*. Consider it another way, thinking back to our waxed cardboard carton. Empty the carton of its contents and the space that once held milk or juice inside is its *volume*.

When thinking about the volumes of the house, most of those words we talked about earlier come into play once again. You probably want a house that has good proportions, that is human in scale, and that has attractive patterns of materials. But let's begin with proportion.

Proportion can be a slippery concept. Consider a square room. It would seem perfectly proportioned, with its identical length and width. Yet as living spaces, square rooms tend to be static while rectangular rooms seem to suggest movement. That's probably because they're more easily subdivided into different areas, encouraging flow. So matching dimensions don't automatically make for good proportions.

Like facades, interior spaces and elevations can be symmetrical, with balanced windows and doors. Shapes have an important impact, too, though the shapes and masses within the volumes of the house tend to be movable elements like pieces

ARCHITECTURAL DESIGN: THE SHORT COURSE

Must you stay awake nights worrying about proportion, scale, symmetry, massing, and pattern?

In a word, no.

All these concepts are part of the language of building. You'll find understanding them is helpful when talking design with architects and builders. None are beyond your understanding, and to flout them in renovating a house is to risk spending good money on a bad renovation.

Yet perhaps the most important word of all when it comes to remodeling work is *continuity*. Remaining true to the existing building isn't everything, but it sure can help. When it comes to planning exterior details like siding and roof shape, try to match the new ones to the old. Roof slope and overhang and the choice of siding are easy enough to match up.

On the inside, keeping the same overall sense of scale, window design, molding treatments, and other basic details can also draw the place together.

In combination, these elements define the massing, symmetry, proportion, and texture of a house. Make them consistent or, if you want to contrast the old, use them to communicate something to the observer other than that no one could agree on what to do. Keep in mind, though, that if you're remodeling a house with a distinct style you either use it or lose it.

of furniture. Concerns like light and ventilation become much more important inside than out. But perhaps most important of all is the interior layout.

LAYOUT. Earlier in this chapter, I made a point of recommending you remain true to your original floor plan. That's because traditional plans often make a lot of sense. There's a basic organizing philosophy that works for most traditional families, in which the home is divided into three main areas. These include the private areas of the house (the bedrooms and attendant bathrooms and dressing areas); the working zone of the house (the kitchen, a utility room, secondary entry area, etc.); and the relaxation spaces, perhaps a living room, dining room, and/or a family room. (See also Chapter 1, page 56.)

As you think about your renovation, keep in mind the invisible lines of demarcation between each area. That new dining room you've been pining for probably doesn't belong immediately beneath the new bedroom for the baby—the two activities are at odds with each other, as happy talk and laughter are great at the dinner table but not so wonderful when you want your child to drift gently off to dreamland.

DRAMA. Another consideration in thinking about your house is harder to quantify than more traditional design factors. But I think it's important for a home to satisfy the normal human desire to entertain and be entertained. There's no one way that the theatrical can be incorporated into a house, but domestic stagecraft can include color, contrast, decoration, and other elements.

One of the favorite dramatic devices of Frank Lloyd Wright was to shift ceiling heights. The visitor to many Wright houses is ushered into a low, dark hall. Moments later, upon moving to another space, the ceiling rises, often dramatically. Cove lighting high on the wall, clerestory windows, vaulted ceilings, or other elements add to the drama. Wright was a master at using the tools of design to add excitement to the experience of a house.

Drawing Conclusions

If you're following the logic of this book, the time is approaching for the design work to begin. My hope is that by this point in the process you feel as if you know your house pretty well. You've identified historic elements, structural liabilities, and have a feel for the house's character and vintage. Presumably you also have a growing list of needs and desires you want fulfilled in the remodeling you're contemplating (though we'll explore that list in the next chapter in more detail).

You may also have begun to hear, to your surprise, a previously unrecognized sound, a chorus of sorts that, as in the plays of ancient Greece, can help guide and inform the action in your own little drama. From time to time, as you think about changing your home, these voices sing in harmony about your obligation to the past. They may remind you that this house was there before you arrived and probably will survive you and generations of others after you. *Do the right thing* is one refrain you may hear. Even if you're not hearing the voices (yet), there are other instructions that other remodelers before you have heard and disregarded at their peril.

TAKE THE LONG VIEW. Develop your plans on the basis of a thorough understanding. Conduct your physical investigation and recognize the style of your house. Try to see your home in context, identifying both its location in time and where it fits in the development of your neighborhood and town. Learn about other, similar houses from local historical societies, museums, or reference works from your bookstore or library.

SAVE ORIGINAL WORK. You've heard the advice before, you'll hear it again. But do listen to it: *Save quality workmanship.* Most old plaster, hardware, doors, windows, floors, and many other elements are probably worth keeping. Even if you think something is hopeless, get a second opinion. Countless remarkable resurrections have been accomplished, often at a cost less than that of reproducing or even simply replacing the original. If the first contractor you contact has an attitude about saving the old (*Geez, that'd be a lot of trouble*), maybe you're talking to the wrong person. One caveat, though: Something that is old isn't by definition better. Bad craftsmanship, even if it's old is, well, just bad craftsmanship. Good work in poor condition is probably worth conserving; shoddy work isn't worth much, whatever its vintage.

TRUST THE HOUSE. Old isn't always better. But when you are stuck, look behind you: The ghost of the builder is there to help. One way to consult the departed builder/designer is to consider what were his or her *original intentions.* Your close examination of the house will have given you some understanding for how the place was originally used, its degree of finish, its patterns, symmetry, detailing, and so on. Refer to that knowledge in making remodeling decisions.

Even if so many changes have been made over the years that knowing what the designers or builders had in mind is difficult, it's often possible to identify what they *didn't* intend. A good example of this is interior brickwork. In apartment buildings, brick was commonly used to construct the party walls that divide one building from another and then was covered with plaster. In the same way, chimney stacks are traditionally of brick that, except for the vicinity of the firebox and mantel, was camouflaged with layers of plaster. Yet in recent years, many walls and chimney breasts have had their plaster coverings removed and the brick and mortar left exposed. The builders almost certainly would be embarrassed to have their masonry work revealed for all to see: their intention was for the regularity of the plaster to obscure the rough masonry. But in an historical irony, we have come to value the signs of the handmade, even when it's poor workmanship. Think about the original context before making such changes.

BE HONEST. Don't try to make a house something it never was. Don't try to make the Victorian look Colonial. Don't try to make solid middle-class housing into a mansion fit for a robber baron. Recognize what you have, respect it, and work with it.

MIXING PERIODS. A challenge to any remodeler is the mixture of times that are (or will be) evident in the remodeled house. If you are restoring a period house to its original appearance, the challenge is to do it with absolute fidelity. But most of us, however, want to make our houses suit our needs.

Changes made over time add a fourth dimension: there is no one date and, in fact, there could be several dates of significance. Among preservationists there is a consensus that later changes can have equal validity to original construction. Good workmanship may have been followed by better workmanship. We've already discussed saving good old work, but don't let any one era dictate all your decisions. Modern conveniences are essential to most people. Even if you're remodeling a house that is only a few decades old, the technology has changed and you will probably be updating kitchen appliances and adding bathrooms. Perhaps you'll be modifying heating and cooling systems. Respect the evolution of your home as you go about changing it. Consider all the earlier changes as equal until proven otherwise; then decide what works for you and what doesn't.

A MAGIC FORMULA? At this stage, you should also be developing some kind of informal formula that you can use to help you make decisions about your renovation. We're not talking about an unbreakable law of nature that dictates *Yes, you can do that* or *No sir, no way.* It's subtler than that. There are variables to be factored in, personal and architectural and economic considerations.

In the simplest possible terms, the best remodeling results from a carefully calculated mix of good old work and appropriate new work. On the face of it, the formula is just simple arithmetic. But there's an overlay, too.

I don't believe every homeowner needs to be slavishly consistent to the original configuration and detailing of the house. I don't take a purist's approach. However, the straightest road to a bad remodeling job is to pay no attention at all to what you're starting with.

Making Plans

Chapter 4

Thinking Through the Design

With a thorough understanding of your existing house, you are now equipped to think about changing it. It's time to define the task and to put some notion of what you want to do on paper.

You need to decide whether the task consists of adding new space, improving existing space, or simply putting unused space to use. You may be adding something entirely new onto an existing home; perhaps you're finishing the unfinished, converting a basement or attic into a livable, finished space; or you may be transforming what you already have in your home or apartment.

Doubling the size of your house with a new addition is not the same as, say, putting a second bath in that small back bedroom, but the steps in the

You probably have a lot more to start with than just a doorway. But even this remnant of a nineteenth-century entryway might prove to be an inspiration to the right customer.

process *are* essentially the same. The bigger the project, the more time, money, and headaches are involved, but it is generally a matter of more of the same elements.

Regardless of the scope of your project, the first step is to decide what you want and need. Thus, you need to explore those desires. The next step toward actual construction, will be to create—or have created—plans that conform to the requirements of local building ordinances. That will be the subject of the next chapter. But in moving toward those plans, you need to make numerous subjective decisions about style and materials and answer a multitude of questions for yourself or your architect/designer.

So consider the questions that follow. They will help you develop a feeling for a design you can live with.

Asking Questions

People with no formal design training—and that describes most homeowners— often have difficulty expressing their architectural likes and desires. They may be able to identify what they don't like—*I really thought her new kitchen was awful, didn't you?*—but articulate and thoughtful men and women frequently get tongue-tied when it comes to describing what they want from a renovation. They hear themselves muttering platitudes like, *I want it to have, you know, a spacious feel . . . and I want it to look great, of course . . . and be light and efficient and warm and friendly and not too expensive . . . yes, that's what I want.* All of which conveys exactly nothing.

Before you seek professional assistance with your design, which we'll also discuss in Chapter 5, I recommend you consider some basic issues. Whether you plan to talk directly to a contractor or to begin by hiring a designer, you will save both of you time and trouble if you have already considered some of the questions he or she will ask you.

This is not a test. There are no right or wrong answers. The purpose is to help you identify what it is you want both for yourself and, in a while, for the professionals you hire to effect the renovation. Don't be in too much of a hurry as you think about these questions. Some of them may seem irrelevant or elementary, but consider how you would phrase your answers if a design professional were to pose the questions. It is what's on your mind that he'll be interested in and you need to be able to communicate your needs and desires clearly.

Another purpose of this exercise is to stimulate your thinking. The questions that follow may get you to consider some key issues that you haven't thought about before. Get other members of your family involved in this brainstorming, too. If you all have to live there, get everybody to contribute.

LOCATION. ***Will your renovated house out-price the neighborhood?*** The underlying assumption of this book is that the house or apartment you plan to renovate exists. So in that sense, location is not at issue here. Yet where your house is affects many other decisions.

I know, I know, you've heard it before, but I still have say it: The three most important factors in determining real estate value are *location, location,* and *location.* As someone considering a remodeling, you would be wise to proceed with this old truism in mind.

In practice, it means that if your house is already the most expensive in your neighborhood by far, you are unlikely to recoup the cost of any remodeling work. Proceed, if you wish, but do it because you are satisfying a need of yours and not because you're expecting the project will enhance the value of your house. On the other hand, if your house is worth less than those around it, good renovation work should make it more valuable.

As you think about your renovation, keep the larger context of your home in mind, too. Different regions and neighborhoods come complete with unwritten rules. In staid old Boston, subdued and tasteful are preferred over the gaudy. In the Florida heat, hotter colors are more welcome. In California, there's a premium on natural materials. If you're a newcomer to a region, consider whether your design ideas conflict with the prevailing tastes. You can do what you want, regardless of what your neighbors think, but you risk paying for the work a second time when you try to sell the house and potential buyers don't like what you've done.

SITE. ***Are there features of your property that you want to use or need to work around in planning your renovation?*** Perhaps extensive landscaping will be necessary, or you'll be moving an existing driveway or adding a new walkway. Elements in the

The context here is unavoidable: These three-story houses are very much the same. If I were to renovate one of them, I'd try to stay true to the original spirit of the streetscape, maintaining the setback, detailing, and other common elements.

hardscape, plantscape, or overall landscape may need to be changed to accommodate the renovated house.

Do you have a site plan? Unless your job involves only the remodeling of interior spaces, you will probably have to file a site plan with the building department. A survey may have been done at the time you bought the property, but if no survey exists, you may need to arrange for a surveyor to conduct one or pay your designer an additional fee to do his own site inspection. Ideally, you should also have a topographical map of the property as you think about the landscape and try to communicate your vision to others.

ORIENTATION. Do you want to reorient the facade of the house toward or away from the street? Perhaps there is a view you want to welcome into your new master bedroom suite, or one you want to fence off so you don't have to look at it each time you wash dishes in your new kitchen.

Depending upon where you live, you may want to employ or avoid the heat of the sun. In the summer, it passes higher in the sky; in the winter its path is lower.

What about the sun? Many successful designs try to locate the kitchen so that it receives east (morning) light, and dining or relaxation areas to take advantage of afternoon sun. If no one in your household cares about a sunny breakfast space, then perhaps it makes more sense to make that the office area. You live there and you understand your site best. Think about how the sun travels around your house and how you would like to see it welcomed into your home.

Light and heat decisions are also influenced by climate. Those of us who live amid snow and brutal cold much of the year welcome the sun. In a tropical or subtropical area, you'll need to minimize the effects of the sun's rays, especially during the hottest hours of the day. Factor the climate into your thinking.

ZONING, EASEMENTS, AND SETBACKS. *What other constraints will you need to deal with?* As we discussed in Chapter 1, you may also have to deal with external dictates. Your municipality may have zoning limitations. There may be maximum heights specified for residential buildings. Setbacks are often established to keep building density down by creating unbuilt areas to act as buffers. Such setbacks require that no structure be closer to the street than a set distance (often 30 or 35 feet). Side boundary buffers of 10 feet or more are common; rear boundaries of 25 feet or more are also usual.

In the same way, easements may prohibit the construction of houses or additions closer than specified distances to natural phenomena like bluffs, streams, or even scenic vistas. Determine whether there are setbacks or easements on the books in your community. And are there right-of-ways or other limitations on your deed? How about utility easements? Except in instances where changes can be negotiated in these requirements—and sometimes they can—you'll have to work around them.

If you do want to make changes, be sure you follow the proper procedures. I know of one well-to-do Pennsylvanian who wanted to fence in his expensively landscaped garden to protect it from deer. He knew that his driveway had once been a through road, but it had fallen into disuse. He had a casual conversation with a town official who told him with a shrug he didn't think a fence would be a problem. So the property owner went ahead and enclosed a large plot of land within a 12-foot tall fence.

Almost immediately, several old-timers in town complained and the town board ruled that once a road, always a road, and that the landowner had no unilateral right to fence it off. Most of the tall perimeter fence remains, but it deters few deer because of a 20-foot gap that must legally remain open. The lesson? Find out who you have to talk to in order to complete the paperwork that is required, and then live up to the letter of the law. In the end, it'll prove simpler.

THE SIZE. *If you are planning an addition, how large would you like it to be?* Will you be adding bedrooms? If so, how many? Will you be adding a family room? A separate dining room? An eat-in kitchen? Office?

Make a list of the spaces you want. How many rooms have you at present? How many are you thinking about adding? Consider the existing rooms and compare them to your vision of the new spaces. Are the volumes you're talking about adding similar to those in the original house? You don't have to mimic what exists but, as we discussed in Chapter 3, houses that look like a unified whole generally appeal to the eye.

THE STYLE. ***What style is your house?*** In Chapter 2, we talked at length about style. Thinking about your home and the changes you would like to make in its architectural context can help resolve a range of problems and questions. Identifying other houses in the same style that have elements you admire can be useful in thinking through the design. Collect pictures, clippings, or photocopies in a folder for reference. Keep a few photographs of your house there, too, for comparing and contrasting.

THE EXTERIOR. ***What establishes the character of the exterior finish of your house?*** Is the siding wood, stone, brick, aluminum, or vinyl? What style are the windows— double hung, casement, awning, sliding, skylights? What about the trim: Is it flat, thin, and nondescript or decorated, molded, carved, or bold? Are there decorative elements you like/don't like such as pilasters, balusters, window boxes, porches, doorway or window decorations?

THE INTERIOR. ***What are your specific room-by-room requirements?*** Every family is different. In musical families, room may be needed for a piano, or an appropriate space designated for trombone practice. Consider the house room by room.

Entry/vestibule area. Is more closet space required? Are there tables, chairs, or other furniture to be planned for? What would you like the floor covering to be? Here and elsewhere in the house, are there special wall or ceiling surfaces or would you like certain finishes? Most new interior wall and ceiling surfaces today are by default drywall construction. Make a note if you want paneling or some other finish. How about the lighting, windows, and doors? Is there another entrance to the house, or should there be, such as a mud room or garage entry?

Kitchen. Lighting is critical in the kitchen. Is it adequate or is that on your list of changes? Will you be changing the floor covering? What about the appliances: Do you know the size and kind of refrigerator you need? A separate freezer? A range or independent cooktop and wall oven? Dishwasher(s)? Are the washer and dryer to be located in the kitchen? Do you want an eat-in kitchen? If so, for how many? Do you want visual access to dining or living areas or for the kitchen to be a discrete space?

Dining room. Is a separate dining room necessary? Do you have pieces of furniture that must be accommodated in the design? What about floor coverings and wall or ceiling surfaces? Seating for how many at the table will be required?

Living room. Are there sofa, chairs, rugs, artwork, or other furniture or decorative elements to be planned for? Is there a fireplace or do you wish to add one? What activities do you anticipate this room will be used for? Do you entertain often? If so, how many people must you allow for? Lighting design can be important here, too, so note your concerns.

Family room. What activities do you anticipate this room will be used for? Are there special furniture requirements (e.g., pool table, projection TV screen)? How about closet or storage requirements? Bookshelves? Computer desk? Phone lines? Have you concerns about floor covering or wall or ceiling surfaces?

Master bedroom. Do you want a private bath or separate dressing room in a master bedroom complex? Is special soundproofing necessary? For your clothes closet, how many linear feet of hanging space do you require?

Children's bedrooms. How many separate bedrooms do you require? How much closet space for each? In addition to a bed and dresser, must each room include space for a desk, dressing table, or computer? Will you need a phone jack in each room?

Guest bedroom. What are the basic requirements: just a bed and dresser? What about closets, television, or phone? Will this room have its own bath? When it's not occupied by a guest, will it have family purposes, such as hobbies, home office, play, or study space?

Bathrooms. How many do you need? Where are they (or will they be) located? One each on the first and second floor? One in the master bedroom complex? A half bath downstairs? Is a bathtub required in a new bathroom? A shower? A circulating or whirlpool bath? What about towel storage? A linen closet? Bidet? Special floor coverings? Distinct wall or ceiling surfaces?

Office or den. Will you need a desk? Chairs? What are your storage or closet requirements? Will there be furniture elements like filing cabinets or bookshelves?

Utility room. What will the space contain? HVAC equipment? Washer and dryer? Hot water heater? Have you additional storage requirements?

Other spaces. Does the photographer in your house require a darkroom? Is there a need for special storage of old files? Is there to be a basement workshop? Do you need a garage? A deck? Greenhouse? Wine cellar? Stable, shed, other outbuildings? Do you dream of a fireplace in the family room?

ROOM RELATIONSHIPS. *Are there some rooms that you would group together, others you would separate?* For example, most people would prefer the master bedroom at one end of the house and the children's rooms at the other. Do you want the nursery adjacent to the master bedroom? Would you put the living room away from the master bedroom? List your priorities.

MECHANICAL NEEDS. Perhaps the best time to update or modify the working systems of the house is while other construction is taking place. Does the house have central air conditioning? How about zoned heating? Will the existing electrical entrance provide adequate power or do you need to upgrade? Is the existing wiring safe? Is the existing plumbing, both supply and drain lines, in good condition?

SPECIAL CONCERNS. *Are you anticipating any changes in the usual patterns of your home?* For example, are you expecting another child? Will some or all of your children shortly be leaving the nest? Will an elderly parent be coming to live with you? If you are remodeling, is your present house energy inefficient, and should you be considering retrofitting it with insulation or another heat source?

Have you considered all of your special needs in specifying your rooms? Keep in mind such issues as privacy, the individual hobbies practiced by members of the household, any contradictory schedules of household members, lighting needs, noise factors, and so on.

THE COST. *How much can you spend?* This may be the most important question of all as, directly or indirectly, the level of investment you can make will determine everything about your remodeling. In Chapter 6, we'll talk about pricing and estimating, but even to open a design dialogue, you need to know what you can spend. The budget frames everyone's thinking as plans are made and construction proceeds.

Most designers and contractors work with tight budgets everyday; they will conscientiously try to work within the limits you establish. But you need to be clear about what you have to spend, what you expect for your money.

The Work to Be Done

At this stage, you should be able to describe in ten words or less the nature of the remodeling you would like to have done. Much more can be said about size, configuration, style, finish, and other details, but in the simplest possible terms, how would you answer a friend or neighbor who inquires, *I hear you're thinking of remodeling?*

In general terms, the options are these:

We're planning a minor remodeling of existing living space. A job of this sort will involve no major changes in partitions or the overall shape of the space being remodeled. The electrical, plumbing, and HVAC services are also to remain essentially unchanged. Such jobs might involve new cabinets, appliances, or even the arrangement of elements in the kitchen; retiling a bath; plastering and painting; adding wainscoting, wallpaper, or other surface finishes; sanding, carpeting, or reflooring; adding or installing bookcases or built-ins; and so on. Minor remodelings may involve a designer, carpenter, or painter, but probably will not require filing for a building permit or hiring plumbers and electricians.

MAXIMIZING YOUR REMODELING DOLLAR

The average American is said to move every five to seven years. As that statistic suggests, you would be wise to think carefully about how you spend your renovation dollars. The odds are that in the not-so-distant future, you will be trying to recoup your expenditure when you're getting ready to move on to your next dwelling.

Not every home improvement or renovation will bring a healthy return on investment. So which will enhance the value of your house? Kitchen and bathroom renovations usually more than pay for themselves. Some experts believe that for every dollar well spent in bath or kitchen renovations, the value of the house increases by two dollars, though some studies are more conservative (one recent survey found that on average sellers recouped better than 90 percent of the dollars they had invested in kitchen remodelings). Painting, stripping, and such cosmetic work typically pay for themselves, but other work is less of a sure thing.

Remodeling the kitchen. Most of us, consciously or unconsciously, tend to think of the kitchen as an indicator of the quality of a house. A well-equipped, efficient, and attractive kitchen makes the potential buyer feel immediately at home. Conversely, an outdated kitchen will leave the buyer thinking it's a problem to be solved. Thus, if you're planning a kitchen renovation, consider both what you want and need *and* what will leave future buyers with the best impression.

Quality is important—both for you and them. Durable and attractive materials like stone counters, hardwood cabinets, and imported tile can help convey a sense of the well-made. Make sure you have ample storage and counterspace. Good lighting is important, too, especially over cooking surfaces, the sink, and food preparation areas. In medium-size or larger kitchen, eating areas, whether at tables or islands, add to the life of a house, involving other family members and guests with the cook's activities. Brand-name appliances are another good way of conveying a sense of quality.

Bathrooms. Bathrooms are second only to the kitchen in maximum benefit for the buck (according to one survey, better than 80 percent of remodeling costs are recouped on average in subsequent home sales). If you have no bath on the first floor of your multistory house, a half bath is an excellent investment—both for your comfort *and* the resale value of the house. Private baths off master bedrooms are also popular, but be wary of an overly large master suite. Some homeowners have discovered the hard way that too many square feet devoted to dressing areas, workout space, and bath-shower-whirlpool combinations can be an expensive waste of space and money. Good tile work and quality fixtures (new or antique) also add value. For a modest investment, handsome towel bars and other hardware can add considerably to the finish. The installation of two sinks can make the new bathroom twice as efficient on a workday morning.

Decks, window and siding replacement, home office installations. In terms of financial returns, these projects are next, recouping on average roughly 70 percent of the costs invested. Decks offer indoor-outdoor spaces that add significantly to living areas for minimum cost. Replacing windows and siding can offer considerable energy savings, as well as make the house more attractive. With more and more small businesses being run from home offices, a well-appointed office space can also be a selling point when it comes time to move on.

Floors, moldings, and woodwork. Whatever the nature of the job, the materials you choose will have an impact on the perceived value of the work. Hardwood floors are good investments. They're durable, warm, and attractive. After the stripped-down starkness of the seventies, moldings, casework, and other woodwork have made a major comeback. Bold cornice moldings can add formality to a room. Chair and picture rails are practical and attractive additions that define surfaces and set off furnishings. Consult with your designer about appropriate profiles and scales for moldings, since they should reflect not only your tastes but the vintage and quality of the existing home.

Lighting. Individual lighting fixtures can be surprisingly expensive, yet a few new light fixtures may be the most cost-effective way of "remodeling" a house. Without changing anything else, a new lighting design can add drama, convenience, and character to a house. Certain kinds of fixtures can draw attention to themselves, while others are almost invisible but emphasize other elements. Good light can also make your life in the house more comfortable. (See also The Lighting Designer, page 180.)

Basement and attic conversions. If you're going to remodel spaces downstairs, be sure that the space is light and dry enough. Your remodeling dollars won't be well spent if the first impression people get is of darkness and damp. Sometimes designers can, however, design imaginative solutions to illuminate downstairs spaces, using a mix of natural and artificial light.

If you're going upstairs, beware of too little headroom. Or of a narrow or steep stairway. If the place is going to feel cramped from day one, consider alternative approaches. Light and ventilation are crucially important, too. Roof windows and dormers can help.

Closets. Think about it: Have you ever heard anyone say they have too much closet space? Unless they intrude on other spaces, closets are always improvements.

Other factors. In this era of fax machines and the Web, more than one phone line and plenty of phone jacks are a small but appealing selling point (and a convenience while you're in residence). Modest landscaping involving shrubs, trees, foundation plantings, stonework, or small perennial beds almost always pay for themselves. Faux building materials like vinyl siding and fake brick make a house look plastic.

Keep in mind the delicate balance between what you want and what the next owner will need. That tension can sometimes be a tie-breaker in the decision-making process.

Another way to save money may be to use architectural salvage. In this picture alone there are the makings of an imaginative addition—the pairs of arch-toped windows, a mantel, paneled doors, and a variety of window sash. One or several of these elements might, at modest cost, add character to a new space.

155

ONE SIMPLE HOUSE

When originally constructed about 1820, this house was pretty basic: a center entrance, gable roofed house. Its only decorative detail was the band-sawn trim that lined its cornice.

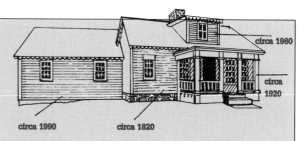

circa 1960

circa 1920

circa 1990

circa 1820

Sometime before 1900, the first of its additions was attached at the rear. In the next few years, other changes were made. A galleried porch was added, probably during the 1920s. A later dormer provided more light and space to the second floor. In the early 1990s, an L was added, as well, nearly doubling the size of the house.

Despite having been built in at least four or five stages, this house has an integrity about it. One reason is that each of the remodelers was wise enough to recognize the importance of that band-sawn trim, and adopted it for the added elements. Like the ribbon on a package, it unifies the whole.

The basic house, circa 1900.
Photo credit: John A. Eberle, Red Rock Historical Society

The house with porch and dormer added.

The house today, with its addition.

We're planning a major remodeling of existing living space. These are bigger jobs, for which a building permit is probably required. In a major remodeling, partitions might be added or removed. This may involve *bearing walls*, these being walls that support the structure above. In most instances bearing walls can be removed or at least modified after structural alterations have been made that safely redistribute their loads. If new plumbing lines or electrical circuits are required or new openings need to be cut in exterior walls for doors or windows, your job will also classify as a major remodeling.

Typical projects of this sort would be the opening of two or more interior spaces into one; the addition of a new bath; a kitchen remodeling in which new plumbing risers or electrical circuits are required; or the installation of a new central HVAC system, electrical service, staircase, fireplace or chimney, or exterior doors or windows.

We're converting unfinished space to living area. It may be in the attic, basement, porch, or garage. But you've decided to add the space to your living quarters. This probably will require building department approval, as there is likely to be electrical work, as well as fire and building code issues.

In the case of an attic conversion, you need to consider a range of questions. Is there adequate headroom (most codes require ceilings that are a minimum of 7½ feet tall)? Do the stairs meet code and safety requirements? Is there adequate light and ventilation? Do you need to add dormers? How about skylights or "roof windows"? Will you need one or more additional electrical circuits? Plumbing risers and waste pipes? How will the space be insulated?

A cramped attic space can, with the addition of dormers (or roof windows), become a livable and even welcoming space.

If you propose to remodel a basement, your list of concerns will be similar, with light and ventilation uppermost. Again, stairs will be an issue, as will electrical and perhaps plumbing lines. Dampness is often a big problem downstairs: If you have a wet basement, converting it into living space may not be the answer you're looking for. With either a *garage* or a cellar conversion, you'll probably need to identify a means of covering a concrete floor.

We're going to put on an addition. Putting on an addition is a bit like building a new house: you'll need new foundation; frame; walls, floor, and roof surfaces; windows and doors; and all the connective tissues, too, like wires, pipes, insulation, and HVAC connections. An addition will certainly require a building permit and I'd recommend hiring a designer or architect to help you think through the delicate matter of integrating the new structure into the existing one.

Drawing and Measuring Your Home

When it comes to architectural renderings, I have two recommendations: First, make a few preliminary sketches yourself and, second, leave the finished drawings to the professionals. This isn't as paradoxical a strategy as it sounds. For a complete novice, making simple drawings can be easy and the benefits great. After a couple of hours spent measuring your house and rendering the spaces on a few sheets of graph paper, I guarantee you'll have a better understanding of the place. And in Chapter 5, we'll talk about communicating all that newfound knowledge to an architect or designer.

Now, though, it's time to sharpen your pencils. . . .

MEASURING THE HOUSE. The key drawing is the floor plan. To draw one, you'll need two tape measures, one 50 feet long and another that's 16 feet in length. (If you don't own two such tapes, they're good investments. Inexpensive tapes can be bought for less than ten dollars each and will be handy later, too, when you're monitoring construction progress, laying out a garden, doing home repairs, whatever).

For the beginning draftsman, quarter-inch graph paper makes the drawing job immensely easier. During this measuring and preliminary sketching stage, you don't have to worry about rulers and square corners. You can rely on the grid to keep you from getting too far off.

Start with a single room. Begin by drawing a rough approximation of its shape on your graph paper. Be sure to mark off all the fixed elements, including windows, doors, built-ins, radiators, fireplaces, and appliances.

Starting at the corners, measure the overall length and width of the room. The measurements should be from wall to wall, not molding to molding. Don't worry about eighths and sixteenths of an inch—round off dimensions to the nearest half inch ($\frac{3}{8}$ becomes $\frac{1}{2}$, $\frac{7}{8}$ the next inch, $\frac{1}{8}$ the previous one, and so on).

Record the measurements on your sketch. Having a helper will save you time. The second person can not only hold the end of the tape but can write while you call out measurements.

Next measure the distances between the elements. Note those measurements on your drawing, too. Now, look again at what you have: Did you miss anything? And check your work: Add the shorter distances along one wall to be sure their sum is equal to the overall length. If the numbers don't add up, go back and measure again.

MAKING A DRAWING. On a fresh piece of graph paper, start anew. This time identify the longest dimension and determine the largest scale you can use to fit the room onto the sheet. Depending upon the room's size, the scale might be four quarter-inch-squares per foot, meaning 1 inch of the drawing represents 1 foot of the actual dimension of the room. That would allow a small bathroom of about 7 feet by 10 feet to fit comfortably onto an 8½-by-11-inch sheet of paper. Two squares to the foot would allow for a room that's roughly 15 by 20 feet, and so on.

Plot the outside dimensions of the room first. Next locate the openings, the

159

HOME-PLANNING KITS

You'll find them advertised in the shelter magazines. Home-planning kits come with a large grid that resembles a game board, and a lot of preprinted symbols for furniture, appliances, cabinets, fixtures, and architectural symbols. You can then recreate your existing house and add to it as you wish. Specialty kits are sold for kitchen and bathroom renovations. There's even a 3-D kit on the market to help you make a cardboard model.

If you have a fear of sketching, a kit may be the answer to thinking through your design.

doors and windows. Put the interior wall thicknesses in, too (they're easiest to measure at the doorways).

Locate the other fixed elements.

USING THE DRAWING. Now that you have a basic plan, you can experiment. I find making little scale models of couches, tables, chairs, and other elements helps in thinking about what you have and what you want to change. Position them in order to see what works for you. In the case of a kitchen renovation, for example, it's a simple matter to photocopy your basic plan and then vary it with different configurations. You can make the room bigger. You can add an L. Or blow out a wall. How about eliminating a closet? Or combining the dining room and kitchen?

One discovery you may make when you draw a room is that your dreams are bigger than the reality. Often spaces that seem large enough to accommodate mixed uses are not, and it's suddenly apparent when you draw in that new kitchen island, breakfast nook, and pantry. They won't all fit. That's one of the purposes of such drawing: You are continuing to educate yourself about your spaces and what you can reasonably expect.

Once you've drawn one room, adding others is more of the same.

These drawings won't make you an artist or designer. Having made them, however, will prove a tremendous advantage as you try to identify for the design professional or contractor you hire what it is you want and expect. These drawings are a first step toward describing in visual terms what you want to do.

COMPUTER-ASSISTED DRAWING. Most architectural firms these days rely on computer-assisted-drawing (CAD) programs. Consumer versions of such software

are available from a number of different publishers. Will they save you time in making basic drawings? If you're computer literate and adept with a mouse then, yes, probably, the investment of time and money (roughly $50 for a basic program) makes sense because, in the end, you'll be able to do additional drawings quickly and move on to other sorts of drafting tasks, too. On the other hand, if you don't often venture into cyberland, it'll probably take a fair amount of practice and experimentation to execute even a simple drawing. It's your call.

Complying with the Code

Another set of constraints you need to keep in mind is the building code. A building code is a collection of regulations regarding building construction that is intended to ensure public safety. Not all codes are identical, however, as they vary from one jurisdiction to another. There are state codes, city codes, and town codes, and more than one may apply to your job. Although the contractors you hire will assume the responsibility for meeting code specifications, a rudimentary knowledge of building codes may be useful as you consider your renovation.

Among the restrictions that may concern you are these:

CEILING HEIGHT. The standard is for a minimum of 7 feet, 6 inches for habitable areas. Exceptions may be made for kitchenettes, bathrooms, and cellar conversions. Keep this in mind, particularly if you're converting existing space in the attic or basement.

FENESTRATION. According to most codes, a room is not a room unless it has a window. This applies consistently to bedrooms, living rooms, and dining rooms, although in some places bathrooms and kitchens may be deemed habitable if they have adequate mechanical ventilation. In some municipalities, no room that is below grade is classifiable as a habitable space.

STAIRWAYS. The requirements for stairways typically specify a minimum overall width. The treads must not be too shallow (from the nosing at the front to the junction with the riser at the rear); the risers should be of consistent height and not too

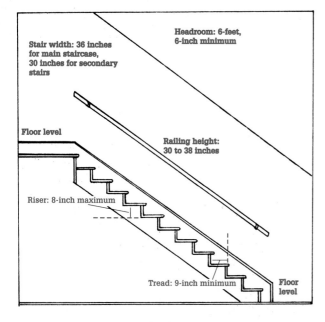

Stair width: 36 inches for main staircase, 30 inches for secondary stairs

Headroom: 6-feet, 6-inch minimum

Floor level

Railing height: 30 to 38 inches

Riser: 8-inch maximum

Tread: 9-inch minimum

Floor level

tall. Angled treads called *winders* (they're shaped like slices of pie and are often used when a stairway changes direction) may be prohibited except on secondary staircases. The rules on railings specify height, strength, and location. If you are converting existing space in an attic or basement, the code may require that you substantially rebuild original stairs that are inadequate or that you add a second run of stairs.

FIREPLACES, CHIMNEYS, AND WOODSTOVES. Most codes specify a clearance of 2 inches between the wood frame and all elements of a masonry mass. New chimneys must be lined, either with clay tile or steel, and be of a specified height with relation to the peak of the roof. Spark protectors may be required at the cap of the chimney; dampers may be specified at the throat. The outer hearth of the fireplace must extend a minimum of 16 inches in front of the firebox; on either side, there must be a clearance of at least 6 inches between the firebox and any flammable materials. The firebox may have to be built with fire brick. Woodstoves must meet similar installation criteria regarding fireproof materials and clearances.

Building code requirements vary considerably, but the code in effect in your area may prescribe commonsense standards like these for constructing a new staircase.

ELECTRICAL CODES. The electrical code is a discipline unto itself and, again, it varies considerably from one jurisdiction to another. Some codes require all wires in the walls be sheathed in armored metallic cable; most permit the use of nonmetal sheathed cable. The gauge of the wire must be suited to the load at one end and to the fuse or circuit breaker at the other; thus, a kitchen circuit with several wall *receptacles* (outlets) will be wired with 12 gauge wire and a 20 ampere breaker or fuse. In new construction, there are requirements regarding the number and location of receptacles, indoors and out; the gauge and type of wire used in different applications; whether electrical boxes can be plastic or galvanized metal; and so on. All receptacles must be grounded (a safety feature that directs any wayward electrical current that results from an electrical malfunction to the ground rather than through

162

you; the third prong on a plug is there for that purpose). Most codes also require ground-fault interrupters on bathroom, kitchen, and exterior receptacles (GFIs are safety devices that function as secondary fuses and will, in the event of a fault in the ground, shut off power to the outlet and prevent electrical shock). The bottom line? Even if local ordinances don't require it, hire a licensed electrician to do the wiring required on your job. In any case, many codes require that you do so.

PLUMBING CODES. Given the variety of needs in a modern house, plumbing codes, too, tend to be complex. And variable, as well, since some municipalities prohibit the use of plastic pipe, others permit it. Some allow it to be used for waste lines only, some for supply lines as well. Lead solder is forbidden for joining copper pipes in some places; in others, it's permitted.

Even after you've established what's acceptable in your area, the language of plumbing can be mind-numbing. There's PVC, ABS, and PB plastic pipe; metal pipes may be copper, brass, black iron, cast iron, or galvanized steel. The fittings that join the pieces together range from couplings and caps to tees and street ells to elbows and nipples. There are unions, Ys, P-traps, straps, and clamps. And that's even before you get into fixtures and faucets and their miscellaneous parts. As with electrical work, major plumbing is best left to the licensed professionals. With HVAC plumbing, wiring, and ductwork? Again, I'd recommend you consult with the pros.

FIRE CODES. Fire codes also tend to be long and complicated, specifying the use of noncombustible materials on the roof, furnace area, and partition walls between an attached garage and the home. Some codes prohibit the use of certain plastic products because they give off toxic fumes when burned; others require that rigid insulation be covered by a noncombustible surface for the same reason. Then there are fire-stop requirements in wood-framed structures, meaning strips of wood must be placed in wall bays between stories and between joists where they pass over partitions to prevent the spread of fire. Smoke alarms are virtually universal today.

THE LETTER AND THE SPIRIT OF THE LAW. Elements of older houses often don't meet current code requirements, having been built before the code was written or enforced. If that is so in your house, you may want to bring into compliance conditions that are dangerous and out-of-date.

Yet that isn't always necessary or appropriate, as most codes, by necessity, take a one-size-fits-all approach. So, for example, antique fireplaces and stairways often don't meet code. Old wooden exterior doors may also fall short. When it comes to existing work that is not demonstrably dangerous, however, only an overzealous building inspector will demand that changes be made. If the code officer asks for changes that you think are unnecessary or would detract from the historic character of your house, explain why you are reluctant to make the change. Or try to reach a compromise. There may be an appeal process as well. Good old work is worth fighting for if there's no issue of safety but merely a desire by the code officer to enforce the building code.

Taking the Next Step

Imagine for a moment that the renovation you've been considering has been completed. After countless conversations with designers, contractors, plumbers, and painters, your house is once again your own. The toolboxes, sawdust, and drop cloths are gone. At last.

Follow the fantasy a step further. You and your family have suffered through weeks of inconvenience but now it's all over except for a few lingering invoices. Friends and relatives, having heard about the ups and downs, the delights and the delays of the process, are clamoring to come over and have a look.

What do you want the first guests who come to see the finished product to think?

I can't answer that question for you. Some people want a jaw-dropping *Wow!* Others want a respectful silence or a few words of admiration. Perhaps you want to evoke surprise, laughter, or envy. But you should think about the impression you want to give others. The key people you have to satisfy are yourself and those with whom you share the house. Yet you may understand your own expectations a little better if you try to see them through someone else's eyes. At the very least, stepping away slightly from your own vision may enable you to describe what you see with a little added perspective. Because describe you must: Next, you'll be talking to the people who will help you make it reality.

Chapter 5

The Working Plans

This may surprise you but, even for the professional, home remodeling is a minefield of economic, architectural, and emotional (that's right, emotional) challenges. Let me explain.

An acquaintance of mine is a nationally known restoration architect. John Mesick of the Albany, New York, firm of Mesick, Cohen, Wilson, Baker, has worked on state houses and stately homes all over the country. His name is associated with works designed by Thomas Jefferson and Frank Lloyd Wright. But there's one kind of restoration he almost never does: He avoids working on homes, on houses that are to be inhabited by people going about their day-to-day lives.

That kind of work, he says, is laden with pitfalls. He reports it's actually easier to deal with a committee, as he often does with museum houses or other

Through old glimmerglass, a house of a certain age gains even more character.
Photo credit:
Hugh Howard

historic structures. Even with a range of competing interests, the complications are fewer than when dealing with a client who plans to live in a house.

"It's all so *emotional*," he says of working with homeowner clients. People simply don't have a critical distance when it comes to their own homes, he says. For John, serving the client's desires is often at odds with what he feels is his first obligation, that being to respect and conserve the historic structure. The man is a genius at what he does. But do you need a restoration architect with the highest standards to address your home renovation?

Probably not. If fact, you're more likely to want one whose top priorities include tending to your emotional needs. Yes, he or she should appreciate the existing structure, too, but you want a listener—as John points out, working on a private home is a very personal process. You'll probably need someone to help you face the ups and down of the renovation process, but that's only one of the criteria.

Before we talk about the others, however, you may be asking, *Why do I need a designer in the first place?*

That's a question worth pondering, too.

To Hire or Not to Hire

*I*f *I know what I want, why do I need a designer at all?* Perhaps you don't. But understand that, strange as it may seem, having an architect or designer is usually *more* important on a renovation job than for new construction. Countless plans exist for new houses—but no two renovations are alike. Your needs and requirements are site-specific and you can't just go out and buy a set of ready-made plans. And you will need plans.

Unless your remodeling is confined to cosmetics, you will need a building permit. Before issuing one, most municipalities require that you submit plans to the code officer. National, state, and local codes require close adherence to regulations regarding wiring, plumbing, structure, and even rubbish disposal. If you are planning on seeking a loan to underwrite a major renovation, your bank may also want to see professionally prepared blueprints. The detailed listing of materials that designers prepare are also necessary for getting accurate cost estimates.

In short, whether you draft them or someone else does, you'll probably need plans.

Do I need an architect or a designer? Most architects happily identify themselves as designers; on the other hand, a self-described designer usually is not an architect. Because they perform basically the same role in a typical remodeling job, I use the terms "architect" and "designer" more or less interchangeably in this book. However, most architects are licensed and have more academic training and professional experience. (See *The Architect versus the Designer,* page 171.)

Can't I just hire a contractor and work out the design with him? Well, you certainly could. People do it all the time. Many experienced contractors are as well equipped to deal with a simple remodeling as an architect. Some have established relationships with local code officers so the red tape is minimal. However, if you have some special needs or your house has some peculiarities, you may want to draw upon the design skill and training of a professional designer.

Some builders are quite good designers, but most are not. Though designers and builders often work closely together, the nature of what they do is fundamentally different. Architects and designers specialize in the abstract, in conceiving suitable configurations, shapes, and spaces. Builders are concerned with the concrete details of materials and fasteners and with the physical work of construction. The architect is a big-picture person, responsible for envisioning the whole. It is the carpenter's and the other tradesmen's jobs to be concerned with the individual parts.

In a sense, asking a builder to be your architect is like expecting an actor to write the play in which he is to perform. Certainly some actors are playwrights, and some builders are fine designers. More often, however, the disparate talents of the designer and builder are found in different people.

Can't I do the design myself? If you have design skills, that's another option. But are you sure that you know enough to do the job? The simplest definition of "design skills" is that you have had the training to execute drawings that are clear and complete enough for the inspector, carpenter, and other contractors to follow. But that's a bare minimum.

A good designer also has a working knowledge of ergonomics (human engineering), local building codes, materials, and costs, plus at least a modicum of *design sense*. That's an intangible. It's the ability to take a practical design problem and devise a solution that is both functional *and* aesthetically satisfying. If your design skills are such that you can draw the plans but aren't so sure you can bring a mix of vision and critical distance to the assignment, getting a pro is probably a good idea.

I'm planning to do the work myself, so why can't I design it myself? Again, you probably can. However, in most communities there are design requirements for significant renovation jobs. This won't apply to work that involves no more than repainting, new countertops, or other minor work, but for remodeling jobs that cost more than a certain sum, or that involve rewiring or new foundation work, the requirements are more rigorous. Which brings us full circle: You'll probably be required to submit plans that bear the stamp of a licensed architect or engineer. Such regulations were established for your protection, as well as that of your neighbors. The experts can help ensure that the work done at your house is consistent with fire and electrical codes and is structurally sound.

What are the other benefits of having a designer or architect on my team? Architects and designers cost money . . . but they can also save you money. In the short term, the savings may be reflected in more informed purchasing of materials and labor, as designers or architects may be familiar with economical solutions.

In the course of the job, there are fewer change orders when a design has been thought through thoroughly, and that is the essence of the designer's job. An architect will begin by asking many questions to elicit as much information from you as possible. This time spent in working through the design to anticipate problems can help avoid the need to make changes during construction that are invariably more expensive. A designer or architect may also help avoid code violations.

In the long term, good design work is as important to the resale value of your house as structural matters. If fact, you will cost yourself money in the future if you remodel your house (or "remuddle" it) by violating the integrity of the house's original design or even if you simply make the sort of small mistakes that often occur in the absence of a good designer. Examples of such mistakes are doors that open into other doors; mixed up window shapes that seem fine from inside but look all out of

THE ARCHITECT VERSUS THE DESIGNER

You will probably have a choice when you look for someone to help design your remodeling project. The most likely candidates will be *architects* or *designer-draftsmen.*

The architect. Architects are licensed by your state. Typically, an architect has passed a licensing examination, has at least a bachelor's degree in architecture, and has spent three years working in an architect's office. A registered architect must take legal responsibility for his or her work.

The architect's formal training involves a varied and complex curriculum. Courses such as strength of materials are just as important as those in design. The architect must know not only how materials look, but how they are used. As a result, he or she should be able to advise you on what materials distinctions really mean (e.g., hardwood versus softwood floors, porcelain-iron or fiberglass bathtubs, etc.) and devise appropriate solutions to the sorts of challenges remodeling older structures often present. The architect can help engineer structural changes, too.

The designer-draftsman. There are no licensing requirements for designers in most states. Theoretically, anyone could hang a shingle out tomorrow and call himself a designer. As a result, it is doubly important that you thoroughly establish the experience and proven abilities of a designer before making your hiring decision.

As a rule, home designers are less expensive than fully trained and licensed architects. But many specialize in certain kinds of work and bring much practical experience to certain tasks. Kitchen designers, for example, design nothing but kitchens; space planners often do commercial, office, or retail spaces.

Other candidates. Your carpenter can also be your designer. For a kitchen renovation, you may find a design consultant at your disposal at one of the "big box" houseware stores. Some of them can very efficiently slot their own cabinets and fittings into a software program and redesign an existing space. You may find plans for similar renovations in books, magazines, and other sources that, in collaboration with your carpenter, you can copy. Yet in many of these cases, too, you'd be better off paying for a few hours of design time to make sure the pieces of the puzzle fit together.

I need to add, however, that degrees and titles rarely tell the whole story. I've heard a lot of horror stories about highly trained but incompetent architects. On the other hand, one of the best remodeling designers I know is a sometime contractor who, having immersed himself in historic architecture and long acted as an intermediary between clients and architects, finally threw up his hands and said, *Hey, I can do that better than those guys can!* And he does.

Find a designer you can afford, whose skills are in proportion to the job you want done, and with a style that suits yours.

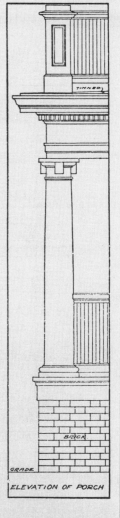

ELEVATION OF PORCH

proportion from outside; ideas adapted from magazines that looked just right in their original settings but seem grossly out of place in your house.

Perhaps the most important advantage of a skilled designer or architect? While the mere presence of one on your team won't guarantee a better finished product, the odds are greater that it will be well thought out. Often remodelings that were done *without* design help telegraph to the visitor, *No designer or architect worked here.*

Successful spaces are the result of good planning. Effective use of light, whether it's through intelligent fenestration or artificial illumination, helps, too. So does the right mix of materials, textures, and colors. The good architect/designer comes to every assignment with a body of experience, design training, and, perhaps most important, an open mind and a fresh eye. With luck, he or she will leave you with a satisfying living space that meets your needs and expectations.

What Kind of Design Help Do I Need?

A designer must be both creative and pragmatic. He or she must have an artist's eye for shapes and color. The designer must be able to envision the space being designed, and to anticipate the traffic patterns, airflow, and seasonal changes. In addition, the architect or designer needs to know the rules and regulations to be met in a given jurisdiction *and* have an accountant's expertise for balancing budgets. As if that were not enough, the designer must also conceive a design that suits the subjective tastes of the client.

While all designers should have each of these skills in some measure, not all designers are alike. Some have a great deal of design training, others have relatively little. Some are especially expert at solving complicated structural problems, others are more adept at devising decorative solutions. What kind of professional do you require? Must your designer be a fully licensed architect? Or will an experienced draftsman suffice? That depends upon the job and the experience of the designer. Consider the following questions. (See also The Designer-Draftsman, page 171.)

How complex is the job? In deciding which professional you need, a key consideration is the complexity of your renovation. One that involves structural change should be reviewed by a licensed architect or engineer who has been trained to resolve the special problems presented by removing beams, opening up cathedral ceilings, or otherwise changing the skeleton of the building and thereby shifting the loads it must bear. Architects and designers alike consult structural engineers when the going gets complicated, but if you are thinking of using a designer-draftsman, inquire whether he will consult an engineer if your design involves out-of-the-ordinary or outsize shapes.

How much design help do you really need? For small jobs, design help may be an unnecessary luxury. An experienced carpenter who has done dozens of similar jobs may have the necessary design skills to see you through a wide range of basic remodelings.

On the other hand, a good architect or designer has design experience to draw upon. When you look at a rabbit warren of tiny upstairs bedrooms in the old house you just bought, you may understand intellectually that there are many possibilities there. But the professional may see immediately that the addition of a dormer here, the removal of a wall there, and presto, in his very mind's eye, a brightly lit studio appears. To you, there are possibilities you can't quite see; to the architect, it's a matter of developing a clear image that can be put on paper. Then you get to review the possibilities.

The bottom line? If your project is very straightforward and requires essentially no imaginative brainstorming, you may be quite satisfied with the standard structure your contractor offers to build for you. But if you want something out of the ordinary, you need a professional to guide you in the design of your new house or addition. And sometimes design professionals pay for themselves simply by helping you avoid costly mistakes and assuring that you get what you want . . . not what you *think* you want.

On the other hand, if you are hiring an architect to supervise a contractor so you can be confident the job is being done just right, what you really need is a "construction manager" (see Hiring a Construction Manager, page 208).

How Much Will a Designer Cost?

The title "architect" conjures up in many people's minds fancy designer houses, monumental homes out of the pages of *Architectural Digest*. And, yes, it's true, people with a great deal of money often hire architects. But it isn't true that you have to be rich to afford an architect or designer.

The designer/architect is paid to perform several different tasks. You will be paying the designer to learn your house, your needs, and to develop a program for your renovation; for him or her to execute preliminary drawings for your review; and then to execute finished drawings once you are happy with the approach. The last part described is roughly half the job, the first two parts something like a quarter each. Should you hire your architect to supervise construction, that may increase the fee another 15 or 20 percent.

Design fees vary tremendously but there is a logic—remodeling a modest kitchen, say, will cost less than designing a large addition. The way fees are calculated varies, too, but most designers will work for a fixed design fee, a percentage of construction, or bill on a per-hour basis.

FIXED FEE. The fixed fee is just what the name suggests, an arrangement in which the architect and the client agree to a single price for the job. They also agree on what the job is so if there is a significant change from the original agreement (say, the addition doubles in size or budget), then the fee may be renegotiated. Otherwise, the fee agreed upon on day one should be the fee the client pays.

PERCENTAGE OF BUDGETED CONSTRUCTION COST. The fee will be a percentage of the total construction cost, generally 10 to 15 percent in residential construction. The greater the cost of construction, the lower the fee percentage should be.

The key word here is *budgeted*. The implication is that if you determine before breaking ground that the total cost is to be, say, $25,000, then it is the architect's job to complete the construction for $25,000, and his percentage will be of that sum. However, if the job ends up costing $35,000, there is no reason why he should be rewarded by being paid the same percentage of the higher cost, especially if he has been in charge of the process from the start. (One exception would be, however, where the cost overrun was the result of the client making changes and adjustments well into the process. In such cases, it is reasonable for the architect to expect additional payment for his additional services.)

Whatever the method of payment, the designer will want, as mentioned above, the bulk of his fee upon completion of the plans. If you do not plan to involve him in the supervision of the project, he'll want it all. After all, whether the designer is to be at your side throughout the process or not, he will have done the bulk of his job by the time the finished drawings are completed.

HOURLY RATE. This is perhaps the most common approach in renovation or remodeling jobs. At your first meeting, you agree to an hourly rate; depending upon the experience of the designer, fees may range from $50 an hour to many times that. If the price is too high, finding a less expensive designer is one answer, though many architects charge a lesser rate for the time spent by draftsmen employed in their offices.

If you opt for this arrangement, consider writing two safeguards into your understanding. First, negotiate an "upset price." We will discuss upset prices for construction contracts in detail in Chapter 6, but the concept is simple and sensible. You and the architect agree on a maximum fee; further, you agree on an hourly rate. Then he keeps track of the hours required to complete the job. If his hourly wages are less than the upset price, you pay the lower sum, but if they are more, that's his problem. You do not pay any more than the ceiling (the upset price) you agreed upon at the start.

The other safeguard (not only for this agreement, but for any agreement, as we'll discuss in Chapter 6) is a clearly stated payment schedule. You should agree to pay the architect for performance. Perhaps a small payment is due upon signing the contract, another on acceptance of the preliminary sketches, and so on. In this way, the architect gets paid as he works, but you also know exactly what you are paying for.

OTHER EXPENSES. It is common for architects to bill separately for extra expenses. These include reproduction costs (photocopying of blueprints), which shouldn't be more than a few hundred dollars and, for a modest remodeling job, much less. There may be a fee for the services of a specially trained structural or professional engineer, if required (an unusual design configuration or an addition to an older home that requires the existing structure to bear some of its weight are two circumstances that might call for such a consultation). The prices for engineering services vary greatly, so be sure your architect gives you an estimate up front. Another cost would be to prepare a survey that indicates the boundaries or contours or other aspect of your property; this might be required if you are putting on an addition. As with engineering fees, get an estimated cost from your architect for such a survey before it's done.

Finding the Right Designer

No other profession leaves such large tracks. The work that architects and designers do is hard to hide: buildings, or parts of buildings, draw the eye from far away as we drive or walk by. Regardless of whether or not we like what we see, houses are too big to ignore.

In the same way, when we enter other peoples' homes, most of us can't help but notice our surroundings. We are wowed by what we like, we cringe at what we don't. Mental notes get made about the dos and don'ts.

Often, such everyday means as looking and asking around help us find good designers, architects, and contractors. You see a design you like, and you inquire of the owner of the place whom he or she hired to create the space you admire. You ask for a fair appraisal of the designer's skill and professionalism. If you like both what you see and you hear, you can call the architect, make an appointment to meet, and get on with it.

A personal reference isn't always so easy, but if a friend, relative, or neighbor has recently had his or her home built or remodeled, ask for an assessment of the designer they used. Chances are you will get an unprejudiced evaluation—they like the result or they don't, the architect/designer was helpful and responsive or he wasn't, and so on. Occasionally you will get an insecure response from someone who isn't really satisfied with what he or she bought but is unwilling to acknowledge it because to do so would be to admit having made a mistake. But generally you'll get a pretty candid earful, and you may also be able to get a look at the architect's work to make up your own mind.

WHERE DO I FIND A DESIGNER? Ask friends, neighbors, or colleagues for the names of designers or architects' names. Ask your real estate broker and attorney.

Remodeling Style: Ideas and Options

Welcome to my house. That's right, this is my home, the one in Cambridge, Massachusetts, that I describe in the introduction to this book. Here's a look at what we see from the street . . .

. . . and at our **commodious and practical kitchen.**
PHOTO CREDIT: SAM GRAY

I've always thought that looking at *before* and *after* shots was a wonderful way of understanding the remodeler's craft. And this sequence is a great example. Believe it or not, this nondescript white ranch house *(top left)* was the starting point for the bold red home in the next three images. And it took more than a coat of Cherokee red paint—note especially the various roof lines and how much interest they add to the remodeled home. DENNIS WEDLICK, ARCHITECT

Sometimes a geometric shape on the exterior—such as a low-pitched roofline—can be reflected in the living space inside. In this Florida remodeling, the roof pitch of the portico is carried indoors to a gracious dining room. ANDREA CLARK BROWN, A.I.A.

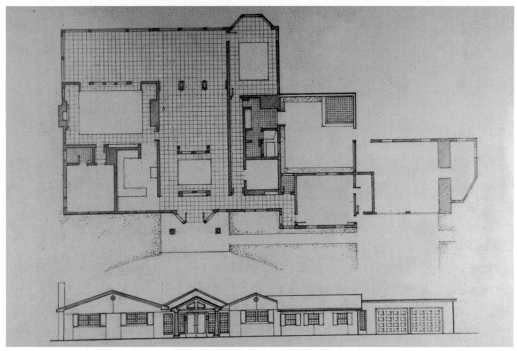

Dining rooms can be luxurious, or they can make you feel like you're enjoying a weekend in the country, as this casual dining room does. Note, too, the way it flows into the rest of this California home, with the kitchen on one end and the sitting room on the other.
TOM GOFFIGON/LT DESIGN

Speaking of kitchens, this apartment kitchen in New York might look familiar to you—both in its existing (*below*) and remodeled (*opposite*) incarnations. That's because this is the space delineated in the architectural plans reproduced in Chapter 5 (see pages 188–195). What once felt very cramped now looks very welcoming. The gridlike appearance on the face of the cabinetry proved one effective means of making this kitchen seem larger than it is. IAN J. COHN/DIVERSITY: ARCHITECTURE & DESIGN

If this stairway looks old to you, then your instincts are half right. In the remodeling done in this house, the existing balustrade was extended—the railing from the newel post on back to the basement stairs is all new. KATE JOHNS, A.I.A.

The classical tradition—so often drawn upon in nineteenth-century American architecture—has been reinvigorated and once again put to practical and decorative use in recent years. ALBERT, RIGHTER & TITTMANN; PHOTO CREDIT: STEVE ROSENTHAL

This antique light adds immeasurably to the character of this unadorned stairwell. Light fixtures are often expensive, but the investment may be worth it in one or another "show-off" space in your house.

Architecture isn't always about illusion, but don't underestimate the value of a little trickery now and again. In this picture, nothing more than a bit of paint and a bit more painterly skill have been employed to create the faux effect of a fabric swag. With the addition of the inexpensive border paper, the overall impact is appealing indeed.

ELIZABETH LAWRENCE PAINTWORKS

If, as the saying goes, God is in the details, then so is good design. Sometimes it isn't all new design, but the old and the familiar. This restored stove integrates beautifully with Fiestaware of the same vintage. Think about the objects you cherish in planning both the design and decoration of your remodeling.

TOM GOFFIGON/LT DESIGN

PHOTO CREDIT: PAUL WARCHOL

The dependable and practical Foursquare can be, well, a little stodgy. But with a wraparound porch to add breadth and detail, it takes on a new grace. DENNIS WEDLICK, ARCHITECT

Thoughtful plantings and hardscape can literally add to the living space of your home. Can't you imagine reading the newspaper on this comfortable patio space on a warm summer evening?

Fences can provide privacy, decoration, and even a sense of an earlier time.
ASHER BENJAMIN

Witness the transformation: You can see the new lighting, the granite fireplace surround, and the sense of order they add to this penthouse living room. What you can't see is that the scored sections on one side of the fireplace house audio and video equipment as well as log storage; the other is simply a matching panel. IAN J. COHN/DIVERSITY: ARCHITECTURE & DESIGN

Frank Lloyd Wright loved to make the doorway to
a home secondary; here, a calculated mix of plant
materials and a circuitous entrance route subtly
add privacy to this entrance.

The Yellow Pages will surely have some candidates, too, as will the Better Business Bureau in your area, and you can always check with the American Institute of Architects (1735 New York Avenue, N.W., Washington, D.C. 20006) for the licensed architects in your area. If you admire work in one of the shelter magazines, seek the architect cited. Ask around at the local lumberyard. Ask a local contractor for a suggestion, although you may have to discount disparaging comments he may make. Architects and contractors are often at odds with one another.

Without too much trouble you can get a list. Once you have a few candidates, however, don't think for a minute you are home free. Now your homework really begins, as not every designer will suit your needs, tastes, and personality.

Yet the decision to hire—or not to hire—should be made only after you meet the designer.

MEETING THE DESIGNER. Make an appointment to see the designer, either at his or her offices or at your home. Keep in mind this is a preliminary meeting. The purpose of this first session is not to settle upon a design scheme, sign a contract, or make any final decisions. Plan on talking about your needs and concerns, and trying to get a sense of the person personally and professionally. The meeting will probably take an hour or more.

You will need to determine whether you can work with him (or her). If you feel uncomfortable for any reason—perhaps you realize that you're both high-strung creative individuals and you don't relish the prospect of hard-fought struggles about every detail—maybe you should continue your search for a designer. You must make a judgment about your needs and the designer's skills and how your personalities mesh.

This hiring decision is, in a sense, the first major decision in what will be a long string of subjective decisions. Yet it may be the most important, because the designer often sets the tone for the work to come. The experience of redesigning and constructing your living space can be immensely satisfying and exciting, and your designer must be a partner in that process. Are you confident that your designer will listen to what you say and try to accommodate your concerns? You will need to trust his judgment, too, so be sure that you feel in your heart as well as in your head that he is well suited to the job at hand.

Other grounds that may be helpful in making the decision are these:

■ **Previous work.** The single most reliable criterion for selecting a designer or architect is his or her previous designs. At the very least, you should review a portfolio of each designer's work. That will give you the opportunity both to evaluate the designer's skills and get ideas for your own renovation.

■ **Checking references.** If you like what you see in a portfolio, arrange to see one or more of the designer's projects first hand. Most designers will provide such references on request and often will gladly take you personally to see a completed project. If you have the opportunity, talk to the clients themselves. Don't be bashful about asking questions of the clients. Inquire about the process. How good were the designer's listening skills? Did he bring good ideas and clever solutions to the process? Was she agreeable to changes along the way? Checking references is simply the best single safeguard you have.

Ask the homeowners how smoothly the job went, how flexible the architect was in dealing with the client's and the contractor's questions and problems. Did the job come in close to the estimated budget? The architect is unlikely to send you to see work that either he or the customer is unsatisfied with, but you can still learn a great deal in looking and talking.

■ **The work.** Make sure the architect does a good deal of residential work. If there is only one house but twenty commercial spaces in his portfolio, that should tell you something. Residential work can be very satisfying for an architect, but it is likely to be more time consuming than profitable.

Keep in mind that experience is not the only indicator of ability. A young, energetic architect may be willing to do more research and may bring fresher ideas than an old pro with an established, staid practice. But here, again, you must rely on your good judgment. Experience is very valuable but not an absolute prerequisite.

■ **Staff.** Try to determine whether the architect has adequate staff and a workload that will allow for the right amount of personal attention to the project from start to finish. Who will do the actual design work? Expect that the architect will delegate much of the work on the finished drawings to a draftsman in the office, but who will be doing the actual designing—the designer himself or someone in the office? If it isn't the person you're talking to, insist upon meeting him or her. Ask the designer how many meetings will be necessary upfront; how many design hours does he anticipate will be necessary?

■ Accessibility. Does the location of the architect's office make it possible for him or her to be available for consultations? If you plan to involve your architect in overseeing construction, will he have to travel an hour each way to get to the job site? A long trek back and forth may mean fewer inspections, or perhaps larger, portal-to-portal billings.

On the other hand, don't reject an architect whose work you like simply because of geography. I know of many instances where designers worked from great distances, in some cases never even seeing the work, before, in progress, or after. It's not ideal, but with a good contractor and a capable designer, it can work.

■ The cost. Talk about fees, too, as it is never too early to broach this subject. Find out before the first meeting whether it's free or if the meter will be turned on as you walk through the door. You probably won't be able to settle upon a final design cost on day one, but don't allow the subject to be shunted aside with assurances like, *That's no problem, I'm sure we can work that out.* Make sure you have a sense of the total cost.

■ Can I talk to more than one designer? The short answer is, yes, of course. This isn't exactly comparison shopping—price alone should not determine whom you hire. But keep talking to designers until you find one that seems to suit your job and expectations.

If you begin by talking to several architects, pick one you like, and then let him or her create a preliminary design for you. On the other hand, if you have a particular design problem, you needn't feel shy about turning two or three architects loose, so long as there is a cap on what each architect's initial presentation will cost. I know of one instance where the owner of a small apartment hired one architect and two designers to create a new kitchen—independently of one another. The result was that the architect and one designer came up with workable solutions (the third solution was of no value, in the homeowner's judgment). And the finished product

THE LIGHTING DESIGNER

When was the last time you looked at the lightbulb rack at your favorite housewares store? There are incandescent bulbs, of course, those glass spheres with necks and threaded metal bases. And fluorescent bulbs, mercury-filled tubes of white glass. And tiny halogen bulbs that give off a disproportionately large amount of light. And there are dozens of sizes and shapes of each.

Even if you're conversant with the bulbs, how about lighting systems? Your house requires some *general lighting,* the basic illumination you require for making your way around the house after dark. In some areas you need *task lighting*, which illuminates countertops, benches, desks, or reading areas. Perhaps you will also want *accent lighting,* which supplements the other lighting, adding emphasis to your favorite painting.

When it comes to fixtures, the lighting game begins to get really complicated. You may need ceiling fixtures, which can be surface mounted or recessed. Pendant fixtures are another option: they can be lantern-shaped, bell-shaped, or a chandelier. Cove or cornice lighting at ceiling level can offer indirect light. How about track lighting? It can be used as general light, to spotlight, or to gently wash a large area. Wall lighting can be dressed up as sconces, surface mounted, or as tracks. Portable area lighting—floor lamps, table lamps, desk lamps—offers as many options as there are shades, stand configurations, and positions in a given room. Projector fixtures can illuminate a specific area of wall. In the kitchen, there are under-counter lights. And there are shelf lights, spotlights, downlighters, minilights, uplighters, narrow beams, diffusers, low-voltage lights, reflectors, and much else. There are literally *thousands* of fixtures on the market ranging in price from a few dollars to many thousands.

Good lighting can have both practical and dramatic effects. You may want, for example, a living room that is cozy and comfortable when you are home alone yet, when entertaining guests, you want deep pools of light in your conversation area or a dramatic spotlight that draws attention to an elegant architectural detail.

Are all these possibilities beginning to blur before your eyes? The range of choices is one reason why people consult design professionals called *lighting designers* or *lighting consultants.*

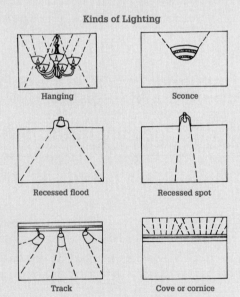

Kinds of Lighting

Hanging   Sconce

Recessed flood   Recessed spot

Track   Cove or cornice

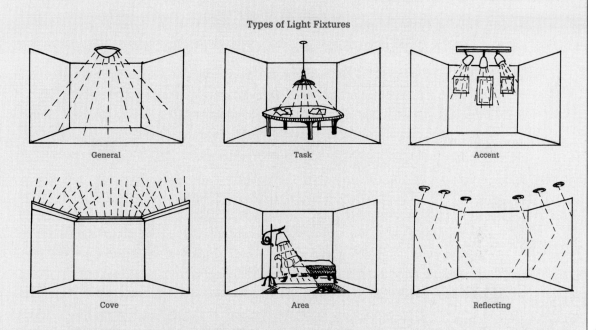

Types of Light Fixtures

General   Task   Accent

Cove   Area   Reflecting

Your architect or designer may be able to help you develop a lighting plan. Perhaps your contractor can, too. However, there are also professionals who, for a fee, will develop a lighting plan tailor-made to your home. Many lighting shops also have qualified people who for no added charge above the cost of the fixtures you purchase, will review your floor plans and create a plan for you.

Whoever does the work, it's important that the lighting not be an afterthought. Mounting switches and fixtures in walls and ceilings is relatively inexpensive early in the construction process, much more expensive later. Cove, cornice, and other lighting that requires special installation should be identified early to avoid wasted time and change orders. Lighting should be part of the original conception, not relegated to the status of finishing touch.

Lighting can help define spaces, emphasize textures, add drama, or simply make it easier for you to see where you're going and what you're doing. For a small added investment, a thoughtful lighting plan can make the difference between a truly successful interior renovation and a merely satisfactory one.

incorporated elements of one of the rejected designs. If you choose this approach, however, make sure you are very clear with the architects or designers about fees and expectations.

TAKING THE NEXT STEP. When your first meeting concludes, agree upon what is to be your next step. Perhaps you will establish a time for a second meeting. If your first session was in the designer's office, the next one may be at your home. Even if you have prepared careful drawings of the existing rooms, the architect/designer will probably want to see the space in person and may confirm your measurements.

DEFINING THE PROGRAM. During initial discussions, the designer will attempt to elicit from you what your goals are. What do you expect the remodeling to accomplish? He or she will ask about your needs, budget limitations, and your design inclinations. The purpose is to define in abstract terms the design task—a process architects sometimes term *programming,* as the result is a *program* for your design.

With the program in mind, the designer can design a structure that satisfies your objectives, working within established limitations, regulations, and other constraints. Some architects spend relatively little time in establishing the generalities of the problem; others like to invest more hours in generalized discussion. But once the designer has a clear idea of what you want and a basic familiarity with the structure to be remodeled, the visualization can begin: schematic drawings that illustrate the scale and interrelationship of the various components come next.

Reviewing the Plans

Different designers have different working styles. Some take the let's-go-for-it approach, and their initial sketches are surprisingly detailed and worked out. Many designers, however, take it one step at a time. Their early sketches are abstract, typically rough pencil jottings meant to suggest an approach that is not so much visual as intellectual.

If your architect begins with rough drawings, you will see little sense of style, dimension, or even shape but will be asked to think about the doodles as representing in a thematic way the nature of the space you are building, the traffic patterns through it, and the relationships of the spaces within to one another. On the other hand, if the paperwork you gave your designer clearly spells out your desires, he may arrive with drawings that are recognizable as floor plans and even elevation drawings and perspectives. Then the discussion can focus in on the details much sooner.

Whatever his or her approach, your designer will probably want to sit down and review the early plans with you. The designer-architect will explain his intent in executing the design as he has, and discuss with you any reactions you have.

If you've given him your sketches or notes, what he gives back to you should be familiar. If at first you don't see in his drawings what you expected to see, focus on what is different. Is the designer's vision better in some ways but not in others? Ask your architect to explain to you his rationale for what he has done.

In part, the point here is to be open-minded. You must give your designer the opportunity to respond to the task you've assigned her. Pay her the courtesy of listening to her as she did you. Your architect will have taken your materials and will have absorbed what you said. She will have applied her own training, experience, and instincts. Even if at first you don't like what she has done, give it a chance.

It is also very important to inquire about anything you don't understand.

THE PRELIMINARY SKETCHES. These should probably look familiar to you. You'll see elements from your existing house you recognize. Even the new parts should, at least in part, reflect your ideas and wishes. If the first sketches do not look like what you were seeing in your mind's eye, try to look through whatever details of finish that the designer has contributed. Do you see the same shapes and relationships you discussed earlier? If there has been a major departure, ask why.

Ask yourself if the design answers your needs: If not, say so.

It's a good idea for you to live with a set of the preliminary sketches for a day or two before giving your designer your formal response. Have others in your household study them, too. The architect or designer will no doubt take notes on your reactions as he shows them to you and as you express concerns about the size of this or the absence of that. However, almost invariably your response a day or two later is more reasoned, thoughtful, and complete than at the moment you are first confronted with new shapes and thoughts and visions.

It creates headaches for everybody to have friends or relatives kibitzing ("I wouldn't do it that way if I were you."), but if you are not confident of your feelings about how the plan is emerging, you may wish to involve one outsider whose tastes are compatible with your own. Take care not to let that person dominate you. It is, after all, your house that is to be renovated.

When you do discuss things with your designer, have written notes to guide you. An elaborately typed and phrased letter is unnecessary, but having a carefully assembled list is important. That way you won't forget something, *and* you will have an idea of the number of issues you are raising. You may even discover before you talk with the architect that there is a pattern to the problems so that one general overall comment can be made that covers a number of smaller issues.

Be candid with your architect. Don't get personal if you really dislike something, but be frank to say it doesn't work for you. If it doesn't work at all, say so, but at the same time be sure your response is a fair one. Just because it isn't what you expected doesn't mean it's bad. It could be better than your original notion—after all, you have hired a professional to do the best job she can, and maybe with her training and experience she can see things you could not. Give the drawings fair consideration.

Be as articulate as you can about why you're not satisfied. The more specific you can be about your objections, the more likely it is that he will be able to make the changes you want in the next set of plans.

As you consider the plans, think about the lives and schedules and habits of the people who will be living there. Imagine yourself in each doorway, seated in every corner. What do you see, in the room, out the windows, looking down the hallways?

Oh, and one other thing: If you do like what you see, don't hesitate to say so. Designers like approval just as much as other people.

PRELIMINARY PLANS. How many sets of plans will you see? The earliest drawings will be the most generalized and are as much for discussion as anything. It may take one or many sets of rough sketches before you are satisfied with the direction the building is going. But once you are confident with the overall approach, it's time to go on to preliminary plans.

If you see several sets of preliminary plans, each set should have more detail than the last and should incorporate the changes you discussed in the previous versions. However, before the preliminary plans give way to the final plans and specifications you should get your architect's best estimates of the total cost. It is never too early to talk about budget (construction budget rather than design fee), as your architect should know from your first session what your financial range is. But at this point it is realistic to get specific about costs.

By this stage, the "working systems"—the electrical, plumbing, heating and air conditioning systems—enter the picture. Specific materials, too, are useful at this point. Doors, windows, wall coverings, and so on factor in here. It is also at this stage (if you are putting on a major addition) for your architect to prepare "outline specs" (preliminary listings of materials and instructions used for purposes of estimating).

Some clients or architects will ask a contractor to join in at this stage. We will talk more about the contractor in Chapter 6, but a contractor can be useful at this time for estimating purposes. In addition, he may be able to offer some hands-on solutions from personal experience to certain problems, solutions that your architect might not offer.

A last act you should perform before instructing the architect/designer to go off and execute the final plans is to study the last set of preliminary plans one room at a time. Be sure you understand what is being done for you. If you get a sketch from your architect and you aren't sure what that 8-by-12-foot bedroom he has drawn really is like, measure a similar room or rooms in your house to get a sense of what it would be like enlarged or shrunken to 8-by-12.

Ceiling heights, too, should be seen and not merely imagined. If you are considering a towering 20-foot ceiling, find one and experience it. You may discover that 12 feet is just as dramatic, or that the floor space in the room you are planning is dwarfed and you feel like you're in an upended shoe box rather than a palace.

Make sure your furniture fits. Check the location of every light fixture and every plug; are there enough of them? Again, imagine yourself living in the space: Does it all seem to be as you want it?

The Final Plans and Specifications

These large pieces of paper are, finally, what you are paying your architect for. The drawings should be fully dimensioned—they're the map the contractor will follow in executing the work. Review the set of plans carefully before you sign any construction contracts (see Contracting the Contractors, page 222). Make sure it is consistent with the last version you saw, and that the corrections you asked for have been made.

Make sure you understand everything. You will cost yourself money later when you want something changed that you, out of ignorance, let pass at an earlier stage. Even substantial changes are relatively inexpensive before the contracts are signed and the hammers begin to swing. The sample drawings reproduced here will give you some idea of what to expect of the final plans.

A second element of the plans are the *specifications* or *spec sheets*. These are detailed descriptions of the materials to be used. Often these days spec sheets are long, formatted lists that came with the designer's CAD program with a few added wrinkles peculiar to your job slotted in. Construction methods may also be specified. Taken together, the plans and specifications will enable your contractors first to estimate accurately what it all will cost and then to construct what has been so laboriously planned.

The spec sheets also require *your* close attention. They should specify a lot of details about required materials about which you may have strong opinions. They'll cite everything from the brand name and model number of kitchen appliances to the thickness and quality of the plywood to be used for subflooring. Spec sheets will often specify decorative items like doorknobs, the maker and kind of paint, and molding sizes and profiles.

In examining spec sheets, look, for example, to see if the new windows in your addition are true divided lights like the old ones are; whether the new bathroom fixtures are good quality brand-name models or just cheap knockoffs. If you don't understand the shorthand, ask questions. Make it your business to know what the spec sheets say—after all, the numbers and abbreviations describe what *you* are buying.

Not that you have to simply accept what's there. In fact, you will find a new use of the words *or equal* in the specifications. Also called *allowances*, "or-equal materials" are typically finish materials like carpeting, light fixtures, or tile. The appearance of the term "or equal" means that if you don't like one of the items listed on the spec sheets, you may substitute something else. The term also implies that you may do so at no cost if your new choice is priced the same as (and thus is equal to) what was specified.

Keep in mind, however, that the allowances specified are usually not top-of-the-line goods. Thus, if you substitute a more expensive set of lighting fixtures in your kitchen for the basic ones specified, your cost will go up from the original estimate. As you review the plans, remember that it's *caveat emptor,* let the buyer beware.

You should have a meeting with your contractor before signing a contract to answer your questions and concerns, so go through the specs line by line in advance of the meeting and make a list of your questions. Look, too, for the abbreviation "NIC," which stands for "not in contract." That means that if you're adding a laundry room and the spec for the washer and dryer says NIC, they're not included in the estimate. They'll be your cost, not the contractor's.

Faucets and light fixtures are a perennial source of friction between homeowners and designer-builder teams. The story usually goes this way. The customer explains to the designer what he wants in, say, his new master bath. Sketches and then working drawings are executed, a contractor is hired, and the work begins. The job is nearly done when the homeowner discovers to his chagrin that the faucet, the showerhead, and the sconces are inexpensive and unattractive. He complains to the contractor, and together they refer back to the specifications. Sure enough, the homeowner is getting exactly what the paperwork specifies. "But they're not good enough," he complains, "I want something better." The contractor says, "Fine, you're the boss. The 'or-equal' clause in the contract entitles you to substitute something of equivalent value." Then the homeowner discovers what he wants will cost two or three or even ten times as much as what was specified—*and* that he has to bear the additional cost himself.

It's happened a million times and will happen again. How do you avoid it? Think about details that are important to you, and make sure your designer and contractor are sensitive to your concerns. Explain your expectations for the level of quality. Then examine the specifications extra carefully.

Some people decide to do some of the shopping and provide fixtures or other components themselves, excluding them from the contract. This can work, but you need to be sure you coordinate well in advance with the contractor and the subs. If something you want doesn't arrive in time, you may find your job delayed or more expensive.

A PORTFOLIO OF PLANS

If the finished job is the ultimate testament to a designer's skill, then the drawings that come first are the dress rehearsal. Thus, the more you can glean from an examination of preliminary and final plans, the better you can anticipate the finished product.

Architectural plans vary greatly, depending upon the project's size, budget, complexity, and other variables. Thus the sample plans that follow may differ from yours in many particulars. Nevertheless, the object is the same: to convey on paper for the contractors in two dimensions how the three-dimensional spaces will eventually appear.

Unless you intend to relinquish all control of the job, you will need to be able to read architectural renderings and, in your mind's eye, superimpose them onto your home. It's a process of translation and having a rule handy as you review the plans may be helpful. It may even make sense to buy an inexpensive architect's scale (a plastic one can be purchased at most art supply stores for a few dollars). That way you can determine how far point **A** is from point **B** even if the dimension isn't on the plans.

Site plan/zoning information. **The boundaries of your property will be indicated, as is the footprint of the house (or, in the case of an apartment building, the entire structure). In addition, any zoning or other restrictions will be drawn in, including setbacks and easements. Necessary site work, utilities, and the vistas that will be visible from the house may also be indicated. A plot plan isn't always necessary if you are simply finishing off existing space in your house, but for an addition or a completely new building, one will be required.**

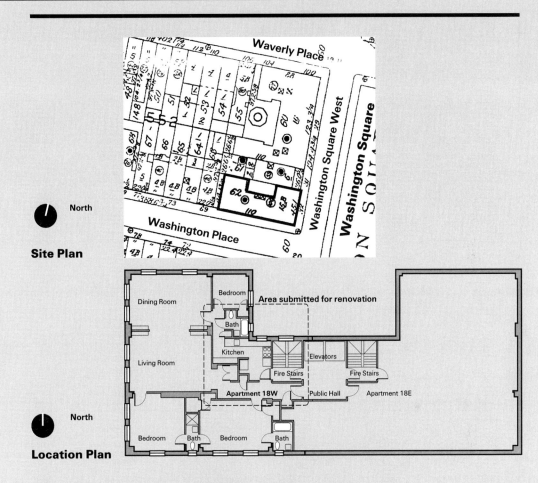

North

Site Plan

Dining Room

Bedroom

Area submitted for renovation

Bath

Living Room

Kitchen

Elevators

Fire Stairs

Fire Stairs

North

Apartment 18W

Public Hall

Apartment 18E

Bedroom

Bath

Bedroom

Bath

Location Plan

1 Site Plan/ Zoning Information
Not to Scale

Apartment 18W	located on the 17th floor of construction
Block No.	552
Lot No.	62, located on the north side of Washington Place, between Washington Square West and 6th Avenue
Zoning District	R7-2
Map	#12c
C of O:	None
Address:	82 Washington Square West

Building Department Notes
No Change in Use, Egress or Occupancy
Controlled Inspections: Final Inspection, Directive 14

Tenant Safety Notes
1. Construction work will be confined to the apartment interior, and will not create dust, dirt, or other such inconveniences to other apartment units within the building.
2. There will be no one occupying the apartment during construction.

Diversity: *Architecture & Design   New York City*

Shockey Apartment

189

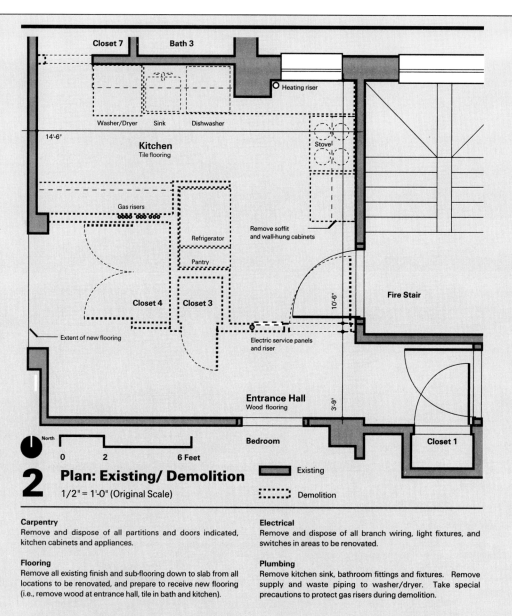

Closet 7   Bath 3

Heating riser

Washer/Dryer   Sink   Dishwasher

14'-6"

Kitchen
Tile flooring

Stove

Gas risers

Refrigerator

Remove soffit
and wall-hung cabinets

Pantry

10'-6"

Fire Stair

Closet 4   **Closet 3**

Extent of new flooring

Electric service panels
and riser

Entrance Hall
Wood flooring

3'-9"

North

0   2   6 Feet

Bedroom

Closet 1

2 **Plan: Existing/ Demolition**

1/2" = 1'-0" (Original Scale)

⬛ Existing

⬚ Demolition

Carpentry
Remove and dispose of all partitions and doors indicated,
kitchen cabinets and appliances.

Flooring
Remove all existing finish and sub-flooring down to slab from all
locations to be renovated, and prepare to receive new flooring
(i.e., remove wood at entrance hall, tile in bath and kitchen).

Electrical
Remove and dispose of all branch wiring, light fixtures, and
switches in areas to be renovated.

Plumbing
Remove kitchen sink, bathroom fittings and fixtures. Remove
supply and waste piping to washer/dryer. Take special
precautions to protect gas risers during demolition.

Existing/demolition. **This is one of several sheets that will be drawn in the format of a** *floor plan,* **meaning the drawing shows the location of the rooms in a structure, showing what you would see if you were to slice through the walls at one height and look down on the truncated structure from above. It's also called a** *horizontal section view.* **Floor plans indicate inside and outside walls, the openings in them (windows and doors), appliances, and plumbing fixtures. In the case of this plan, elements that are in situ are illustrated, as well as what will need to be removed to accommodate the desired changes.**

190

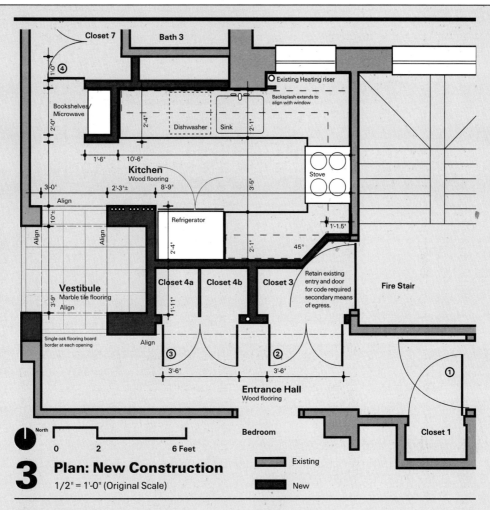

3 **Plan: New Construction**
1/2" = 1'-0" (Original Scale)

Existing

New

Walls

New gypsum board walls on steel studs with batt insulation to match existing at locations specified. Composition of wall, usually 4" thick, comprises one layer .625" gyp. bd. each side of steel stud, spaced @ 16" oc, with perf-a-tape and sealant top and bottom, and sound attenuation blanket within. Yellow pine base molding, 6" high x .75" thick, to match existing profile. Caulk continuously along the top edge. Finish paint on site.

Ceilings

New gypsum board ceilings on black iron substructure to elevations specified. Composition of support structure: 1/4" or 1/8" diameter hanger rods not to exceed 4'-6"oc, fastened into slab with expansion shields; connected with GAT clip 481.5L, Cat. No. 16.59 SM to .5" cold rolled No. 475 carrying channel not to exceed 4'-6"oc; furring channel and clip connector; 5/8" gypsum board firecode type X.

New construction. **This floor plan describes for the general contractor the final arrangement. This will help establish the scope and detail of construction work for the contractor and owner and, in fact, will also become part of the contract documents.**

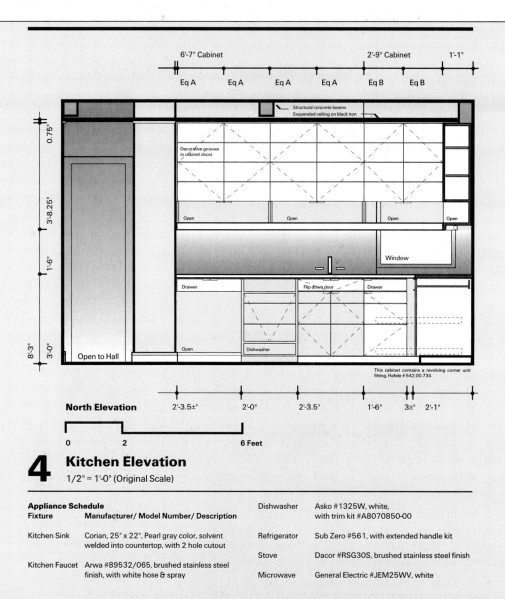

North Elevation

0   2   6 Feet

4   Kitchen Elevation
1/2" = 1'-0" (Original Scale)

Appliance Schedule		
Fixture	**Manufacturer/ Model Number/ Description**	
Kitchen Sink	Corian, 25" x 22", Pearl gray color, solvent welded into countertop, with 2 hole cutout	
Kitchen Faucet	Arwa #89532/065, brushed stainless steel finish, with white hose & spray	
Dishwasher	Asko #1325W, white, with trim kit #A8070850-00	
Refrigerator	Sub Zero #561, with extended handle kit	
Stove	Dacor #RSG30S, brushed stainless steel finish	
Microwave	General Electric #JEM25WV, white	

Kitchen elevation. The plot, foundation, and floor plans are all sectional views from above; elevations are different. An elevation is a view of the completed exterior or interior of a building, from the point of view of an observer looking straight at the wall. However, an elevation is a two-dimensional drawing and has no perspective. An elevation indicates patterns, proportions, scale, relative positions, and materials, but does no more than suggest what the actual construction will finally look like. The number and variety of elevations you need will vary depending upon the design. In this instance, the elevation reproduced portrays the renovated kitchen and specifies wall and ceiling finishes.

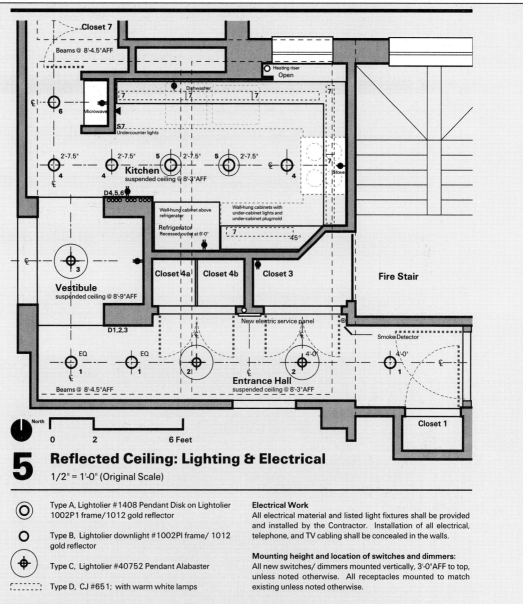

5 **Reflected Ceiling: Lighting & Electrical**

1/2" = 1'-0" (Original Scale)

◎ Type A, Lightolier #1408 Pendant Disk on Lightolier 1002P1 frame/1012 gold reflector

○ Type B, Lightolier downlight #1002PI frame/ 1012 gold reflector

⊕ Type C, Lightolier #40752 Pendant Alabaster

⌐⌐⌐⌐ Type D, CJ #651; with warm white lamps

Electrical Work

All electrical material and listed light fixtures shall be provided and installed by the Contractor. Installation of all electrical, telephone, and TV cabling shall be concealed in the walls.

Mounting height and location of switches and dimmers:

All new switches/ dimmers mounted vertically, 3'-0"AFF to top, unless noted otherwise. All receptacles mounted to match existing unless noted otherwise.

Reflected ceiling: Lighting and electrical. If necessary, there will be additional floor plans for each of the mechanical tradesmen, namely the plumber, electrician, and HVAC contractor. In the case of this set of plans, for example, the locations of multiple ceiling fixtures, kitchen cabinet lights and plugs, along with other electrical components are indicated. The more complex the job, the more electrical, plumbing, and mechanical plans there will be.

193

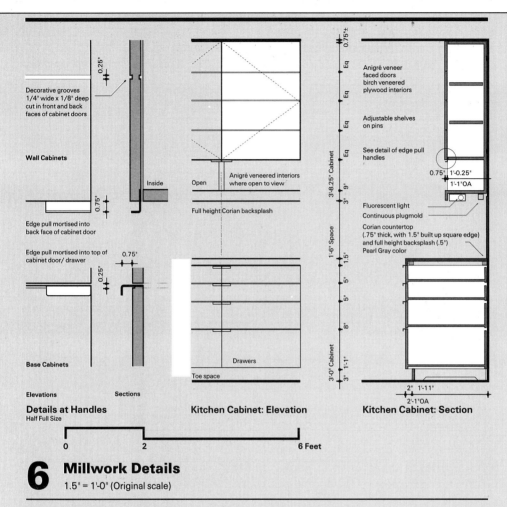

Decorative grooves
1/4" wide x 1/8" deep
cut in front and back
faces of cabinet doors

Wall Cabinets

Inside

Open

Anigré veneered interiors
where open to view

Full height Corian backsplash

Edge pull mortised into
back face of cabinet door

Edge pull mortised into top of
cabinet door/ drawer

0.75"

Base Cabinets

Drawers

Toe space

Elevations   Sections

Details at Handles
Half Full Size

Kitchen Cabinet: Elevation

Anigré veneer
faced doors
birch veneered
plywood interiors

Adjustable shelves
on pins

See detail of edge pull
handles

0.75" 1'-0.25"
1'-1"OA

Fluorescent light
Continuous plugmold

Corian countertop
(.75" thick, with 1.5" built up square edge)
and full height backsplash (.5")
Pearl Gray color

2" 1'-11"
2'-1"OA

Kitchen Cabinet: Section

0   2   6 Feet

6 Millwork Details
1.5" = 1'-0" (Original scale)

Millwork Construction
AWI standards for custom grade construction.
Exteriors of cabinets shall be faced with anigré veneer;
interiors of cabinets and adjustable shelves therein shall be
birch plywood with anigré edges.
Countertops and full height backsplashes shall be completely
fabricated from Corian, .75" thick for countertops with 1.5"
built-up square edge, .5:" thick for backsplashes, with integral
sink; all in Pearl Gray color

Millwork Hardware
All exposed hardware to be brush finish stainless steel. Refer
to schedule for complete specifications.

Millwork Finish
All exposed wood surfaces shall be finished with two coats
precatalysed nitro cellulose lacquer, clear satin finish, a
sample of which shall be submitted for approval.

Millwork details. **The finished plans may be accompanied by a variety of other drawings illustrating important elements of the construction that require additional visual explanation. These *detail sheets* will typically show sectional drawings to guide your subcontractors with anything from the shape and dimension of the cornice molding to the installation and configuration, as in these plans, of the cabinetry in the kitchen.**

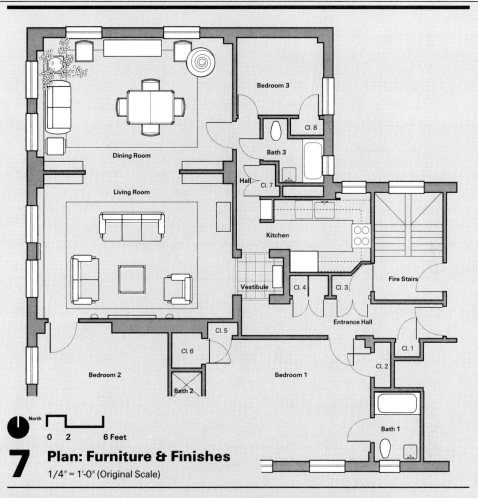

North 0 2 6 Feet

7 Plan: Furniture & Finishes
1/4" = 1'-0" (Original Scale)

Paint Specifications

Preparation
All surfaces shall be prepared in accordance with manufacturer's published specifications - i.e., sanded, spackled smooth, free of loose dirt, dust, and oil - thoroughly dry prior to commencement of finishing. The painter shall be responsible for insuring that the surface is properly prepared. One coat of primer throughout, and two coats of finish paint throughout.

Ceilings: Color #857
Primer: Latex Quick Dry Prime Seal
Paint: Regal Wall Satin (Latex flat finish)
Walls: Color #855
Primer: Latex Quick Dry Prime Seal
Paint: Regal Wall Satin (Latex flat finish)
Base Molding: Color #857
Primer: Alkyd Enamel Underbody
Paint: Satin Impervo Enamel (low-lustre finish)

Furniture and finishes. **This floor plan provides the contractor with guidance about finished surfaces; in these plans, the prime and paint procedures are specified.**

So have a look at the plans herewith. Thanks to the magic of the architect's skills and his or her CAD program, your space, too, can appear (on paper) before your very eyes. And after you have reviewed the plans, have a look at the photographs in the second photo insert to see how the finished product described in these drawings actually appears.

UNDERSTANDING COSTS

Frank Lloyd Wright was once asked if he could design a $10,000 house. The question was asked many decades ago, so it wasn't so absurd as it sounds today.

Wright replied that yes, he certainly could. But he added a qualifier: One thing he couldn't do would be to design a $20,000 house for $10,000.

Wright could sound like a wise guy at times, but those remain wise words. In fact, the same principle he espoused underlies a simple formula you might keep in mind as you think about the estimated cost of your project.

Budget = Quality of Materials × Size

It's deceivingly simple but it's practically a law of nature. Especially if you are concerned with cutting dollars out of your budget, you will have to shrink the house or compromise on some of the materials. True, there are other extraordinary options that we will discuss later (being your own contractor, for example) but in general this formula is painfully accurate.

If you discover you can't afford to do what you want to do, then think about reducing the size of the job or finding cheaper alternatives.

GETTING ALONG. Crucial to working with an architect—and eventually with contractors you hire to do the actual construction—is mastering the art of compromise. No matter how reasonable you think you are and how professional your designer is, the two of you are going to feel differently about some things. If he's any good, he's going to have some ideas that are new to you, and they may come as a big surprise.

Compromise has been the key to more than a few political careers and good marriages, not to mention a few billion working relationships of all kinds. But compromising and giving in are not the same thing.

Compromise implies movement, a movement by both sides of an issue toward a middle ground. In the case of an architect who has presented you with a possibility you simply don't like, you can of course take a tough position and say, "No, it isn't acceptable; change it." You're the person with the checkbook, you've got to live in the place, so make up your own mind.

On the other hand, you have hired the architect to help you. He can do so in a number of different ways, but only if you let him. So hear him out. Consider carefully what he is saying. He may give you a series of design arguments using some of those words we talked about in Chapter 3, such as *proportion* and *balance*. He may also be thinking of your pocketbook: small-seeming changes can significantly affect prices. Listen first, then make up your mind.

The ladders, the tools, the staging, and the unfinished exterior of this house send the message *Construction Zone*. Photo credit: Hugh Howard

Chapter 6

Contractors, Contracts, and Costs

Dankmar Adler—architect and partner of the great Louis Sullivan in the firm of Adler and Sullivan—once remarked that he would rather hire a crook who knew how to build than hire an honest man who didn't. "I can police a crook," Adler said, "but if a man doesn't know good work, how am I to get it out of him?"

I'm not sure I agree with Adler's reasoning. But I do know that hiring well is one of life's key skills—and a crucially important one when it comes to remodeling work. The right contractor can make the process go smoothly with a minimum of disruption to your life, while the wrong one can cost you money, peace of mind, and leave you with an unsatisfactory result.

While the timing varies, sooner or later you'll need to shop for a contractor.

Or, perhaps, for several subcontractors. You or your designer may invite the participation of builders during the planning stages or you may decide to wait until the plans are completed. That's a judgment call best made jointly by you and your designer. If you're working on a strictly limited budget, earlier consultation with a contractor to get estimates may help keep the focus on cost control. On the other hand, fewer inhibitions during the design stage may lead to more creative solutions to your particular remodeling if budgetary constraints allow.

Supposing that the time has come to find a contractor . . . who conducts the search?

Many architects will be happy to run interference for you. They can handle the finding, hiring, and estimating. The argument for this approach runs like this: If your architect does it, he or she will save you time (if he's minding the store, you don't have to). He knows whom to call to get quotes on a job. He may be able to get services and attention you would not since he can offer contractors consideration for future jobs. Since his business regularly involves soliciting and reviewing bids, he should know what to look for. He's negotiated building contracts before, and has probably spent many hours resolving disagreements—since they are inevitable, his help may be valuable. He can inspect along the way. He can help decide on the inevitable small changes that occur in the course of construction. He can serve as a valuable buffer between you and the contractor.

If this sounds ideal, talk it over with your architect (or designer, though not all designers have the training and experience to perform all these services). Understand, however, that you will have to pay your architect a substantial additional fee. These additional services are not free.

Supposing you decide for financial or other reasons that you won't be handing over the reins to your architect, an alternative is to leave the supervision to the general contractor, whom we will meet shortly. Or you can be your own general contractor (see Being Your Own General Contractor, page 206). Yet another option is to hire a *construction manager* (see page 208). But before you decide which path to take, let's take a closer look at the other players in the construction process.

The General Contractor

A *general contractor* or *GC* is hired to take a set of plans and turn them into a building. He'll orchestrate the comings and goings of the workers, order materials, inspect the work done, coordinate an ever-changing schedule, and handle a lot of the paperwork, which will include material bills, payroll, and issuing invoices to you, the homeowner.

The GC will also arrange for the subcontractors—the excavation contractors, plumbers, electricians, dry-wallers, tilers, roofers, and foundation crew, whatever and whoever is needed. It is the GC's responsibility to make sure the subs do their jobs on time and in strict accordance with the plans.

As with an architect, you sign a contract with the general contractor that obligates you to make certain payments at specified points during construction. In return, the GC assumes responsibility for the entire building process. The GC makes a profit by marking up the labor and materials costs by a percentage. That percentage varies considerably. The typical range is 10 to 30 percent.

THE CARPENTER-BUILDER VERSUS THE CONSTRUCTION COMPANY. Many GCs began their careers in the building business as carpenters but at some point decided they wanted to run their own companies and assumed overall management responsibility. In a large construction firm, the GC is actually a company rather than an individual, and an individual *project manager* will assume day-to-day responsibility for a given job. The project manager may or may not have hands-on building experience but does have business training. Increasingly, the tools of the GC's trade consist of a notebook computer and a cell phone rather than a hammer and a circular saw.

The carpenter-builder GC probably has only one or two jobs going at a time, while a construction company will need more and larger jobs to pay its overhead. The carpenter-builder may have a desk at home that functions as an office and a workshop in a converted garage or basement. The construction company will have an office with an accountant, payroll clerk, and other staff; trucks and miscellaneous vehicles; a warehouse or other building that functions as the base of operations with equipment, materials storage, and workshop equipment, and a variety of other accouterments of a good-size business.

The large and small general contractors each have certain advantages. You may be able to shape a more flexible working relationship with the carpenter-builder than with a larger company. On the other hand, the construction company probably has a much greater capacity and can do a broader range of work. If your project is large, you may benefit from the larger crews of a construction company.

Logic might suggest that the smaller contractor will be able to give you the best price, but despite the extra overhead costs at the larger concern, there are also some economies of scale. In general, though, the odds are that as a small, one-time buyer of construction services, you'll do better with a carpenter-builder for your remodeling. He is accustomed to dealing with individual owners, may have more time and patience for your special concerns, and he may well price the job a little cheaper, too. If you're in doubt, get both companies and carpenter-builders to bid on your job.

When hiring a smaller general contractor, determine how much experience the head man has. If the candidate you're thinking of hiring is a carpenter who's just branching out and trying his hand at being a carpenter-contractor, think carefully before making the hiring decision. He may master his profession quickly, but the truth is it's actually a new line of work, one that requires fewer building skills and more business sense. If your remodeling job is modest in scope, hiring a rookie GC may work to your advantage, since many people starting out on a new career have a pride in accomplishment that fades over time. Make sure you are confident he has the scheduling, budgeting, and other skills to handle the expanded duties.

THE SUBCONTRACTORS. Subcontractors get their name from their relationship to the general contractor. When you hire a GC, he will contract with individual subcontractors to complete specified tasks for specified prices.

You may need several subcontractors or none, depending upon the nature of your remodeling job. Among the subs that may be needed for a residential project that involves extending an existing foundation are a surveyor, earth-moving subcontractor for excavation and site preparation, and foundation contractor for the footings and cellar walls (though another sub, a mason, may be hired to build the walls if they are to be of block). Electrical, plumbing, and HVAC (heating, ventilation, and air-conditioning) subcontractors may be necessary and, depending upon who your GC or carpenter is, roofing, drywall, painting, and clean-up contractors may also work on your job. Usually any vinyl flooring, tile, and countertop needs can be filled by one contractor, while another will sell and install your carpeting. If there is landscaping to be done, you may need one or even several additional subs to plant trees, lay walks or patios, build walls, seed the lawn, and so on. Depending on local and state requirements, at least the electrician, plumber, and surveyor will be required to be licensed. Electrical, plumbing, and other inspections should be the responsibility of the appropriate subs.

If you have a general contractor handling your job, he'll be in charge of hiring, scheduling, paying, and supervising the subs. If you are your own GC, you'll be hiring them yourself (see page 206).

Hiring Decisions

The routine for hiring a GC is not radically different from that of hiring a designer. You want to hire someone with proven skills, somebody you can work with, and someone with a sound business sense for schedules and managing personnel. If your architect is supervising your construction, he handles the hiring of the GC for you.

If you are on your own and you don't know where to begin, ask for recommendations from friends or acquaintances who have had home construction done. Personal references are always best. Personal to you, that is, not to the contractor—sometimes people refer a favorite nephew or the son of a friend out of regard for their relationship rather than a knowledge of the person's skills or qualifications. You will probably do best hiring a local contractor with an established business and reputation.

If the referrer has had work done by the contractor, ask for an assessment of the work. Did the contractor finish at or near the budgeted price? If not, were the change orders reasonable? Was the work completed on schedule? Did the contractor willingly return to correct problems? Would they use him again? Are they happy with the finished product?

Another source of contractors is your local lumber yard(s). Not houseware stores where nails are sold by the dozen, but real building supply houses where contractors do their bulk business. The proprietors of such places know who the reliable contractors are. They know which contractors pay their bills on time, whose orders are always confused, and which ones are always returning merchandise.

MEETING THE CONTRACTOR. Once you've identified candidates, you will need to meet and talk with each of them. The contractor will need to see the plans and will want to examine the structure to be remodeled. Only after looking at the existing home or apartment and reviewing the changes to be made can an estimate be prepared (see Getting Estimates, page 212).

CHECKING REFERENCES. When you meet them, ask each GC for four or five local references. That's a perfectly reasonable request, and no reputable contractor should hesitate to provide them. Getting the names and numbers, however, is only the beginning—next, you need to make a few calls.

Telephone the previous clients, identify yourself as a homeowner in the market for building services, and ask the key questions: *Did the GC in question finish the job on time? Is the completed job satisfactory? How much did the price change along the way? Were the workers neat or did they leave a hopeless mess behind?* If possible, ask if you might be able to take a first-hand look at the work, too. Only by inspecting it yourself can you judge the caliber and acceptability of a contractor's work. You may get additional insights into the contractor from talking with the clients in person, too. Lessons previous customers learned may be helpful to you.

Call the local Better Business Bureau and ask if there are any complaints on file against the contractor(s) you are thinking of hiring. A call to the local building department inquiring about their professionalism and courtesy may be revealing. Ask each contractor who his primary supplier of materials is, and then call that supplier.

A quick call to a local credit bureau is also a good idea. Ask how long the company has been in business. If you uncover any pending suits or liens, walk away. You don't need the problems that can occur when a contractor is in litigation, like the sheriff arriving to impound the contractor's tools—or your building supplies. It happens.

Other sources for references are banks and subcontractors. Ask the GC who he has dealt with and call them, too. The banks can tell you about his fiduciary responsibility and the subcontractors about how well organized he is.

Another word of caution: Treat your contractors, subs, and the other people you hire with appropriate respect. They're not your employees, they are businesspeople from whom you are buying services. A modicum of courtesy and basic consideration will be rewarded. That goes for the men and women who work for them, too.

On the other hand, resist the temptation to get too friendly with any of your contractors. Keep your relationships strictly professional. They aren't your friends: again, these are people with whom you have a business relationship. Invite them to dine with you *after* the job is done. A friendly but professional distance is appropriate until then.

Being Your Own General Contractor

There is no mystery to being a general contractor, though some skills with people, finances, and general good sense are required. For someone who has never done it, a willingness to ask questions, some of which may seem elementary or even silly, is necessary. And a knack for solving problems is certainly helpful. I wouldn't recommend that a novice act as his or her own contractor if the job is large—say, a new house or a large addition—but an interior remodeling of moderate size can be quite manageable.

Yet that still begs the real question: It isn't *Can I do it?* It's *Should I do it?*

The best argument for trying to be your own contractor is the payoff. Contractors are, after all, in business to make a profit, so adding 20 or 30 percent to the cost of materials and labor as profit is perfectly reasonable.

If you are your own GC, you don't have to pay anyone that percentage.

On the other hand, there are arguments against being your own contractor. For example, if you aren't satisfied with the finished product, you can't complain to your GC that the job isn't good enough and refuse to make the last payment. You would be talking to yourself because *you* are the general contractor.

That may be the biggest single reason not to be your own GC. If you hire someone to do the job for you and then something goes wrong, it probably won't be your problem because GCs are paid to solve problems and get the job done. When you hire a general contractor, you are paying for his experience, competence, ability to anticipate problems, and, more than anything, for his willingness to assume final responsibility for the whole job. And he'll get the permits, do the scheduling, and handle disputes between subs and suppliers.

So if you opt to do the GC's job, you'll have some sleepless nights. Should major problems arise, you won't have the same simple recourse to call your lawyer and tell him, "Sue the damn GC, it's his fault." Acting as your own contractor does not mean buckling on a tool belt and swinging a hammer all day.

Being your own contractor can mean you increase the odds of getting exactly what you want. GC's make money by executing each job simply and efficiently so they can get on to the next one. Changes along the way and variations from the usual that make a job last longer can be the cause of irritation and uncooperativeness from a GC. Thus, if you are very detail conscious and plan to be looking over everybody's shoulder anyway, it may make sense for you to be your own GC.

According to a 1996 survey conducted by the Consumers Union, roughly half of the reader respondents used a GC to oversee their renovations. The degree of satisfaction was roughly the same for those who did and those who didn't. Perhaps the average *Consumer Reports* reader is more careful and savvy than the average person . . . but perhaps you are, too.

Now let's talk about the key elements of the job.

HIRING SUBCONTRACTORS. This will be your responsibility, and it's a crucial one, since these are the ladies and gentlemen who will actually remodel your house for you. They're the carpenters, plumbers, electricians, and other tradespeople who translate the plans into your living spaces. As with any manager, the key skill is finding the right personnel.

The most important player will probably be your carpenter. He's the person who will shape the structure that defines the spaces. He builds the framework that will be the matrix for the electrical wiring, piping, vents, phone lines, and insulation. He'll return after all that has been roughed in and cover it with finished surfaces. The carpenter is the pivotal player and should be hired first.

JOB QUALIFICATIONS FOR THE HOMEOWNER/CONTRACTOR

Ask yourself whether you have:

The time. No, it isn't a full-time job. You probably won't need to spend more than two hours a day during construction. Yet you must be on call for surprises and emergencies. Is your workplace close enough to your home and is your schedule flexible enough that you can make the trek to the job site during working hours? How about at lunch hours? Are you accessible by phone most of the time?

The commitment. Don't take on the job of general contractor on a whim. You probably won't be able to hand it off to someone else partway through without costing yourself most of the money (or more) you were hoping to save.

The personality. All right, now let's really talk. You will have to be a manager. That means you will need to be tough at times with your subs. Yet you can't interfere with their work. It's a fine line. Do you have enough patience, critical distance, and savvy that you can both let the pros do the work they know how to do better than you yet know instinctively when to step in?

HIRING A CONSTRUCTION MANAGER

A construction manager is another alternative to hiring a general contractor. It may be a good way for the homeowner who has no building experience to get some of the benefits of being his or her own contractor yet, at the same time, to have a pro at hand to lend confidence and guidance.

One key difference between hiring a GC and a construction manager is financial. In a traditional homeowner-GC arrangement, the contractor calculates his costs, gets estimates from subcontractors, and then marks them all up a percentage to give you a single price. In contrast, the construction manager won't give you one price; your checks won't all be payable to just one payee. Instead, *you* will hire all the contractors and there will be no middle man to mark up costs. You will pay the construction manager a fee, but that will be less than the GC's markup would have been. You should end up ahead.

With a construction manager, you sign an agreement specifying that his (or her) fee is a percentage of the total time and materials costs. A typical fee of 10 to 15 percent would translate, on a job with a time and materials cost of $50,000, to a construction management fee of $5,000 to $7,500 for the manager's services.

Another advantage of the construction manager is that you will retain a high degree of control and involvement in the process. The construction manager is essentially a consultant who lends a professional hand. The construction manager will help solicit bids, review estimates, coordinate schedules, and oversee construction. But you will be closely involved with every step along the way.

The basic service provided by architects usually includes some routine construction supervision, but for an added fee, many architects will assume the construction manager role. Some carpenters and small general contractors will also work on a manager/fee basis. But whoever does it, the estimating, negotiations, scheduling, and supervision are the manager's responsibility.

What's the downside? A general contractor assumes responsibility for a job; a construction manager does not. Disputes, poor workmanship, and other difficulties become *your* problem. It's only fair, really: you save some money and assume some of the risk. But if you find an experienced construction manager with good references and negotiate a thorough and fair contract, the chances are good you won't have major problems.

Whatever arrangement you decide upon, remember you're the boss. Insist that the work be up to your standards.

The carpenter will be your primary sub, so ask him for help in finding an electrician, plumber, or mason. And don't worry too much about cronyism here. Most carpenters can be counted on to recommend people they like to work with but few will recommend subs who don't know their jobs. They know which are the guys who mess up the schedule and who do sloppy work and make trouble for everybody else. They don't want those headaches any more than you do.

PROFESSIONAL HELP

In order to be assured that you're not embarking on a trip straight to debtors' prison, it's a good idea to consult a lawyer and probably to seek other guidance as well. These counselors won't be wearing flannel shirts and work boots, and they may never even visit your home, but your attorney, accountant, and insurance agent can be important players.

The real estate attorney. You may resent it, but the fact is we live in a world where good legal counsel is essential to conducting business. While you might like to think of the home renovation process in warm, emotional terms, it is also true that buying construction services is to sign a series of contracts. By definition, you're entering into a string of business deals.

The bigger the job, the more you need a lawyer to look out for your interests. Your banker, the contractor, the architect, and each of the other players will have different concerns. Their counselors—and they'll probably have them, even if you don't have contact with them directly—cannot be counted on to protect you.

Even if you hire a GC or use an architect to supervise the whole process and never visit the site, you will need legal guidance for reviewing contracts and checking out zoning restrictions and numerous other matters. You may find that an experienced real estate attorney can help in ways you have never considered. He's seen his clients through most of the hassles you've never faced before, so his experience and advice can be invaluable, whether it is in negotiating the right contract at the start, resolving a misunderstanding in the middle, or resolving a dispute long after the job is completed.

If you have an established relationship with an attorney, be sure he is well versed in real estate law. Does he do a reasonable volume of real estate law? Even if he was your college roommate, check it out because real estate law has its own complexities and can get just as arcane as any other area of the law. And mistakes can be very expensive. If you don't have a suitable lawyer awaiting your call, try calling a couple of nearby real estate agencies or mortgage departments at local banks and ask them for references. The local bar association is another potential source; ask for the chairman of the real estate committee.

Other professionals. If you have an accountant who prepares your taxes, get his or her opinions and guidance early. Sit down with the accountant and discuss your budget, loan arrangements, the cash flow of the project (you expect which bills in which month, which are this year, which next), and your income. There may be tax credits (some credits are available for rehabilitation of older buildings), certain tax advantages, and other issues that could save you money.

Even though your contractors should provide you with Certificates of Insurance describing their insurance coverage, you should also consult with your insurance broker. As you improve your house, you may wish to up your coverage for the added property value. You might also wish to check your liability coverage to be sure it is adequate. Should someone fall and break a leg, you—as well as the contractor—might get sued and you'll want adequate insurance protection. Construction sites have many potential dangers and you should minimize your risks, both physical and financial.

To find carpenters or subcontractors, ask friends and neighbors. The Yellow Pages are a good source, too. Another option is to visit job sites in nearby residential areas. Walk right in and ask for the head carpenter, plumbing contractor, or the electrician. The chances are excellent that you'll come away with a business card, a phone number, or possibly an appointment. You may even get an estimate on your job if you have the plans with you and the boss has an hour to kill.

Another good source of subs is supply houses. Ask at plumbing, electrical, or tile shops that deal with the trades. You should get a couple of names. Ask other subs for the names of the tradesmen they respect and with whom they've worked.

Check each sub's references (customers, suppliers, banks, and others). Get several subs to estimate on the big jobs and at least two on the small ones (replumbing an existing bathroom during a remodeling is a small job, plumbing two new baths, a laundry room, and a hot tub in a large addition is a big one). Do your homework on the people you are hiring before you hire them.

When it comes to dealing with subs, keep in mind that most of them bid a lot of jobs and some take on virtually every one they are offered. The bad news is that you, as a one-time customer, may get a place toward the bottom of their priority list, well below the GC's who are going to be building many houses in the future and therefore may be continuing customers for the subs' services.

You need to steel yourself for the frustrations and scheduling hassles but, on the other hand, you're not taking on the world all alone. Your subs will also be key allies in getting your job done. They are there not only to get your house built, but to help you do it. You may be surprised to find the pride that many individual operators in the construction business take in their work. Try to use that pride and spirit to your advantage. Good planning on your part and constant communication with the various subs are both essential.

Many states and municipalities require that general contractors be licensed and properly insured before they can legally hang out a shingle identifying themselves as GCs. However, no such requirements exist for the homeowner acting as his own GC. If after you do it yourself you like it so much you want to do it again for someone else, then you can find out what the requirements are.

INSURANCE. When you act as your own GC, you'll need a builder's risk or fire policy. In most states, prices tend to vary only slightly from company to company

> ## OPEN A SEPARATE CHECKING ACCOUNT
> **Unless your project is very small or you've one professional to manage everything for you, open a separate checking account for the duration of your construction project.**
>
> **Keep your day-to-day household and other finances discrete from the new account. Deposit all loan proceeds or other construction funds directly into the account. Pay all your contractors, suppliers, designer fees, and other expenses by check from that account.**
>
> **The separate account will make it easier to monitor costs and identify your available balance at a glance. It may also help discipline you into thinking of the project in a more businesslike fashion. Construction projects have a way of assuming a life of their own and you want to be sure to be on top of the process. The separate account can help.**

because they are usually closely regulated, but check with the insurance agent who handles your homeowner's policy to determine the paperwork required and the cost. You will want to arrange for the insurance to be effective the moment the building materials arrive or the first worker sets foot on the site, whichever is earlier. If you have a construction loan, the bank will probably insist you have a valid insurance binder on hand at the time you close on the loan. When the work is finished, you can then amend the policy once again to standard homeowner's coverage.

Don't take the decision to be your own general contractor lightly. Don't let the possibility of saving a substantial amount of money blind you to the potential for complications and conflict. You may find a great deal of satisfaction at having managed the whole process yourself, but you should also be confident that you have the time, interpersonal skills, organizational abilities, and just plain desire to stay the course, even when the going gets a bit rough. And it will—no construction project is without its ups and downs, its setbacks and frustrations. For many people, the markup a GC adds to the actual costs of construction is a fair price to pay to manage the process. There is a potential for savings, but there must also be an investment on your part of time and commitment. You'll have to coordinate the activities of the subs, establish schedules, pay bills, and perform a number of other functions. But there's another role you will have to assume as well.

As GC, you're the person with the "buck-stops-here" sign on his desk. The decisions, large and small, are yours to make. There'll be professionals around to help answer questions and advise but, finally, yours is the voice of authority.

Getting Estimates

The first task you will put before your contractor will be preparing an estimate for the cost of construction. You will have signed off on the plans—so you can hand them off to the contractor. Or perhaps your designer/architect will, if you have elected to hire him to manage construction.

As we discussed in Chapter 5, the plans will probably come complete with spec sheets. This isn't your last chance to make changes in them, but if there are fixtures, appliances, or materials specified that aren't to your tastes, there's no time like the present to adjust the specs. In order to prepare an estimate, the contractor(s) will begin by doing *takeoffs*. Takeoffs are lists of materials contractors prepare using the plans and specifications. Each takeoff will detail the quantity, quality, size, and other identifying characteristics of the required materials. A carpenter's takeoff, for example, will list boards, lumber, plywood, nails, and other goods; the plumber's takeoff will include pipe, fittings, fixtures, and miscellaneous supplies.

Before you hand over the plans, take another look at the spec sheets. Make sure that all the items specified are what you want. You'll get what's there unless you speak now. Don't take for granted that the "or-equal" language will protect you (as we discussed earlier, an allowance won't allow you to substitute a more expensive item for the one specified; see page 187).

I've said this before and I will again: Changes are better made sooner rather than later. This goes for buying goods as well as the actual work on the building. It may go without saying that if you change your mind after the carpenter has built a wall, it'll cost you money to demolish the wall and build it somewhere else. But it's also true that if one of your subs has ordered the materials specified, then you own them. He may be able to return them although there may be a substantial restocking charge. He may even be willing to buy them back from you, but probably at something like fifty cents on the dollar. The better approach is to revisit the specifications sheets at this stage and affirm that what is specified is what you want.

The plans and the spec sheets are all you need to solicit bids, whether you're looking for one number from a GC or prices from each of several subcontractors. The plans will be divided among the trades so that the carpenter, electrician, plumber, and the rest will be able to estimate the labor and materials required to complete

ESTIMATING HINTS

Get at least three estimates for each job. Whether it's the whole job or only one subcontractor's portion of it, only when you have a basis for comparison will the outrageously expensive estimate stand out. And remember, the cheapest isn't always the best. If one price is much less than the others, there's probably a reason why.

Get your job estimated during the off-season. This won't help in Southern California where construction work isn't seasonal, but in the snow belt you may well get a better number from a contractor during the idle months when he wants to line up work for the first day of spring. Even if a contractor's prices don't vary much from season to season, he'll almost surely have more time to devote to working out the estimate carefully and maybe even to helping you brainstorm about costs and technical concerns.

HOW TO CUT COSTS

What if the sum your construction estimates total is greater than you had budgeted? Sit down with your designer, especially if he took part in the creation of that original budget. Review the estimates with him or her and see where the unexpected overages are.

Have separate meetings with both the architect and GC. Ask each for strategies for cost reduction. The first approach should be to work within the design you have. Can certain materials be changed to less expensive ones? Is there a portion of the job that can be postponed a year, such as leaving one of the new rooms as raw space until that next baby you're thinking about having is more than simply a thought?

If none of you can devise a way to trim the existing plan, is there a logical portion of the design that can be dropped? The second bay in the garage? Do you need that extra deck off the second bedroom? When it comes to design changes, your designer is essential.

If you get contradictory advice from the contractor and architect, ask both of them to meet with you at once. Get a brainstorming session going. They can make their cases to each other, as well as you. Yours is the deciding vote.

A word of warning: *Don't* be penny-wise and pound-foolish, as the saying goes. Don't eliminate something very important to you just to trim the budget. That could defeat the purpose of the whole project. If you have a number of potential cuts from the project, make a priority list, and do your cutting from the bottom up.

Try to take a big-picture approach. Don't end up compromising the whole just to save the hot tub. Consider adding later what you can't afford now.

their parts of the job. You give them the paperwork they need, and they will respond in kind, providing you with written estimates of what they will do for how much.

If you have a general contractor, he'll do all the calculating for you. He'll prepare takeoffs, and get materials estimates from suppliers. He'll scratch his head and sharpen his pencils to figure out the labor required. He'll get estimates from subcontractors for electrical, plumbing, HVAC, insulation, drywalling, or whatever other portions of the work he'll job out to others. Then he'll total all the numbers, add his profit, and give you one price for the whole job, which you may then be able to negotiate.

If you are assuming the responsibility for dealing with the suppliers and subcontractors, you'll have to solicit bids, review and compare them, then calculate your own bottom line. But the principles are the same for reviewing estimates, whether you're looking to hire one contractor or several.

REVIEWING ESTIMATES. The key in reviewing estimates—and ideally you should solicit three for each task—is to be sure all are comparable. Read them carefully. While each of the estimates you're comparing should have been prepared on the basis of the plans and specifications you provided, the estimates themselves may not be identical. Occasionally a tradesman will substitute for this or that item. It may be an improvement, it may save you money or it may not, but be sure you know what has been changed. Sometimes mistakes get made, too, and the sooner they are identified, the better.

The estimate should refer specifically to the specs, perhaps in lawyerish language like, "This estimate prepared per specifications and plans submitted by Client and attached hereto . . ."

Consider a simple estimate done by a carpenter for a deck you are adding to your house. Say you are using a plan you found in a home design magazine, and it came with a spec sheet. You hand copies of the plans and specifications to the carpenters you've asked to bid the job. Each carpenter will examine the site to determine what site preparation is necessary, note what changes will be required to adapt the plan to your home, and then go off to work up a price. Each one will share the materials list of lumber, nails, and other materials with a clerk at his favorite lumberyard. Usually in a matter of minutes, the yard will hand over (or fax back) an itemized list of materials and unit costs. The contractor will then figure how much labor, other costs, and profit he needs to add to it, and will provide you with a written estimate with the price, payment schedule, and other terms specified.

As a rule, the cost estimates you get for a particular job should be in the same range, plus or minus 10 percent of the middle figure. However, if one is very high, that suggests the contractor doesn't want the job. Be happy for him, that means he's got plenty of work.

One rule of reviewing estimates is that the cheapest isn't always the best, while the most expensive isn't always best, either. If one estimate is very low, that isn't necessarily wonderful news. Check that estimate very carefully, reading its details against your plans and specifications. The contractor may have misunderstood the job, specified cheaper materials than you want, or changed something that is crucial to you. In the case of a deck, for example, he may have estimated costs using pressure-treated decking rather than the redwood you saw pictured in the magazine. Don't just sign on the dotted line in order to save yourself that money. In the end, it may not be a saving at all.

If your designer provided cost projections, compare them to the estimates. It is unreasonable to expect that his or her numbers will match up exactly with the estimates, but the designer's budgeted costs should be in the range with most of them unless specifications have been changed significantly. If none of your estimates are in the range the designer said they should be, meet with your architect or designer and try to find out why. Even if it is just a matter of his making a mistake, he should know about it. And he just may be able to point to something that the estimators missed that accounts for the discrepancy.

Estimates often become a part of the contract between you and the contractors and we'll discuss contracts shortly. But now that you're preparing to spend money on your house, let's talk about whence that money will come.

Footing the Bills

If you have the cash on hand to pay for your remodeling project, you needn't read this section. Most people, however, need to borrow money to underwrite their job.

The best option is usually a mortgage loan. That's because the interest on a home mortgage is tax deductible. There are several varieties of mortgages that can provide the funds for a home renovation project, but each depends upon how much *equity* you have.

UNDERSTANDING EQUITY. Equity is the net value of your property after all indebtedness held against it has been deducted from its gross value. Allow me to translate.

Suppose you want to borrow $25,000 to improve your $100,000 home. You need to determine what portion of the home you own outright and what percentage of its value is still due to the bank. If your original down payment was, say, 25 percent of the purchase price, and your pay-down on the principal since then equals another 25 percent, you own the remaining 50 percent, or half your house. That would mean you are an excellent candidate for that loan, since most banks will loan up to 75 percent of the value of an existing house.

Even if you have not owned your house long enough to pay down the mortgage significantly, if the value of the house has increased, you may still have substantial equity you can borrow money against.

There are a number of ways you can draw upon that equity. The two principal ones are *first mortgages* and *second mortgages*.

FIRST MORTGAGES. For the home renovator, negotiating a new first mortgage is one way of underwriting the remodeling job. In practical terms, this means you will apply to the bank for an all-new mortgage. If the bank approves the loan, some of the proceeds will be used to pay off the existing mortgage. After deducting closing expenses and fees (see Closing Costs, page 218), whatever is left over will be paid to you. Typically, a new mortgage makes especially good sense when the interest rate you are paying is at least one percentage point higher than the rate you would be paying on a new mortgage.

If you bought your home using money borrowed from a bank, the loan you obtained was probably a first mortgage. The rudiments are simple. You borrow the money, having promised to pay it back (with interest) in a specified number of payments at specified intervals. In return, the bank considers your house to be collateral for the loan, making it a "secured" loan. That means that should you fail to make the agreed-upon payments, the bank will have the right to foreclose, assuming ownership of the house.

Not all first mortgages are the same, of course. There are conventional mortgages, which are *fixed-rate, self-amortizing mortgages*. "Fixed-rate" means the interest rate established at the time the loan is granted stays the same throughout the term of the mortgage; "self-amortizing" means that at the conclusion of the mortgage's term the loan will have been paid off (i.e., "amortized"). The conventional thirty-year mortgage continues to be the most popular mortgage, in part because homeowners know that, even as the financial markets rise and fall, their payments will remain the same.

Another type is the *adjustable-rate mortgage.* Conventional mortgages were the rule until the mid-seventies when interests rates skyrocketed and the adjustable-rate mortgage (ARM) became commonplace. The ARM, too, is self-amortizing, but a "rollover" mortgage (as the ARM is sometimes called) allows the bank to adjust the interest rate during the term of the mortgage. The initial interest rates for ARMs are generally lower than with conventional mortgages. However, the bank will revisit the rate at specified intervals and adjust it with respect to some preestablished index. The frequency of the adjustment varies; some lenders do it as frequently as every three months, others wait as long as five years, although once a year on the anniversary of the day you closed on the loan is typical. The index varies, too, though Treasury securities are one commonly used point of reference. The mortgage contract signed at closing will specify the initial interest rate, how often it can be adjusted, the index to be used, and also the *caps,* namely the maximum amount the rate can be increased in a year and over the life of the loan.

Is a conventional to be preferred over an adjustable-rate mortgage? That depends. In recent years, the prime rate and other indicators have remained low, meaning fixed rates have been relatively low, while ARM interest rates have tended to increase quickly from the initial rate. In the past when rates were high, the opposite was often true.

One rule of thumb is, when rates are low (significantly under 10 percent), a fixed rate is probably the best deal in the long term. However, there's a corollary theory: If you are fixing up your house fully expecting to resell it in the near future, the ARM with its lower initial rate may make more sense.

SECOND MORTGAGES. A second mortgage is exactly what its name suggests: it's an additional mortgage to the first mortgage you are carrying. Typically the holder of the second mortgage will have a claim on the property in the event you fail to make your payments. At the time a house was initially purchased, the seller may have agreed to hold a second mortgage, but for the homeowner planning a renovation, the most likely source of a second mortgage is a lending institution.

The most common form today of second mortgage is a *home equity loan.*

Again, the determining calculation is how much *equity* you have. To go back to our original example, if your house is worth $100,000; if your unpaid principal is $50,000; then your equity is $50,000. With an equity loan, many banks will allow you to borrow up to eighty percent of the value of a house, meaning an additional $30,000 might be obtained in this example. Some banks will offer even more—up to 100 percent of a home's value in some instances.

In the case of a second mortgage, the first mortgage is unaffected by the second one, which is sometimes called a *wrap-around loan*. In a transaction independent of the first mortgage, you apply to a financial institution to lend you money (often it is the bank carrying the first mortgage, but credit unions, home-finance companies, and even some brokerage houses also make home-equity loans). If the loan is approved, you will close on the second mortgage just as you did on the first one, executing a mortgage contract that specifies the amount of the loan, the term of the agreement, the payment terms, the interest rate, your obligations to care for the property, what happens in the event of default, and so on. The interest rate is usually variable (see adjustable-rate mortgage, page 217) but fixed-rate equity loans are also available from some institutions. Home-equity loans are usually repaid over terms of ten to twenty years.

Some home equity loans are for a fixed sum—say, that $30,000 cited in our example. If the bank approves your application, you leave the closing with a check for $30,000, or whatever sum is left after closing costs. An alternative is an *equity line of credit*. With a line of credit you leave the closing with a checkbook rather than a single check. You then write checks for the money you need as you need it, up to the maximum amount of loan. Many homeowners find this a very satisfactory way of going about a renovation—in part because they pay interest only on what they've borrowed.

The interest rates on equity loans are typically two or three percentage points higher than on traditional mortgages. But the closing costs are lower.

CLOSING COSTS. Costs vary from one state to another and from bank to bank, but the costs may include lawyer's fees (possibly yours *and* the bank's); recording fees; mortgage, transfer, or other taxes; points on the loan (fees calculated as percentage points of the sum being borrowed, meaning two points on a $100,000 loan would represent a fee of $2,000); title insurance; filing fees; application fees; appraisal expenses; the cost of a credit report; and so on.

With a traditional mortgage, all of these expenses are usually borne by the borrower; with an equity loan, the bank pays for many of them. When you apply for a loan, most banks routinely provide an estimate of the total closing costs. Ask for a breakdown if one isn't offered. If the amount of equity you have in your home is limited, closing costs can make the negotiation of a mortgage too expensive to justify. Do the numbers to be sure.

OTHER OPTIONS. In addition to mortgages, there are other loan options that might suit your particular financial circumstances.

Credit card advances. If your renovation will be modest in cost, you may want to avoid the paperwork and expense of loan applications and simply draw a cash advance from one or more of your credit cards. Keep in mind, however, that the interest rates are generally rather high (often more than twice that of mortgages). As always, do the arithmetic: Calculate how long you are likely to carry the bloated credit card balance, how much the interest charges will be for that period, and therefore what the relative cost would be compared to an equity loan. You should also figure into the calculation that interest paid on home equity loans is tax deductible while interest on a credit card balance is not. In general, credit cards are an expensive way to borrow money.

Personal loan. A personal loan is a relatively simple transaction. You file an application with a lender, he checks your credit and indebtedness, and he approves or disapproves the application. The loan is not secured by your home, and the decision to approve (or disapprove) the loan is made on the basis of your credit rating, income, and an overall assessment of your financial health. The rate will typically be a good deal higher than for a mortgage; the term shorter; and the interest is *not* tax deductible. Given these disadvantages, a personal loan should be well down your list of options.

Balloon mortgage. A balloon mortgage is one in which a large or "balloon" payment of the remaining principal is due at a specific date. Payments are made along the way, often of interest alone though in some cases token principal payments are made as well. Balloon mortgages are more common in real estate transactions for commercial or multifamily dwellings. However, if your home renovation involves more than simply enlarging or remodeling your home for your family—if, say, your improvement includes the addition of an apartment or a commercial office space you expect will produce income and you're planning to sell the whole complex within a few years—a balloon mortgage may make sense. Talk to your banker or accountant about the options.

Construction loan. In order to construct an all-new house, few banks will issue a standard mortgage. Instead, the bank will grant a construction loan that, after the house is completed and the certificate of occupancy granted, will be converted to a more traditional first mortgage. In most cases, a construction loan isn't the best route for a home renovator. However, if you are radically remodeling the house and the cost of the construction is substantially greater than the equity you have in the house, a combination construction loan and mortgage may be your best strategy.

A construction loan is a bank's way of paying out the construction money gradually. They don't want to put too much money at risk; rather, the bank is interested in assuring that their investment—namely, your house—is constructed according to the agreed upon schedule and terms. Under the terms of a construction loan, the lender will pay in installments, with payments due at specific points in the construction process.

On a construction loan, you pay only interest on the money lent to you. In fact, most contractors (who often finance their businesses through construction loans) regard the interest payments as a cost of construction rather than an out-of-pocket cost. That is, they anticipate making the monthly interest payments to the bank out of the money advanced by the bank.

A construction loan works like this. When a bank approves a loan, there will be a specific disbursement schedule that specifies that a certain percentage of the loan proceeds are due upon completion of the new foundation, more upon the roof being finished, more at the time the windows are put in place, and so on. You construct your addition, and the bank pays you according to the schedule when they see that its strictures have been met.

GETTING A LOAN

Loaning money is at the heart of a bank's business. But to stay in business, the bank must do it carefully, lending it to people who can be trusted with it.

A bank will establish your "trustworthiness" on numerous grounds, most obviously on the basis of your finances. The three key determining factors are your income, your credit record, and your assets and liabilities.

Income. The rule of thumb used at present for borrowing money is that your monthly mortgage payments should not exceed 28 percent of your gross monthly income. If you have other indebtedness—car payments, credit card balances, student loans, or others—the total of those installment debts plus your mortgage payment should not exceed 36 percent of your gross income. In calculating income, the bank will be concerned not only with your salary or average weekly paycheck, but with all sources of revenue, including stocks, bonds, trusts, income from part-time employment, child support, and real estate.

If you are confident of a substantial increase in your income in the near future (for example, if your business has grown at a constant rate for each of the past five years), the projected future income is also an argument that can be used to persuade a bank you are a good risk.

Credit record. If you have previously applied for and been granted a mortgage and have subsequently paid some or all of it off, you are a better risk than someone who has never borrowed money in his life. Other evidence that you are a good credit risk are a prompt payment history on previous personal loans, credit cards, and department store bills, and the timely liquidation of other indebtedness.

Assets. The lender will be calculating not only what you owe but also what you own. Do you own your car? Another house? How about other valuable belongings? Stocks and bonds or other liquid assets? Are you vested in a retirement plan?

Other considerations. If you own or control a business or have substantial financial resources of your own, you may already have a relationship with a particular bank. Try to use it to your best advantage. If you get the feeling you are not getting your due, go to another bank and make it clear that you are interested in not only a loan but might also be interested in shifting other business their way as well. It might help.

Credit unions. If you're a member of, or are eligible for membership in, a credit union, it may be another source of funds. Most credit unions are not-for-profit institutions that exist to serve their members, both helping to save and to borrow money. Inquire of the loan officer or manager at the credit union about the rates, terms, and other details. Often credit unions loan money to members at very favorable terms and with less paperwork than the same transaction would require at a traditional bank. The interest, however, will not be tax deductible.

WHICH LOAN IS THE RIGHT LOAN? The right loan is the one that best suits your particular financial circumstances. In most cases, the key determinations are these: *Does this provide enough money to do the job?* and *Can we afford the monthly payment?*

Answering these questions can be tricky. If you have little experience in these financial matters, seek the counsel of such professionals as your attorney, accountant, or the real estate broker who handled the purchase of your house.

Your banker can also help. The loan officer can be more than just another person across whose desk your paperwork travels from time to time. You don't have to be best friends with him or her, but, on the other hand, you are an amateur in the business and the more professional advice you can get, the better off you will be.

When the time comes to apply for a loan, do it in person. If possible, talk to the person who approves the loans or who screens them, and try to get a sense of how helpful he or she is inclined to be. You don't want someone who will gossip endlessly about the petty details of other people's deals, but you do want someone who will listen to your questions and give you straight answers. Make sure you get all the attachments and instructions and a clear understanding of the processes of approval and payment.

Another suggestion? After you've talked with you banker and identified what you think is the best strategy, sleep on it. Have a couple of additional conversations, perhaps with your lawyer or a close friend whose business acumen you trust. To borrow money is to assume large and often long-term responsibilities and shouldn't be done casually.

Contracting the Contractors

Do you need contracts? *Yes* is the short answer. Contracts are a crucial part of the paper trail that will help assure that you get what you want. This pathway begins with your preliminary drawings and moves on to the designer's sketches and then to the working drawings. The estimates lead to the contracts and, eventually, the road will be papered with your canceled checks and the Certificate of Occupancy. It's a story with a beginning, middle, and conclusion—and if parts of it are omitted, the ending might not be a happy one.

Contracts are legal documents that specify the responsibilities of the parties. A contract will define the work to be done by each contractor, the sums to be paid by you, and other terms. The documents will probably be drawn on standard forms that you, the contractor, and perhaps your attorney will negotiate and execute.

Contracts should always be in writing. In most states, a contract is not binding if it's not in writing. It's only logical: If the understanding isn't written down to start with, when an argument arises later, how do you know whose recollection is right? Get it on paper.

You may never look at the contract again after you've signed it. However, since the contract in a legal sense defines the relationship you have with your contractor, you probably will refer to it occasionally as the job progresses and you make payments. When there are disagreements, you will also refer to it since it provides a framework defining expectations, payments, and schedules.

Obviously the word *contractor* comes from the word *contract*. Let's say you've met with the contractor, described the job, he's prepared an estimate, and you've agreed upon the other terms of the agreement. The contract that results obligates the contractee (that's you) to pay the contractor for the agreed-upon work.

Both parties should sign the contract, and both should be bound by the terms and conditions spelled out in the agreement. In general that means the contractor will be obliged to provide specified materials and to perform certain services for you. In turn, you will be required to pay for those goods and that labor.

A contract should, however, specify in as much detail as possible the work to be done. If the estimate was prepared on the basis of the plans and specifications, they should become a part of the contract, too. If the estimate was prepared without a formal set of specifications, now is the time to get specific. The materials to be used should be listed, not only the quantity but also brand names and model numbers and dimensions and weight and quality and color and other details. A schedule for the work should be specified, as well as the prices and the terms of payment.

Most often renovation contracts begin life as estimates. If you are adding a deck off your kitchen, the contractor may arrive at your home one evening, discuss with you the job to be done, inspect the site, and then retire to his calculator and clipboard. He'll probably use a standard estimate contract form, and may well before your very eyes write down your name, address, a description of the work to be done and the materials to be used, and then sign the sheet and hand it to you for your consideration. He may ask you to sign right then and there and also advance a portion of the price. He may promise to begin work in the morning. It can be that simple.

Do you want to sign on the dotted line? Use your own judgment: It may make sense to hire him, you may want it done right away, you may have done business with this fellow before and know him to be trustworthy. In general, however, I'd suggest that you might be better off if you take your time and give the decision proper consideration.

Whether the job is large or small, the price modest or mind-boggling, there are basic questions to ask of the contractor and about the contractor.

■ Does this contractor do quality work? The only way to know is to check out some of his previous jobs/references.

■ Is the price fair? Unless you have two or more comparable estimates, you probably can't make that judgment. Getting at least three is a good practice.

■ Is this piece of paper fair to you? Particularly if the document is long and packed with tiny print, get your lawyer to have a look. (If the cost of the work being contracted for is small, you may not want to spend the time and money in getting your lawyer to review it. It may not make sense if the attorney's fees will be greater than the contractor's price. One common rule of thumb is have an attorney review any contract that will cost you more than what you make in a week.)

■ Do you understand every word? In many states, the law requires that contracts be written in plain language, but whatever the case in your area, take care to understand what you are signing. Don't be fooled by complicated locutions like "heretofore" and "notwithstanding" into agreeing to something you don't mean.

■ Does the contract incorporate every piece of paper that has gone between the two signers of the contract? That includes the plans and the specifications you gave the contractor and the estimate and any changes he gave you in return. Remember, only written representations will stand the test of most courts.

PAYMENT TERMS. You should never pay more than a fraction of the entire cost of the job before work begins. Advancing 10 or perhaps 15 percent of the estimated cost is reasonable. In general, the principle to follow is that monies should change hands on the basis of progress, not talk or paperwork.

If the contractor demands a disproportionately large payment up front, find another contractor. Good sense also suggests that at least 15 to 20 percent of the total should be withheld until the job is done, and all payments in between should be made only on completion of specific portions of the job, although as major material purchases are made, more money should flow. The payment of bills is your best single method of controlling quality. You pay when the work is done properly and not before.

KINDS OF CONTRACTS. Contracts vary greatly. Those you agree to with banks for loans will have a lot of language describing the financial ifs, ands, or buts. With bank contracts there isn't much to negotiate as it's likely to be a standard contract. With builder's contracts, every deal is different and there will be many details to discuss.

There are also numerous kinds of contractor contracts. Some set a total price in advance so you know exactly what the final price will be; others are more flexible. There's no one right approach for all jobs, so here are your options.

The Lump-Sum Contract. For a straightforward job without a lot of frills (the use of made-to-order materials, for example, to execute a straightforward design), the lump-sum contract is often best, both for you and the contractor. Your contractor will look at your plans, the specs, and probably the existing building, too. Then he'll give you a price. If no changes are made after his estimate is submitted, he will be obligated to hold to that price.

The lump-sum contract is simple and establishes before construction begins what the cost will be. However, if you elect to go with this method, make sure you get three or more estimates. When you get a lump-sum estimate, you won't see a breakdown of materials and labor costs, so it is impossible to tell from the estimate whether the contractor's markup for profit and overhead is ten percent or fifty percent. If you have several estimates, you have a basis for comparison.

While this may seem an ideal arrangement, many contractors doing renovation work won't agree to a lump-sum contract. There are too many unknowns: What if they discover structural problems? Or have difficulty finding new materials to match the old ones? Insect damage often isn't identified until the walls are opened up. Contractors don't want to find their profits entirely eroded by an unpleasant discovery they couldn't have made before starting work.

Cost-plus or time-and-materials contracts. This method of payment means that you and your contractor will agree on a percentage—say, 10 or 20 percent—for his fee. He will then charge his actual costs for time and materials plus the percentage. A job with materials costing, say, $50,000, with an agreed-upon fee of 20 percent for the contractor, would then cost you $60,000.

The most obvious disadvantage of such cost-plus contracts is that the more the contractor spends, the more he makes. There is no incentive for him to keep costs low, as there is when a price is established up front that he knows he has to live with. On the other hand, when it comes to jobs involving retrofitting an older house or where there are necessarily some unknowns (perhaps your final decisions on materials haven't been made yet), few contractors will give you a lump-sum price. They can't estimate on what they don't know.

Make sure you check your contractor's references doubly carefully if you decide upon a time-and-materials arrangement.

Upset price. One way of establishing an upper limit while retaining the flexibility of a cost-plus arrangement is to get the contractor to agree to do the work on what is known as an "upset price" basis. This means that you both agree to a maximum price before he begins the job. Then he proceeds on a cost-plus basis. Upon completing the job, if the price is less than the upset price in the contract, you pay less; if it is more, it's his problem, and you pay no more than the upset price.

Hourly rate. Some smaller contractors may ask to work for hourly wages rather than for a fixed fee. They may say that in the end it will probably be cheaper for you.

Well, that's possible if rather unlikely. It is recommended that you insist upon establishing a price up front. That way you won't have any surprises down the road. In addition, you avoid having employees and the extra paperwork required.

Draw. Some contractors, especially smaller subs with limited working capital, will ask for a *draw arrangement*. Though every draw is a little different, the basic idea is to negotiate a fair balance of payment for work done. The two of you might come up with an estimate for the entire cost and a schedule for the work, then divide the total price by the number of weeks required for completion. The contractor would then be paid that fraction of the price at the end of each week. This approach requires careful monitoring in case there are delays. It's only fair as long as the work progresses at the agreed-upon pace.

Such arrangements are fair to both parties, so long as work progresses as scheduled. Make sure, however, in the case of jobs that require inspections by the building department that the bulk of money due on completion of various stages is paid only after the inspections have been made. It should be the contractor's responsibility to handle the inspections. In a typical case, a plumber might ask to be paid 50 or 60 percent of the total price when the "rough-in" is completed. That's fair enough, as long as the work has passed inspection. You will have to use your instincts and good sense about what portion of a given job is done (if you have an architect or construction manager guiding you, he should make these decisions), but if it's a quarter complete, don't pay a third. A quarter is a quarter is a quarter.

An excellent clause to negotiate into a contract is one that states that, should the completion of your job be delayed for an unreasonable time, you may then use the unpaid balance of the contract to hire someone else to finish the job. The clause must specify what is the expected schedule (thereby defining what is "reasonable"), and may also require notification (i.e., that you must advise the contractor he has a few days or a week to get his act together or else). But it does provide you with an option in the event you find yourself wedded to an untrustworthy contractor.

Liquidated damage clauses. For practical purposes, *liquidated damage clauses* are penalty clauses (in fact, by law in some jurisdictions, these clauses are not enforceable as they are held to be penalties). Liquidated damage clauses do make their way into construction contracts from time to time but, as a rule, they create as many problems as they solve. If a contractor is going to be late and there is a penalty clause in his contract, you can bet he is going to blame the delays on someone else. And who is to say he's wrong?

A RECIPE FOR RENOVATION CONTRACTS

All contracts you sign should begin with the parties to the agreement. Yours and the contractor's names and addresses should be stated up front, along with the date the agreement was drawn and a brief statement describing the work to be done.

The rest of the ingredients are these:

The stages. The stages in the process should be identified and the job described in some detail (more is better). If the job requires cutting into the existing structure (to install electrical or plumbing lines, for example), the contract should specify whose responsibility it is to patch and repaint.

The site. The area and the limits of the job should be specified here (new shingles on the house, not on the attached garage?). Who's responsible for the trash removal? The term "broom clean" may be useful. You might want to insert the phrase, "The job shall not be deemed completed until the premises are broom clean and all trash and unused materials removed."

The materials. Detail is important throughout the estimate, but nowhere more than here. The specifications should include brand names, dimensions, style, color, weight, and other identifying characteristics of all the materials to be used.

The warranty. Is there a warranty? If there is one for all the work or even a part of it, it should be spelled out here. Oral representations are more often forgotten than remembered.

The liability. A copy of the contractor's insurance certificate should be attached to the agreement and mentioned here, along with words to the effect that the contractor will not hold the homeowner responsible in the event of any personal injury or property damage.

The schedule. When does the work begin and when is it to be finished? Put in specific dates.

The cost. The total cost and the schedule of payments belong here. As a rule, you should pay for work that's completed, and paying less now and more later gives you maximum leverage.

More often than not, penalty clauses succeed only in creating arguments. Putting a specific schedule in the contract is important and probably as valuable as a penalty clause.

Change orders. *Change orders* are not part of the original contract, but are formal amendments to that agreement. They are issued when something about the job changes: materials are switched, the design amended, or some unanticipated complication appears.

THE INSURANCE CERTIFICATE

When you hire a GC, subs, and other on-site workers, ask whether they have insurance coverage. Each should have a blanket policy that covers them—and you—in the event of personal or property loss. (Such policies are often referred to in shorthand as PL/PD for personal liability/personal damage insurance.) You don't want to be at risk for a liability claim in the event of any personal injury or property damage. Be sure as well that the contractor has workman's compensation to cover his employees in the event of an injury. Ask him to be sure that his insurance certificate cites the workman's comp coverage, too.

Ask each contractor to provide you with a copy of his Certificate of Insurance together with his or her estimate. When you sign a contract, addend the copy of the contractor's insurance certificate to the agreement, together with words to the effect that the contractor will not hold the homeowner responsible in the event of an insurance claim. Just to be safe, call the insurance carrier cited on the Certificate of Insurance to make sure the insurance coverage is in effect. If the contractor has missed a payment, the coverage may have lapsed.

If the contractor doesn't have insurance coverage? Preferably, get another contractor. At the very least, discuss with your insurance broker adding construction coverage to your homeowner's policy.

Change orders don't have to be complicated, but if the job changes, then the change orders must be done. They are a key part of the paper trail you are creating in order to control your project.

Managing the Money

A renovation project requires more than the skilled handling of different sorts of people. Good management is always a matter of good decisions, no more, no less. Some decisions have to do with personnel, but many have to do with money.

Any successful manager—whether the person is managing a bank, a factory, or a construction company—knows that making good decisions depends upon having the right information at hand. The trickle-down of this principle for you, the homeowner, is that you'll be poised to make good decisions only after you've done your homework. Which means that, in addition to collecting soft data like reputations and weighing your own feelings and considerations, you've assembled the hard information, namely the estimates.

Before you sign up any contractors, collect all your estimates, loan documents, plans, specs, and any other associated paperwork into one place. Designate a drawer, briefcase, or better yet, an entire desk to the work of managing your renovation. Make it your HQ during the process.

You're going into business, so you need to be businesslike. Before most businesspeople embark on a new venture, they'll put on paper a budget that spells out the capital at hand, the anticipated costs, and whether the budget balances. You should do the same.

You don't have to be a CPA to do this. In fact, one sheet of paper should be enough to summarize the entire process. Put your costs in one column, your revenues (e.g., cash on hand and loan proceeds) in another. Leave columns three and four blank.

The estimate sheet doesn't have to be fancy, but it should be complete and accurate. Check the totals at least twice. You might also have one of your professional advisers review it and your paperwork with you, especially if you've never prepared a budget before.

Take a financial precaution, too. After you've totaled the costs, add a line at the bottom for miscellaneous unexpected expenses. Then take 15 percent of the whole cost and add it to the original total. It's a rare construction project that comes in at the price budgeted, no matter how carefully the process is managed. That additional 15 percent will give you a cushion for cost overruns.

Having totaled all the budgeted expenses plus a fudge factor, does your bottom line tell you that you can afford to proceed? If not, you may need to look for other sources of money. Or you may need to rethink what you are spending (see How to Cut Costs, page 213).

Even if the budget does balance, don't abandon your estimate sheet. As you sign contracts and pay bills, enter the real costs in the third column and keep a running balance in the fourth. By monitoring progress in this way, you'll be the first to know when your budget is in trouble, and you can take immediate steps to solve the problem.

If something comes in under budget, don't get so excited you go out and spend the money on something else. Construction jobs always have ups and downs (building materials are commodities traded daily, so their prices change from day to day). Savor the good news, but expect some other expense to come along and swallow the surplus.

Estimating Checklist

C ost overruns are certainly common in renovation work, but there are steps you can take to try to anticipate some of them.

Below is a long—yet hardly exhaustive—list of costs common to renovation projects. You probably won't have to add a line item for each of these for your job, but if you see one you think you'll encounter and it doesn't appear on your budget, find out why. Is it part of the contractor's overall price? Or a sub's? Don't assume: Ask the question, then put the representation in writing.

Here goes . . .

SITE PREPARATION. Do you need to arrange for tree removal or clearing of other vegetation? How about demolition of existing hardscape (patios, walls, etc.). Will precautions be necessary to prevent soil erosion during and after excavation? Are there landscape features (like mature trees) that need protection?

EXCAVATION. Your estimates should specify what is to be done, which may include digging the foundation hole, hauling off unwanted fill, back filling after the foundation is done, and final grading. If there will be drains in or around the foundation, your excavation contractor may install them, so references to crushed stone and drain tile should appear on the estimate.

FOUNDATION. Has the foundation contractor figured in pouring the footings, walls, pads, bulkhead access, and/or slab? Are there poured concrete walkways in the plans *and* in the estimate? What about insulating the foundation? If your designer has specified it, the cost should be included in the price. What about sealing the foundation with an asphalt-based or other sealer? Is that included in the price? Is other drainage or waterproofing necessary?

FRAMING. If the builder has prepared his estimate on the basis of careful specifications, the estimate should cover framing the walls, floors, and roof with a specified grade of lumber. Green lumber might cause headaches down the line, shrinking as it dries. Kiln-dried hem-fir is the norm, but you might want a higher grade of Douglas fir. In some urban areas, steel studs are required by the fire codes. The exterior walls should be covered with sheathing and the roof with a subroof of plywood, oriented strand board, or roofers. If the design calls for laminate or steel beams, steel columns, or roof trusses, check to be sure the builder has incorporated those into his estimate.

ROOFING. The builder, or a roofing subcontractor, should specify the materials to be used (asphalt shingle, cedar, tile or slate, per the specs), as well as flashing and roofing paper. Particularly in homes in colder regions with dense layers of insulation, ventilation is also important. Are there roof or soffit vents specified?

EXTERIOR FINISH. There'll be a layer of material wrapping the exterior of the house, perhaps building paper or house wrap (see page 54). The type of siding should be specified (clapboard, shingle, brick veneer, board and batten), and the material (perhaps pine or cedar) as well as the pattern. The door and window trim, the corner boards, the trim at the eaves (fascia, soffit, frieze, or rake boards) should be consistent with the specifications or clearly described in the estimate. In cases where you want your addition to blend with your original house, you and the contractor may be well served by a general description like, "Siding and other exterior trim will be done in materials and a manner consistent with existing exterior finish."

MASONRY. If there is a chimney, fireplace, stone or brick facing on the foundation, a mason will need to provide an estimate to you, the GC, or the construction manager. It should specify the type of brick or stone. Ask to see a sample.

INSULATION. Again, the specs should be your guide but whether insulation is required in your climate to keep the heat in or out, insulation is a sensible investment. The kind, thickness, and R-factor of insulation for the walls, floors, and ceilings should be specified, along with the vapor barrier for interior surfaces.

ELECTRICAL, PLUMBING, AND HVAC. The building code and the code enforcement officer are your allies here for safety and health concerns. Look for consistency with the specifications (query any variations). Make sure that you see, at least in a catalog but preferably in person, any fixtures or appliances specified. Verify model numbers, colors, and sizes. If additional capacity for hot water, heating, or cooling will be required to service your added space, do your estimates include the prices for a hot water heater, furnace or boiler, air-conditioning components, or other equipment?

WINDOWS AND DOORS. Doors and windows should be highly functional yet they also contribute significantly to the appearance and character of the house. Make sure that your estimates describe doors you like, and that quality lock sets and weatherstripping are included. Are they of a kind and quality consistent with those in the existing house?

INTERIOR TRIM, STAIRS, AND CABINETRY. Window and door trim, baseboards, other moldings like chair and picture rails, and cornices should be specified. Review the sizes, grades, manufacturers, and model numbers of cabinets; if the millwork is custom, make sure the specs include grade and type of stock to be used. If you are adding a stairway, ask to see sample or catalog descriptions of the stair components, including the treads, balusters, and railing.

KITCHEN APPLIANCES, HARDWARE, AND OTHER MATERIALS. Check the specifications carefully to be sure you know exactly what you're paying for. Affirm that what you expect is what you're getting. Sometimes it's best to exclude these from the contract altogether. Shop around on your own and get some deals but *stick to the specs*. Changes in appliance sizes, for example, can wreak havoc with cabinet orders.

OTHER COSTS. Does the estimate include rubbish removal and cleanup? How about painting, interior and exterior? Prime plus two coats of paint are a minimum; on new wooden floors, the finish should be at least two and preferably three or four coats of urethane.

Have you figured in such landscaping expenses as topsoil, seeding, planting, and relandscaping? Landscape costs are often overlooked. That can mean a handsome renovation has little visual impact from the outside because its setting is a tangle of weeds or a bland expanse of lawn. Do your estimates allow for even modest plantings or walks and walls to accent the architectural attributes of your house?

Some jobs require painters with great balance and the agility of a cat.

You may not want to spend a penny more than the sums already in your estimates, but if pieces of the puzzle are missing, the finished work will end up looking incomplete, too. Have the hard conversations now rather than later. You have much more leverage before the work begins than after it's finished and most or all of your money has been paid out.

Decision Making

Over the years, many homeowners have told me the hardest part of managing a construction job is making all the decisions that are required. There are so many to make in any construction job, including design judgments, hiring options, material choices, and money matters.

"I just felt overwhelmed," one man told me recently. "Our designer took me to a tile store and there were *thousands* of beautiful tiles to choose from!"

No one can decide for you whether to use the Italian or the Mexican tile, or which contractor is the right one. You will need to identify the fixtures and finishes you like from the choices you are given. Often, you need to make these decisions expeditiously, or you'll hold up progress.

As you confront tough choices, consider a couple of rules of thumb I've formulated over the years to help me to frame difficult decisions.

Don't let cost be your sole criterion. While budgetary considerations are often key factors, don't let dollars dominate. Especially if the difference in price is small, think about other issues such as quality, durability, and convenience. Spending a little more may mean a lot in the long run.

Don't labor too long over any one decision. As any good manager will tell you, no decision should require more time to make than it takes to collect the relevant information. So learn what you need to know, listen to your advisers, and make reasoned and prompt decisions.

Take a little time for the big calls. On the other hand, you shouldn't allow yourself to be strong-armed, particularly with the big decisions. We've all heard stories about the piece of real estate that had to be bought right then or it was gone, and such stories are sometimes true. But don't believe it if someone tells you that the job they are going to do for you has a today-only price tag on it. It's often just part of a hard sell.

Rather than getting talked into a deal that may not be right for you, tell the person trying to sell you their goods or services that you made your grandfather a death-bed promise you'd never make up your mind about a significant purchase until you had considered it overnight. Chances are you'll get the extra day, and you'll feel more comfortable with the decision.

Decisions don't have to be forever. We all second-guess ourselves sometimes, and it's no crime. Don't be afraid to admit you made a mistake, but correct it immediately upon realizing it.

Consider this instance: When adding a downstairs half bath, a friend of mine bought some cranberry tile. The sample tile she saw in the shop was beautiful. But when the tile arrived, she realized an entire wall of the cranberry tile would be overpowering. My friend's contractor immediately called the tile store and determined they could return the tile if they paid a 35 percent restocking charge. They decided to make a change. In retrospect, that extra hundred dollars was a small price to pay to get what she wanted.

Be wary of trend setting. Remember foil wallpapers in the seventies? They came and went like the common cold. Clients of mine spent a huge part of their budget papering a vast large stair hall and vestibule. The effect of all that mirrored paper was dramatic but it cost a fortune to do. Unfortunately, it also proved detrimental later when the house was put in the market. Not only were the sellers unable to recoup the cost of the expensive renovation, but some buyers were really put off by the foil paper. Keep in mind that one of the pitfalls of cutting-edge design is that it may affect resale.

Do what you want—but do it with both eyes open and one eye on the future.

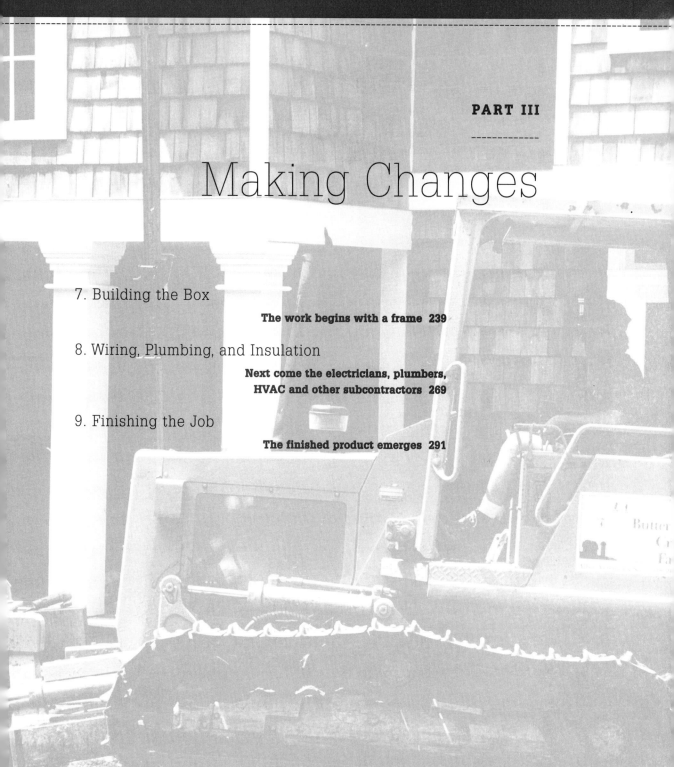

Making Changes

Chapter 7

Building the Box

My adrenaline really starts to run when the noise of construction rings in my ears. As a remodeler, getting a demolition permit from the town was always like Derby Day—*let the fun begin!*

The calculations, the contracts, the drawings, and all the talking can finally give way to the action of building. In a sense, the construction phase of your project officially starts the moment you hire the builder to do the work. With the plans spread before you, you can imagine what the finished spaces will be like.

But the process seems much more real when the men and women of the crew arrive in their vans or pickups. Depending on the job, you'll see anywhere

Renovation is about working with the old yet making it new. The black uprights that frame the firebox are part of a slate mantelpiece that will be reinstalled once the flue work has been completed. Above, the old brick, which dates from the construction of this mid-Victorian house, gives way to a new block chimney, which is, in turn, to be boxed in by fireproof Durorock and plaster attached to metal studding. All in all, it's a modern fireproof retrofit that will retain the character of the original.

from one or two workers to dozens of them. The materials may fit neatly into the trunk of a single car, or require repeated visits from flatbed trucks. It may require hours or days or weeks or months to finish the work. The price may be a few hundred or a few hundred thousand dollars. That all depends on the scope of the job.

If you're putting on an addition, you'll need a hole in the ground for a new foundation. There may be demolition to be done, to remove portions of the structure that will be changed in the remodeling. After the demolition debris has been carried off, carpenters and/or masons will build walls. A roof will rise atop the walls and you'll see the new shape of your home emerge in broad strokes and coarse materials.

If your remodeling job is limited to work within the existing building, there will be fewer steps, perhaps, but the process is much the same—some demolition, some construction, and the spaces begin to emerge.

When the rough construction is completed, the volumes of the house will be approximately those you will see at the end of the process. The spaces won't look the same—the skeleton of the house will be visible, there'll be tools and materials everywhere, and few surfaces will appear finished. The work site will be ready for the next set of workers to arrive, the subs who'll fit the working systems into the skeleton like the nerves and muscles and other tissues of the human body (see Chapter 8, Wiring, Plumbing, and Insulation). All of that will then be hidden behind the plaster, paint, and patina of the completed project (see Chapter 9, Finishing the Job).

In the following pages, read those portions that apply to your renovation (for example, if no new foundation work is required at your home, skip over The Excavation and Foundation). But don't make the mistake of thinking that, having hired all the right people, you can sit back and let them do their jobs. Your attentive eye is a necessary presence on the construction site. You don't have to be there every minute, and perhaps not even every day. But periodic visits are the only way you can monitor the process. Even if you're less interested in the structure of the place than you are in the finished product, remember that what lies beneath the smooth plaster and decorative moldings will have an impact on their final appearance. The better you understand the process, the more you can anticipate problems and communicate effectively with your designer and contractors.

Remodeling Style: More Ideas and Options

Never underestimate the decorative value of color. The welcoming quality this house exudes is a result of its color and the simple patterning of its fence and porch detailing. ANDREA CLARK BROWN, A.I.A.

This is a lesson in sensitive additions. This nineteenth-century house already had a wing put on early in this century *(opposite, top)*, but the current owners still needed more space. The architect decided to balance the old addition with a new one *(opposite, bottom)*. The result is this nicely proportioned front facade *(above)*. KATE JOHNS, A.I.A.

Here's another sensitive addition: The lower roofline, the deep setback, and the careful plantings at this house make a generous addition to a not-so-large house seem very much in scale.

This Greek Revival Style structure isn't old; it's a new guest house on the property of a Federal Style home. Its of modest size (about 1,000 square feet of living space) and nestles nicely into the mature trees and naturalized setting.

Windows can serve a multitude of purposes. In this single instance, an oversized window grid provides light, ventilation, display space for a collection, and a two-way view. It also gives the interior space of this Los Angeles house a more open and spacious feel. TOM GOFFIGON/LT DESIGN

There's something about wood that suits a kitchen. In this modest country home, the warm wood tones are the dominant design element. DENNIS WEDLICK, ARCHITECT

In this kitchen, hardwood cabinets are part of a diverse mix of textures and materials: Note the granite counter-tops, the tile splash, and that the upper cabinets are painted to match the walls. ALBERT, RIGHTER & TITTMANN

If you have a
view, use it. In this
Washington State
home, the breathtaking
view of the Pacific adds
a natural beauty no
designer would want
to compete with.
DAVID HALL, A.I.A./
HENRY KLEIN PARTNERSHIP;
PHOTO CREDIT: DAVID HALL

Space sometimes can
be "borrowed." In this
modest space, a
grander sense of height
and depth was
achieved by turning
the upstairs hall into a
balcony that overlooks
the living room below.
DUNCAN STROIK, ARCHITECT

The cook wanted a country kitchen—and behind the deceptively simple geometry of this gable end is a gracious skylight-lit space.

When photographed in the slanting light of a late fall afternoon, this reproduction inset panel and window surround with pilasters speak for the dramatic interplay of light and shadow that traditional moldings and decorations can bring to a house.

The resemblance of this structure to a Shingle Style carriage house isn't accidental. In fact, this compact structure houses a comfortable guest house, neatly disguised along the drive to the main house. ALBERT, RIGHTER & TITTMANN

This bathroom is a highly successful exercise in geometric patterning. The felicitous blending of various tiles and glass blocks use color, light, and pattern to dramatic effect. IAN J. COHN/DIVERSITY: ARCHITECTURE & DESIGN; PHOTO CREDIT: PAUL WARCHOL

This master bath has his and hers sinks, a view of the surrounding countryside, and a clawfoot tub, all in what was once a low-roofed attic space. The result is a timeless feel to a brand-new space. KATE JOHNS, A.I.A.

A simple hallway doesn't have to be ho-hum. As you can see in this transformation, a nondescript space can be made into an approach that tells the visitor that something interesting is about to happen.

THOMAS BITNAR, A.I.A.

The destination turns out to be a grand public space, in this case an architect's office. On the third floor of this tall Victorian home in Montana, demolition and reengineering of the roof loads made this generous space possible. THOMAS BITNAR, A.I.A.

It's the fond dream of many people to have a fireplace in their bedrooms. In this Indiana home, the tall ceilings make for a very comfortable space to sleep plus a cozy place to sit, relax, and enjoy the view. MALCOLM WOOLLEN, N.C.A.R.B.; PHOTO CREDIT: DAVE DERKACY

This house fits nicely into the seascape on this island setting. But once you reach the porch
with its pergola, your eye is immediately drawn to the view. That view, in fact, so appealed
to the owners that when they remodeled their home, they constructed their bathroom—and
the bath in particular—to take advantage of the vista. The walls roll back so that, when the
day is warm, there is an unobstructed view of the water from the tub.

DAVID HALL, A.I.A./HENRY KLEIN PARTNERSHIP; PHOTO CREDIT: DAVID HALL

In an earlier era when agriculture was a way of life for most people, most homes had barns and other outbuildings. Some homes still do, although not all are so dramatic as this garage-greenhouse building added to a home in Westchester County, New York. IAN J. COHN/DIVERSITY: ARCHITECTURE & DESIGN; PHOTO CREDIT: PAUL WARCHOL

The Building Permit

There is one last piece of paper that you'll need: a building permit. A general contractor usually handles the permitting, but if you are managing the process, you'll need to assume the responsibility. While a permit may not be required if your job is small, you should know which side of the line you're on. Call or visit the building department in your community and find out. Usually there are clear guidelines regarding total cost (permits will be required for jobs costing more than a specified sum) or the nature of the work (if there is plumbing, wiring, or structural work required, then a permit must be issued).

To obtain a permit, you will need to submit copies of your plans and specifications. Many states and municipalities require that the drawings bear the stamp of a licensed architect or engineer. In some communities, separate permits are required for electrical, plumbing, and other building tasks. Before the time comes to file, you should find out what paperwork is required, but you can safely anticipate you will have to provide the building department with at least one set of the plans, along with your address, a general description of the work to be done and its approximate cost, and an explanation of what the space will be used for. The cost estimate is necessary because the building fees in many communities are determined on the basis of a sliding scale depending upon the cost or size of the construction.

Don't be tempted to be cagey and try to get by without a permit when one is necessary. If the building inspector were to find out you have an illegal job going on, he'd probably come knocking on your door pronto. You might then be subject to fines, an order to stop work until further notice, and a whole host of expensive and time-consuming headaches. Once you managed to get the job back on track, you would also have given the inspector a right to be extra exacting in enforcing the building code. Even if you didn't get caught in the act, renovation work that hadn't been properly inspected could produce headaches later, too. I know of real estate transactions that have been held up indefinitely and certificates of occupancy that have been revoked where houses have had illegal renovations and significant code violations.

In short: Playing by the rules will cost you a few dollars in fees but is definitely the appropriate strategy.

The Excavation and the Foundation

Before the building of an addition can begin, site preparation may be necessary. Are there any garden plants, shrubs, or other vegetation you want to remove and set safely aside for later replanting? If there's a tree in the way, you'll need to arrange for its removal. Any other obstacles to the process—an old patio, say, or a stack of firewood—must be moved out of range before work can begin. Depending upon where the work is to be done with respect to the street, additional preparation may be required to clear a path for the equipment and materials to reach the work site.

If you're building a large addition, the arrival of a surveyor may signal ground will soon be broken. With a smaller job, your designer or contractor will probably begin the process by marking out the extent of the new, enlarged footprint of the house.

STAKING OUT. The plot plan will guide whoever it is that does the staking out. For a large project, a transit will be used, an instrument that establishes elevations and levels and points, to help precisely locate where the new excavation is to be done. When the staking out is completed, there will probably be stakes and connecting strings that mark where the excavation is to be done. Perhaps lines of lime will crisscross the ground, extending beyond the actual location of the foundation or cellar hole to guide the men with the earth-moving machines.

Don't faint dead away upon seeing the plot staked out. Even large structures can seem diminutive when reduced to strings or lime lines struck across the ground and viewed under the canopy of the sky. Your new, expensive, and carefully imagined space may suddenly seem rather small. So prepare yourself.

After you've managed to keep your cool on first look, take a second and closer peek. It probably makes sense for you to extend your tape measure from corner to corner. Think of it as a warm-up exercise for the job to come. Your purpose is to make sure the new foundation abuts the old structure where it's supposed to be and otherwise matches the plan.

THE EXCAVATION. Now the noise can begin. Diesel-powered earth-moving machines arrive a day or so later. Often a back hoe will be enough, though for big

jobs there may be a bulldozer (call it a 'dozer) with a wide blade. Or an excavator, a descendent of the steam shovel, with its long arm and the bucket at the end. None of these machines move quickly; they weren't built for speed. But they'll shift gargantuan quantities of soil and, if necessary, tree stumps and miscellaneous boulders. They will leave you with a foundation hole dug to a depth of at least six inches below the frost line.

The *frost line* is the depth to which the winter frost penetrates the earth. In the northern United States, that means the foundation must be at least 3 or even 4 feet below grade; in southern regions where subfreezing temperatures are rare, the foundation may virtually sit on the surface. The base or "footing" of a foundation must

The long reach of this small excavator is perfect for opening a small hole next to an existing foundation.

243

be beneath the frost line to prevent the frost from thrusting portions of your foundation upward and causing your house to settle unevenly (which would result in cracks in the foundation and, eventually, cracks and other damage upstairs in your home). The deeper frost lines in northern areas are one explanation for why full basements are more common there.

The potential problems during the excavation process are too many rocks (if it's solid ledge, blasting may be required); too much water (an underground stream or spring may require special drainage); or even soil problems. Some soils simply aren't firm enough to bear the weight of a structure without additional support, typically an enlarged concrete footing (see below). In parts of the country where soil problems are common, your designer or architect will probably have suggested you test it in advance.

Speaking of soil problems, you may need to protect the soil you have. You may even be required to construct fences, stake hay bales, or employ other means to prevent soil erosion in the event of a heavy rain.

THE FOUNDATION. Once you have a hole in the ground, the foundation can be built. The first step is the *footing*, usually a base of cement wider than the wall to be constructed on it that will distribute the weight over a larger area to prevent settling. (For a house built on piers, foundation pads for the supporting posts to rest upon are necessary.)

The walls come next (after the concrete sets, which takes an average of three to five days). The wall may be of cement block or of concrete poured into a wooden form that is removed after the concrete has set. Setting up the forms for a poured foundation will take a portion of a day; the forms will be stripped two or three days later. Stone foundations are almost unheard of these days, though for aesthetic reasons some concrete foundations are built with a small shelf set into the portion of the foundation that will be above grade (i.e., not buried) onto which a veneer of brick or stone can be laid to hide the less attractive concrete.

After the concrete forms have been removed, perforated piping (called *drain tile*) is laid outside the wall at its base in damp climates. These pipes will be pitched to allow the water that enters them to drain off and away from the foundation.

The earthmoving equipment will then return and backfill around the cellar hole. The soil on the surface must be graded so that when there is rain the water will

Some foundations need repair. In this case, a mason is repointing the mortar joints that hold the old fieldstones in place.

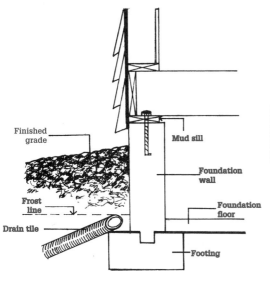

Finished grade

Mud sill

Foundation wall

Frost line

Foundation floor

Drain tile

Footing

Viewed in section, a typical foundation wall is little more than a big foot and a sturdy leg that support the structure above.

BUYING BUILDING MATERIALS

If your designer has specified all the fixtures, appliances, and building materials needed for the job, you may not have to do any of the buying. If you have a general contractor on the job, he or she may handle the ordering and delivery of goods. Yet in most jobs, the homeowner, by choice or force of circumstance, ends up going shopping. Perhaps the goal is to save money; maybe it's to make sure one or another product is to your taste. On the other hand, if you are acting as your own general contractor, you'll need to arrange for buying and paying for a wide range of materials.

Whether you're buying one light fixture or truckloads of lumber, you should keep in mind these considerations:

Discounts. When you begin shopping, ask each supplier—the lumberyard, the electrical supply store, the plumbing supply house—whether they give a *builder's discount.* As a remodeler, you are a de facto builder, so you should act like one and get the benefits. Your suppliers probably won't complain (after all, you are not asking for anything more than many of their other customers get), though if your project is a relatively small renovation, don't be surprised if the answer is no.

Some suppliers have monthly minimums to qualify for builder's discounts (typically, a thousand dollars or more at the lumberyard). Some suppliers have a scale, with deeper discounts for the contractors that do a big volume of business. If the supplier tells you that the preferred builders' terms are not available to you, ask why not and what the required qualifications are. Discounts vary greatly, but a 10 percent discount on lumber and millwork is common, while with lighting fixtures the savings are often much higher. Ask the question.

Delivery. Many suppliers will deliver at no charge. Make sure to establish that they do, and if not what the charges will be. If there is a delivery fee, shop around a bit to see whether other suppliers charge one.

Beware of "sidewalk delivery." A familiar concept to apartment dwellers, it means that your giant new refrigerator will be delivered only as far as the sidewalk—even if your kitchen is on the third floor. That may (or may not) be acceptable to you, but if it is, you'll need to know when the truck is coming and arrange for the manpower to bring the goods inside.

Schedule. When ordering materials, consult often with your GC or subs about the schedule. There's little point in having materials piled at the work site waiting to be used, since the sooner you get them, the sooner you have to pay for them. Stacks of goods can also be very inviting to thieves—in the jargon of the business, they have a tendency to "walk away." On the other hand, you need to be sure that supplies are available when they're needed in order to keep the job on schedule. If the materials aren't on site when required, work will quickly come to a halt.

When researching options, ask suppliers about availability. Find out when you have to order that special tile and odd-size window in order to have them available. Cabinets and heating equipment are most likely to require the longest order time, and their absence can, again, slow down the job.

Payment terms. **You can pay for goods at the time of purchase. Most suppliers will take a local check or a credit card. However, you may want to open an account. If so, the supplier will check your credit (it'll probably ask which bank loaned you money and for other credit references). Having established you are a worthy credit risk, most suppliers will then offer at least a thirty-day term in which to pay, meaning that goods that arrive this month at your house won't have to be paid for until next. That can be helpful in managing the flow of cash during a renovation. Find out exactly what each supplier's terms are as some suppliers also offer a 1$\frac{1}{2}$ or 2 percent discount for speedy payments.**

These days building materials most often come new from the factory, but for some renovations, old-style goods can often suit the existing home *and* save a few precious dollars.

naturally flow away from the house rather than into its foundation. Done by a bull-dozer or other earthmoving machinery, this work is called cutting and filling, as the blade of the 'dozer serves to cut off the tops of the high spots and fill in the low ones. If you are planning on landscaping work later, now is the time to give the yard at least an approximate shape while the heavy equipment is there filling in around the cellar hole.

The foundation won't be completed in day; a week or two to complete the various steps is usual. But once your foundation is ready, the carpenters can begin their work.

Rough Construction

If you are simply reshaping existing space, you don't have to worry about a big hole in your yard. You also won't have to be concerned about the framing of the building or the roofing (unless, that is, you're adding a dormer or otherwise amending the existing roof, in which case you should be sure you read the roofing and siding section, below).

DEMOLITION. Yet almost every remodeling job requires some preliminary demolition. Those kitchen cabinets you've always hated will be removed. Perhaps the cracked tiles in the old bath will be sledgehammered and shoveled into a dumpster.

Make a point of being present at the work site—or having your architect or designer be there—as demolition is about to begin. It's essential that everyone understands exactly what goes and what stays. Sometimes the meeting of the minds you and your designer reached doesn't get communicated clearly. Plans alone may not be enough, so you (or your designer) may want to apply spray paint or masking tape to guide the workers. Even if your general contractor understands, the laborer who actually wields the tools may not. Over the years, I've seen a lot of jobs where the wrecking bar removed or ruined something that was supposed to remain intact. The best renovations are those where you can't tell where the existing structure ends and the new work begins. Don't let a window frame or an old door you're planning to reuse get tossed into the dumpster.

Even if it didn't start in this house, this mantel will look the part.

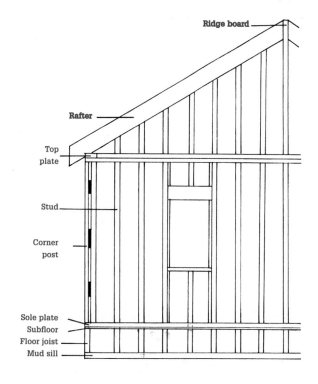

Ridge board

Rafter

Top plate

Stud

Corner post

Sole plate
Subfloor
Floor joist
Mud sill

THE ROUGH FRAMING. Once the demolition has been completed, the process of building anew can begin. The carpenters will construct the wooden framing for any new walls, floors, or ceilings. In some municipalities, certain structures are required to have walls constructed of brick, steel, concrete, or other materials specified for fireproof construction. Most single-family homes, however, utilize a traditional wood-frame construction, so carpenters will handle the rough construction.

While the framing work is going on, you will probably hear some words that are not part of your usual vocabulary. A *stud* is a vertical wall member; a *joist* is a horizontal floor support; a *post* is a larger vertical member, often at a corner; a *beam* is a large horizontal member that supports the structures above.

The basic structure of a wood-frame house, from mud sill to ridge board, isn't so arcane or complicated as it may at first seem to the untrained eye.

Framing doesn't demand the kind of precise (and time-consuming) attention to detail that finishing work does, so inspecting the work site after the workers have

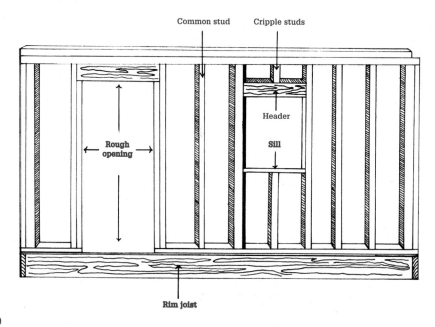

Common stud   Cripple studs

Header

Rough opening

Sill

Rim joist

been there only a day or two can be very satisfying. New spaces seem to emerge almost overnight, and you can suddenly get a sense of how the rooms will appear and relate to one another. With a small remodeling job, the demolition and rough framing may be completed in a day, but don't jump to the conclusion that the job will get done much faster than expected. Framing is often uncomplicated and goes quickly. Most of the decisions will have been made already.

A new window opening has just been framed into the wall of this old shed building. When the finished surfaces are applied, the new and the old will blend nicely together.

Sometimes the demolition and framing will take longer than expected. In the case of many older homes, only when the wall or ceiling surfaces are opened up in preliminary demolition are structural problems apparent. Your carpenter may uncover areas of insect damage or decay caused by dampness. That will mean the replacement of deteriorated structural elements that are required in the new design.

Structural problems may also result from poor construction many years earlier, or plumbers or other tradesmen who gutted members while retrofitting bathrooms or heating and cooling systems. Shoring up structural weaknesses may be necessary. They'll take time and probably cost *you* money as most estimates are based upon no unexpected obstacles.

INSPECTING THE JOB. Your job is *not* to supervise the men and women at work; the contractors and the subcontractors do that. Your job is to examine what's been done, approve or disapprove, and determine when payment is due.

On the other hand, while the carpenters are constructing new walls, opening up new windows or doors, and doing other framing work, you and/or your designer or construction manager should spend some time measuring and inspecting carefully to be sure that the partitions as constructed coincide with the plans. I'd recommend, however, that you put your tape measure to use after hours. There's no need to insult the carpenters, although they know as well as you do that, no matter how experienced they are, they're still capable of making a mistake. Walls do get built in the wrong place, openings set at the wrong height.

You may think there's a discrepancy between what you see and the plans. You may find yourself very disappointed with something—perhaps you just hadn't imagined the kitchen would feel so small. In either case, now is the time to raise the issue. Discuss the differences with whomever is supervising the construction. If your designer is in charge, ask him to have the hard conversation with the contractor/carpenter. But raise the issue as soon as you recognize it. Unbuilding gets more difficult with every nail, every board, every stage in the process. In a polite but firm fashion, raise the red flag, even at the risk of causing a small delay in construction.

Changes will probably cost you money, but this is your home. If there'll be delays or added costs, ask yourself whether the problem will quickly fade—or will you be unable to forget about it and experience a pang of regret every time you walk into that room as long as you live in the house? As the old saying goes, speak now or forever hold your peace.

Speaking of old wisdom, if you believe in tradition, you may want to perform an ancient ritual at the time the ridge board is raised on your new roofline. (The ridge board is the uppermost horizontal piece of lumber to which the angled roof members, the *rafters*, attach at the peak of the roof.) Early colonists in North America placed an evergreen bough at the roof's highest point. The evergreen was a symbol of permanence and an appeal for good luck.

Living In, Moving Out

Do you want to live in a work site? Do you want the sawdust sneezes every morning and plaster dust on your blue suit at the office?

Demolition is loud, dusty work and a taste of things to come. At best, the mess is a hassle and, you may discover, too much to live with. If you haven't already made arrangements, it's not too late to go live someplace else for the duration of construction. Think about it this way: you know how black clothes always seem to attract lint or dandruff? Then how will you feel if your whole life has lint on it? The lint will actually be sawdust and gypsum dust, but believe me, it'll be omnipresent. If you have the option, live somewhere else. At least figure out with your contractor when in the process the plumbing won't be working, the roof will be open, or other basic comforts unavailable to the residents, and arrange to be someplace else then. If you plan to stay in the house, you need to expect the arrival of workers at an early hour. Some may want to work into the evening, too. The life of the house will be disrupted. Prepare yourself and your family.

If your remodeling is the sort that won't take more than a day or two—refacing the kitchen cabinets, say, or adding a deck or patio—then moving out of your home is probably quite unnecessary. On the other hand, if you are putting on a big addition or if major plumbing work will put your bathrooms out of commission, you should make arrangements to live someplace else for a time.

This is an important quality-of-life issue. Don't just dismiss the notion of moving out as too expensive. Don't resign yourself to living with the mess, noise, and disorder without giving the alternatives due consideration.

Look at it this way: A prolonged home renovation project is a tremendous disruption in the life of a household. No, it isn't up there with such stressors as a major illness, a death in the family, or a job loss, but it is among the most stressful circumstances a relationship or a family can face. Everyday patterns and schedules will be out the window. Financial worries are inevitable. Especially with small children, there may be significant safety concerns. The peace and quiet of your home sweet home will be shattered.

Now, you do have some options. Staying with friends or family is an inexpensive one. Taking a room (or rooms) at a nearby hotel is a more costly alternative. For a major job that will take a month or more, renting or subletting an apartment or house nearby may make sense.

How about going on vacation while the work is being done? I know people who've done that and come home to completed work, relieved at not having had to live through the process. But I also know others who returned to a job that was less than perfect, and who have regrets that they weren't there to supervise construction. Don't go away for the duration of construction unless you are comfortable with leav-

Remaining in your home during a renovation may mean sharing it with the likes of this—and despite the buckets, bricks, plaster, shovel, and other debris, this is one very neat work site.

ing the supervision entirely to your designer, contractor, or construction manager.

If you insist upon taking the grin-and-bear-it approach, do yourself a favor. At the very least, develop a back-up plan that will allow you to escape for a few days. Perhaps it's simply a matter of segregating a small sum to pay for a few days in a motel when the frustration peaks. Have a conversation with an old friend whom you've been promising to visit—a weekend away will give you a break from the action.

In talking the construction process through with your contractor, ask him what he thinks. If you learn the house really won't be habitable for a time, add another line item to the budget for alternative living accommodations. Your marriage or relationship, even your mental health, may depend upon it.

Up on the Roof

The basic box is usually completed within a few days or, at most, a few weeks. The timing depends upon the size and complexity of the job—and any unexpected surprises. The wooden skeleton is covered with exterior-grade plywood or another sheet material. It's called *sheathing* when it's on the walls, but when the same or similar material is on the floor it's called *subfloor*. Building terminology isn't always logical.

The finished roof is usually next, and there are a wide range of choices. Material options include asphalt, wood, metal, plastic, clay, stone, and clay tile. You can buy shingles, rolls, panels, or strips. You can have virtually any color or texture you want. You may be able to buy a new roof for as little as a $.50 per square foot or as much as $10 a foot.

THE SQUARE. Before we talk materials, let's talk terminology. Roofers don't usually use the measure "square feet," rather they talk in *squares*. A square is their basic unit of measurement—one *square* is 100 square feet in area, the equivalent of a 10-foot by 10-foot square. The roof of a typical two-story, 2,000-square-foot house with a gable roof will consist of less than 1,500 square feet of roofing area or about fifteen squares.

THE COST. A number of considerations will affect the cost of a new roof. The price of the material is the starting point, but other factors also must be considered. One is the condition of the existing roof—if old materials must be stripped off and if the supporting structure needs repair, that will all cost money. The shape of the roof is another contributing factor. A gable roof with few or no breaks in its planes (like chimneys, vent pipes, or dormers) makes for a simple roofing job. A house with multiple chimneys, intersecting rooflines (the points of intersection are called *valleys*), turrets, skylights, or other elements will cost significantly more to roof.

THE MATERIALS. Not every roofing material can be used on every roof. A flat roof or one with a low slope may demand a surface different from one with a steeper pitch. Materials like slate and tile are very heavy, so the structure of many homes is

FACTORY-MADE FLOORING AND ROOFING SYSTEMS

Most of the wood-frame houses built in the last hundred years have been assembled of dimensional lumber, the standardized two-by-fours, two-by-sixes, two-by-eights, and the rest that you encounter at your lumberyard. You shouldn't be surprised to learn, given the finite number of trees to be harvested, that new products have been developed that take better advantage of the trees we have. Thus, a number of factory-made wood products have begun to appear at the construction site.

Trusses. Perhaps the most common variety of prefabricated structural members are *trusses*. Trusses are carefully engineered arrangements of triangles that can carry large loads over broad spans. They're most often used in home construction to form the triangular gable roof, but other roof shapes and even interior floors are being framed today using trusses.

Trusses use the inherent rigidity of the triangle. Most are assemblages of two-by-fours. At the same time that they conserve materials, they also give the designer the option of creating larger uninterrupted spaces. Trusses are fabricated elsewhere, delivered to the job site on a flatbed truck, lifted into place by a crew or even a crane, and nailed in place much like traditional solid-wood joists or rafters. The costs are roughly comparable, especially when savings in labor are considered.

Laminated-veneer lumber. Made of thin layers (*veneers*, roughly $1/10$ inch thick) of wood that have been glued together, LVL is extremely strong and stable. Unlike the veneers in traditional plywood, all the layers in LVL are glued together with the grain in parallel. This produces a very consistent and uniform product suitable for use as beams, joists, and headers.

LVL actually costs a bit more than solid lumber but there can be labor economies in its installation. The price may also come down as these products become more commonplace, but one argument for the use of LVL is the material's uniformity (there's less spoilage than with solid lumber, where a loose knot, check, or twist can render a piece unusable). Another is its strength—structural members made of LVL can reach across much broader spans. LVL can also be purchased in lengths of 60 or even 80 feet, allowing the builder to span an entire structure without overlapping joists.

LVL comes in two basic configurations. As their name suggests, *I-joists* are a cross between steel I-beams and traditional wooden joists. When looked at in cross section, they have the shape of the letter *I*. The vertical portion is called the web, the horizontals the flanges. I-joists are made of LVL and can be used both as joists and rafters. *Micro=Lams* are structural lengths of LVL without flanges that are used for rim joists, headers, ridge beams, and other applications.

The advantage of all these members is they're strong but light. One man can lift, and two men can position, lengths of 60 feet or more with ease. Trusses and LVLs are all very stable when kept dry in

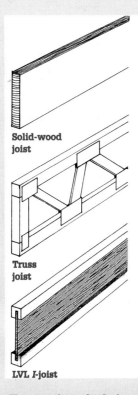

Solid-wood joist

Truss joist

LVL *I*-joist

These are three of today's choices for framing a floor. One is a length of lumber, milled from a tree; the truss is a factory-made assembly of two-by stock; the third looks as if it was fabricated of plywood but it was actually made of specially manufactured laminated veneers.

Often an old wooden frame requires modern components. In this 1870s farmhouse, the owners wanted a wide open span in their kitchen, so several I-beams were sistered to the existing frame to carry the weight of a bathroom and room partition above.

delivery and installation. Shrinkage is minimal, unlike with traditional kiln-dried lumber where shrinkage routinely separates baseboards from floors and cracks plasterboard walls when moisture content is too high. Trusses have the added advantage that their open structure makes the installation of wiring, plumbing, and HVAC systems easier.

Don't be surprised if your designer specifies trusses or LVL in designing your addition, particularly if you are creating a broad open expanse within the house.

inadequate to carry the load. Consider the following options, then talk with your designer and get estimates for the job.

Asphalt shingle. This is the most commonly used roofing surface, probably because it's the least expensive and requires a minimum of skill to install. It's made of a fiberglass medium that's been impregnated with asphalt and then given a surface of sand-like granules. Two basic configurations are sold, the standard single-thickness variety and thicker, laminated products. The standard type costs roughly half as much, but the laminated shingles have an appealing textured appearance and last roughly half again as long (typically 25 years or more, versus 15 years plus). Prices begin at about $50 a square, but depending upon the type of shingle chosen and the installation, can cost many times that.

Wood. Wood was the main choice for centuries, and it's still a good option, though in some areas fire codes forbid its use. Usually made of cedar, redwood, or southern pine, shingles are sawn or split. They have a life expectancy in the 25-year range (like asphalt shingles) but cost an average of twice as much.

Metal. Aluminum, steel, copper, copper and asphalt, and lead are all durable—and expensive—roofing surfaces. Lead and the copper/asphalt varieties are typically installed as shingles, but others are manufactured for seamed roofs consisting of vertical lengths of metal that are joined with solder. These roofs start at about $250 per square but often cost two or three times that.

Tile and cement. The half cylinders of tile roofing are common on Spanish Colonial and Mission styles; cement and some metal roofs imitate tile's wavy effect. All are expensive, very durable, and tend to be very heavy.

Slate. Among the most durable of all roofing materials is slate. Not all slate is the same—some comes from quarries in Vermont, some from Pennsylvania and other states—but the best of it will outlast the fasteners that hold it in place. Hundred-year-old slate, in fact, is often recycled for reinstallation with the expectation it will last another century. But slate is expensive—typically prices start at about $800 a square—and very heavy.

MAKING THE CHOICE. More often than not, the existing roof of your house will determine your choice of roofing material. Should you be considering other options, you'll want to consider not only the cost but the color, texture, weight, and durability of your alternatives, as well as what traditionally has been used on houses like yours.

INSTALLATION NOTES. Whatever your choice of roofing surface, you will probably need *flashing*. Flashing is a crucial part of all exterior work, both on the roof and siding. Flashing is metal (aluminum or copper, occasionally lead) or plastic film. It is applied in strips to areas where dissimilar materials adjoin, such as the intersection of the masonry chimney and the roofing shingles, where the siding abuts the window frames, and so on. Good flashing work is essential to keeping a structure watertight, as the most likely place for leakage to occur is where different materials meet.

Whatever the choice of roof materials, the coursing should be regular to the eye and parallel to roof edges. From one course to the next, the joints should be staggered to prevent leakage. Beware of a contractor who relies on tar for joints. Except with certain roofs where a membrane is used, tar is a lazy expedient that should not be used for a new roofing surface.

For most roofing, a material like building felt (a.k.a. tar paper) is rolled on before the shingles are nailed in place. With cedar shakes, however, lengths of furring strips (sometimes called "cedar breathers") will be laid across the roof in order to allow the roof to breathe. In snowy areas, a membrane called a snow and ice shield may also be laid (see Avoiding Ice Dams, page 260).

Closing Up the Box

On the exterior of the walls, a layer of a water-repellant material will probably be applied, especially in cooler climates. Think of your addition as a gift package, and just like a tie or child's toy, it needs to be appropriately wrapped. In the case of a building, however, the material won't be colorful paper. It'll be one of several products described as *air-infiltration retarders*.

In the past, papers impregnated with asphalt (tar paper) or rosin were applied

AVOIDING ICE DAMS

Many homeowners in the northern United States are all too familiar with *ice dams.* These are thick accumulations of ice that form over the eaves of a house. Water then collects behind the dam and gradually works its way beneath roof shingles through a cycle of freezing and thawing. The result can be leakage into the living areas of the home, which in turn can produce sagging plaster, stains, and other damage.

Low-pitched roofs are the most likely to be affected, but the cause is a warm roof. Heat escapes the living areas of the home and rises, warming the blanket of snow on the roof. As the snow melts, it flows down the slope of the roof only to refreeze on top of the unheated roof overhang. The ice builds up, the thawing and freezing cycle continues, and the flow begins.

Ice dams are preventable. If new roofing is being added at your home, make sure that proper precautions are being taken. The keys are these:

Ensure adequate ventilation. The roof needs to be vented both at the eaves (usually in the soffits) and at the peak, either in the roof itself or via vents in the end walls of the house. An air space above the insulation in the ceiling or attic then allows cold air to move freely, keeping the roof cold and preventing the snow cover from melting. When a roof is being constructed, inexpensive Styrofoam baffles may be installed to ensure that there is a passageway for cold air from the eaves to the peak.

Seal off the house. Proper insulation of the attic rafters or ceiling joists is another part of the solution. So is a tight vapor barrier to prevent moisture from passing from the living areas into and through the insulation.

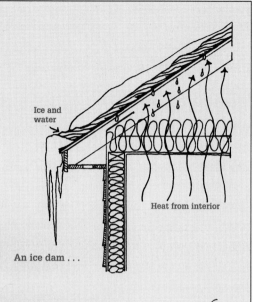

Ice and water

Heat from interior

An ice dam . . .

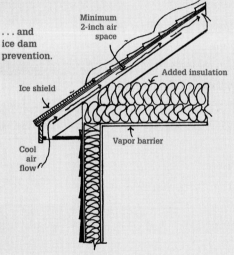

. . . and ice dam prevention.

Minimum 2-inch air space

Added insulation

Ice shield

Vapor barrier

Cool air flow

Install a snow and ice shield. There are a number of products on the market that, when installed immediately on top of the subroof and beneath the shingles covering the overhang of the roof, will prevent water from working its way into the home. A snow and ice shield consists of a bituminous membrane that seals the roof, forming a continuous barrier to water.

260

to the exteriors of houses, after the sheathing went on but before the siding did. More recently, proprietary products like Typar and Tyvek have superceded such papers. The new house wraps are high-tech sheets of olefin fibers that are stapled in place. This clever extra skin allows moisture vapor to escape the wall cavity yet also stops wind from moving freely into the wall.

The house wrap should cover all wall surfaces. Flaps should fold in at windows and doors. An important step that is sometimes omitted is the application of a specially made seam tape over joints between sheets of the wrap and around windows and doors. Without it, the wrap will not form a complete air barrier.

WINDOWS AND DOORS. Windows and doors tend to be key unifying features in an addition. The chances are good that you and your designer will use doors and windows that match or at least resemble those in the existing house. However, in selecting any new windows, there are a number of issues to consider. Among them are these:

Wood or clad windows. The windows in most older homes are made of wood (though metal casement windows have also had several bursts of popularity). On the other hand, many new windows have their exterior surfaces clad in aluminum or covered with vinyl. The advantages of the vinyl and aluminum is they do not require painting; the disadvantage is they don't look like wood and therefore may not match the existing windows.

Energy efficiency is another issue, and the basic rule of thumb is that the more layers of glass, the greater the insulation value of the windows. Your basic single pane window has an R-factor of about one; thermal glass (two panes) doubles the R-factor; if a Low-E coating (*E* is for *emissivity*) is added (a coating that helps reflect heat back, quite like a mirror reflecting an image), you gain another R or so; the same is true if argon gas is sealed between the panes in the airspace, as that limits heat and cold transfer. A typical insulated two-by-four stud wall has an R-factor of about ten, so you can see how a window space can account for significant heat or cooling loss.

The window industry uses another unit of measurement, the *U-value*. The U-value actually measures the heat lost—it's the inverse of an R-value. An R-value of two equates to a U-value of one-half; U-values lower than that have higher insulating value.

While there's no sign, the evidence here reads, "Mason at work." That's a flue coming through the floor, one that serves a generous fireplace in the parlor below. The old line in the house had deteriorated and had to be replaced.

All of which is to say that, as usual, professional help and some shopping around is recommended when you make your decisions about which windows to use. The same is true with doors, too, though the options aren't quite so bewildering. In general, I recommend attempting to match existing windows and doors unless you are building new spaces that are intended to contrast with the original house. And keep in mind, too, that in heating regions of the country, tight and well-insulated doors and windows almost always pay for themselves over a period of years in energy savings.

SIDING AND TRIM. As with the windows and doors, your guiding principle should be the existing finish on the house. But by this stage, you and your architect/designer, along with your pocketbook, will long have decided what the materials will be. If your construction project is a remodeling or an addition to an existing house, then presumably you will have chosen the same or a compatible material to what is already there.

FIREPLACES AND CHIMNEYS. Should your project involve a new brick fireplace or chimney, the masons will be at work during much of the framing. Depending upon the complexity of the masonry mass, it can take a few days or a few weeks for the stack to make its way, course by course, from the footing at ground level out through the roof.

Some Notes on Closing Up

There'll be surprises along the way, some of them delightful and some not. But here are a few matters for which you should be prepared.

WRITING CHECKS. Pay for completed work. And you should only pay for work that is correctly completed, since a paid invoice leaves a contractor or sub no incentive to return and fix the problem. So make sure the work is right before writing the check.

INSPECTIONS. You won't be the one inspecting the work: His title may be *building inspector* or *code enforcement officer*, but for jobs of any size, he'll make periodic visits to the site to ensure you are in compliance with the building code. Typically inspections are required for new foundations; at the completion of the rough framing; after the plumbing and electrical services have been "roughed-in"; when the electrical and plumbing work is completed; and when the house is ready for occupancy. In some municipalities, the amount and installation of the insulation will also be checked.

Some communities require more, some less, but usually before the Certificate of Occupancy is issued the inspections must be completed. The nature of the job is also a determining factor as, obviously, if your project involves no plumbing work, then no plumbing inspections will be required.

CHANGE ORDERS. Consider the story of the homeowner who, upon realizing during construction there was no linen closet in the new master bedroom complex, asked that one be added. He identified a place, thinking the shallow niche at the end of a hallway would require a minimum of change to the plan. Yet when the bills came, the total cost worked out to $1,900. To this day, the homeowner refers to the closet in disgusted tones as "that *nineteen-hundred-dollar* closet!"

Strange as it may sound, he wasn't ripped off. The installation was more than a matter of simply framing in an extra door. There was electrical work to do, too— several electrical boxes had to be moved, a light fixture added, a switch line run to control it. The door itself had to be special ordered, because it was an oddball size. Then the interior of the closet was fitted out with state-of-the-art shelving. In an addition with an average cost of about $100 per square foot, that closet had a square foot cost of more like $250.

My friend made two mistakes: First, he didn't anticipate the need for the closet during the planning stages. But I've already scolded you about the importance of thinking things through first.

Second, he didn't execute a change order when he changed the original plan.

Again, a change order is a sort of contract amendment. It incorporates the change into the basic agreement, describing the change, its price, necessary materials, added labor cost, and so on. The creation of a change order means that everybody's on board, no one is surprised later. You have the bad news of the cost increase, and the contractor proceeds. No surprises.

Change orders aren't inevitable, but they are very common. In order to manage the expense of change, follow two basic rules. First, if someone is managing your construction for you, ask him or her to negotiate the change orders with the contractor(s). There may be inexpensive solutions to a problem. Second, get the change order in writing. Casual conversations have a way of being remembered differently months later.

MISTAKES. Errors get made. Details get forgotten. Misunderstandings occur. That's life.

Perhaps the prefabricated countertops arrive, and they simply don't fit. When the appliances are removed from their boxes, one is mint green, the others white. A partition wall is built in the wrong place. The windows or doors don't fit the rough openings. The tile, the moldings, plumbing fixtures, the cabinetry . . . there really are many things that can go wrong.

What do you do?

THE CONSTRUCTION SCHEDULE

How long do the steps take? No two jobs are the same, but here are some reasonable estimates of what will be required for each stage. Do keep in mind, though, that even the best organized job will, occasionally, have quiet days when work is on hold because of scheduling conflicts, delays in deliveries, and the rest.

STEP / TASK	TIME REQUIRED
1. Surveyor staking foundation location	½ day
2. Excavation and, if necessary, clearing and tree removal	1–2 days
3. Footing and foundation work, including time for curing concrete, installing drain tile, waterproofing, back filling, etc.	2–3 weeks
4. Framing	1–3 weeks
5. Roofing and flashing work, chimney installation	1–2 weeks
6. Window, exterior door installation, siding, trim	2–4 weeks
7. Electrical, plumbing, other rough-ins (overlaps with Step 6) and insulation	1–2 weeks
8. Walls and ceilings	2 weeks
9. Finish work: interior trim, doors, floors, cabinets, painting, set fixtures, etc.	2–8 weeks
10. Punch list, final inspection, etc.	1 week

Get upset if you must, but keep the anger to yourself. Walk around the block. Have a glass of water. Listen to a Mozart concerto. Get cool again, then solve the problem.

If you've put an architect or construction manager in charge, talk to him or her first. Go through channels. Whatever the explanation, you will find a problem or two or twenty as you examine progress on your renovation.

Mistake prevention? Meet often with your builder and designer. Review construction progress, costs, and schedule. What deliveries are due? If there are delays, determine the cause. If people are waiting for materials, what's the holdup?

THE LOG BOOK. Keep a daily log as things proceed. Even if you're not a gifted photographer, buy a cheap disposable camera (make sure it's a model with a flash attachment; they cost less than ten dollars and the quality of pictures is much higher). Take pictures of the job as it progresses.

Later—after the job is completed—you may find a journal useful in settling disputes, large and small. Your notes and pictures may jog your memory and other people's when there are questions of who said or did what to whom and when.

Even if you don't need it, it's a good insurance policy. Plus you'll have a record of the process. When friends and relatives come to admire the finished product, you can show them before and after, as well as in-progress shots. Most people are fascinated. It's both businesslike and fun.

A closing thought? At some point when you won't be interfering with the workers, spend an hour walking through what will be a typical day for you in your new space. Do it on a Saturday or a Sunday, when you have the place to yourself and some uninterrupted time. Literally go through the paces of a typical day: Walk to the bathroom, from the morning shower to breakfast. Carry out a usual work and recreation schedule, the other meals and entertaining and the activities of a day.

Try to imagine what it will be like living in the new space. There should be a growing sense of anticipation. And it's completely normal to have concerns about costs, schedules, and a million other things. But keep in mind your last chance to correct any unanticipated problems is rapidly approaching.

Chapter 8

Wiring, Plumbing, and Insulation

When the framing is completed, the electricians, plumbers, and HVAC subs can begin their jobs. The carpenters may still be at work outside finishing the siding and trim, but inside the house, the electricians will be drilling holes in the studs and joists through which to pull their wires. The plumbers will be running large pipes for the wastewater leaving the house and smaller ones to deliver a supply of water in. Heating pipes or ducts may be snaking their way to new locations. If you have a security system going in or specialized phone installations, the appropriate pros will arrive, too, to bury their wiring in the wall cavities. If your design involves a fireplace or chimney, the masons may still be at the work.

Rewiring can produce a Medusalike mass of wires.

This is an interim stage in the building process. It follows the basic shaping of the spaces and precedes the finishing of the interior walls and floors. It's during this phase that all the components of the mechanical systems that will eventually be hidden behind wall, ceiling, and floor surfaces must be put in place. It's a time when several trades will come and go often, working in tandem to rough-in the basic systems.

The Electrical Rough-In

The plans, as usual, guide the work. For the electrician, there'll be a separate drawing that will map out the location of every switch, plug receptacle, and light fixture. Special-purpose circuits such as for an electric range in a kitchen, a room-size air conditioner in a bedroom, a clothes dryer, or other appliances will also be indicated.

The size of the lines required will be specified. For light fixtures, 15 amperes is usually adequate; for plugs, 20 amps is preferable. (In simple terms, *amperes* or *amps* are a measure of the power or flow of electricity; the number of *volts* identifies the rate; and *watts* are the power actually used). An air conditioner might require 30 amperes at 240 volts (rather than the 120 volts needed for powering your toaster or bedside lamp). An electric wall oven might need 50 amps at a voltage of 240. Most major devices (like a water pump, hot water heater, furnace, range, or refrigerator) have separate lines (*dedicated circuits*) with separate breakers.

The anticipated electrical load on a given circuit will dictate the size of the wire required. But the plans and specifications will determine for the electrician

270

THE THREE P'S IN SUPERVISION

As your renovation or construction project is going on, you will have to deal with the workmen. Even if you feel comfortable with them—and especially if you don't—it is important that you keep a couple of considerations in mind.

The professionals. These men and women are pros in their own worlds. You need them. You wouldn't dream of buying a car and assembling it yourself, would you? In the same way you leave a mechanic to do his job himself, let the carpenters and electricians and plumbers do theirs. Watch if you wish, but don't interfere.

Perspective. Step back, count to ten, think before you speak. Speak your mind but with a little perspective. Don't violate chains of command. Yes, you're the boss but unless you are also acting as your own GC, you are not the only boss.

Patience. Be polite and complimentary. Even if you are not totally satisfied with the work, you are better off finding something good to say about part of it (to the fellow wielding the hammer, as well as his boss) and then, through the proper channels, for the problem areas to be corrected. It is human nature to want to do better work for someone who appreciates it and, conversely, to be less inclined to work for the person who doesn't know how to do anything but complain.

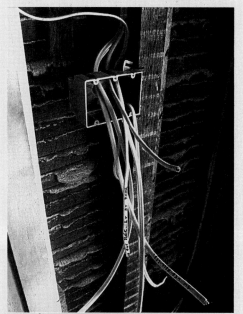

The electricians begin by pulling the new wires through the frame of the house. Because they have carefully labeled each one, the workers can come back later and make the preliminary connections.

the wire size and the number of fixtures or receptacles on each line. It's the job of the electrician—and the electrical inspector—to ensure the wires are correctly sized and properly located.

The wires will extend from the existing electrical panel unless the remodeling requires that the power of your *service entrance* be increased. The entrance is

Here are signs of the old and signs of the new at this house renovation. The giant cast-iron radiator is being relocated. On the baseboard at its old location, there'll soon be a once unheard of *four* phone lines, as marked with the tags on the window apron.

the combination of the electrical meter outside and the service panel, typically inside your cellar or garage, where the feed lines enter from the power lines on the street. There'll be a main circuit breaker (or, in older installations, a fuse) that is the switch that controls all power entering the house. Smaller breakers or fuses then control individual circuits.

When the electrical rough-in is completed, there'll be a new nest of wires that extend from the panel to new boxes attached to the framing where plugs, switches, and fixtures will later be mounted. The boxes for plugs will be at a consistent height near the floor, the switches at a level of 3 or 4 feet. Wall and ceiling boxes will be located for lights. All these boxes will be set carefully so that when finished wall surfaces are later put in place, each box will sit neatly behind the plane of the wall.

During the rough-in, wires should also be run for phone and cable TV. If you are planning on a built-in sound system or intercom, this is the time for the rough wiring for those systems as well. The alarm installers, too, will do their preliminary work, should you be installing a security system.

Your job isn't to check wire sizes or to look for code violations. Your concern is with what's there and, perhaps just as important, what *isn't* there. If you want a phone in a particular location, running the line and installing a box at this stage is a matter of a few dollars. Later on, with finished surfaces in place, the price goes up by about a factor of ten. You need to think through one last time all your electrical, cable, phone, speaker, and other needs and communicate your wants to the crew on hand.

The Plumbing Rough-In

Plumbers work with three basic categories of supplies. There are the *supply pipes* that deliver the clean water into the house and to the plumbing *fixtures*, such as the sinks, toilets, and washing machine. It's the *waste pipes* that drain the water and other waste from the fixtures.

THE SUPPLY PIPES. Starting with the service line from the source—perhaps you have a municipal water supply, maybe a well on your property—the supply pipes extend into the home. The main cold-water pipe, called the *trunk line*, then divides, sending water both to the water heater and to the many branches that supply the fixtures in the house. The cold water supply is paralleled by a hot water trunk line and a second set of branches that provide the supply of hot water to the fixtures that require both. As with the blood vessels in the body or the branches on a tree, the pipes step down in size as the extremities of the system are reached.

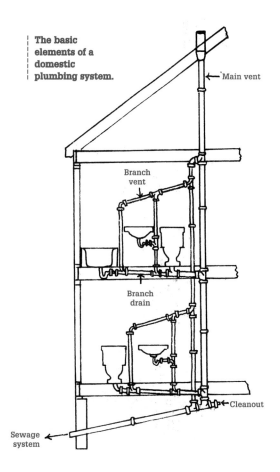

The basic elements of a domestic plumbing system.

Main vent

Branch vent

Branch drain

Cleanout

Sewage system

273

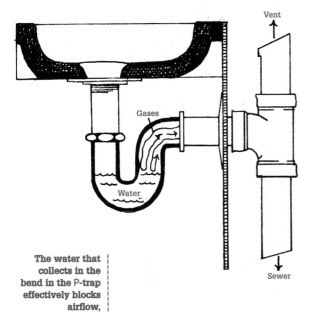

Vent

Gases

Water

Sewer

The water that collects in the bend in the P-trap effectively blocks airflow, preventing sewer gases from entering the home.

Supply pipes can be iron, copper, or one of numerous varieties of plastic. Copper and plastic pipes are the rule today, but your plumber will look to the specifications to indicate what your job requires. In general, copper is more durable and expensive, plastic cheaper and easier to install. Whatever the material used, the pressure in the system is maintained at all times, so the pipes must be tightly joined. With copper, the joints are soldered, with plastic they're fastened with a solvent cement.

THE WASTE PIPES. The waste system is not pressurized. It is dependent upon gravity to function, so all waste pipes must slope downward, away from the fixtures and toward the sewer or septic tank, dropping at a rate of at least ¼ inch per horizontal foot.

The waste system must also be vented, which means that the plumbing system will have a pipe that extends upward and vents outdoors, typically through the roof. That will allow the water and waste in the system to flow smoothly out to the sewer or septic tank. If there were no vent, the system would drain slowly or not at all, not unlike a water-filled straw when you seal one end with your finger. Vent pipes also allow septic gases to escape.

Every plumbing fixture must have its own *trap*, a U-shaped space built into the fixture (in the case of toilets) or in an adjacent pipe. The trap remains filled with water at all times, acting as a barrier to sewer gases that would otherwise rise up through the pipes and enter the living spaces of the house.

THE FIXTURES. While most of the decisions regarding the pipes will be made for you by the designer, plumber, and the building code, you will determine what plumbing fixtures you want. The choices vary tremendously: basic sinks and toilets, for example, can be bought for less than $75, but high-tech designer models can cost many times that. As a result, you will probably let your pocketbook be your guide.

Ask your plumber what models he recommends. He probably has a supplier that stocks one of the major national brands, like American Standard or Kohler. Most manufacturers' lines start with economy models and step up to fancier designs. You will be able to choose color (keep in mind that today's cutting-edge palette may look dated tomorrow), style (the range is Euro-moderne to funky neo-Victorian), and from different materials. Unless you are striving for a strong designer look, recognizably traditional designs in understated colors are probably the safest choice.

PUTTING THE PIPES IN PLACE. The usual order of things calls for the plumber to install the waste system first. Its pipes are large and ungainly, and it's easier to work the smaller supply pipes around the waste pipes. At the locations where the fixtures will later be set, the plumbers will stub off the pipes, capping the ends of the supply lines where they protrude through the floor or wall. By capping off the ends of the pipes, the plumbers will also be able to

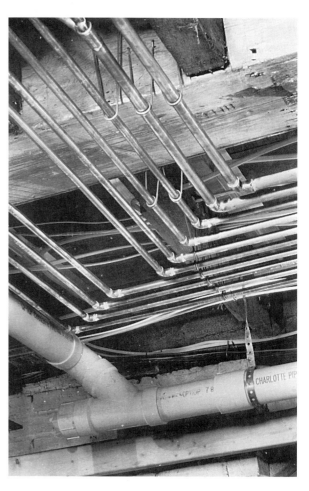

Heating systems with multiple zones require an impressive network of pipes, carefully hung and arranged to serve different areas of the home.

pressure-test the system to be sure there are no leaks. Plumbers and electricians often work side by side.

(Note that if the foundation of your new structure is simply a slab, much of the plumbing rough-ins will have to have been completed before the slab is poured, along with any portions of the mechanical systems that will be buried there, such as steam or electric lines.)

Once the rough-in has been completed, the plumbing will be inspected, usually by the code enforcement officer. He'll check to see that pipe sizes meet code (minimums are specified for trunk lines, bath, shower, sink, and other supply lines, as well as for waste lines from individual fixtures). The inspector will also check to be

FIXTURE OPTIONS

It's your call when it comes to selecting toilets, sinks, and other plumbing fixtures for your renovation. But a couple of very popular options might figure into your thinking. One's an old standard that's been reborn, the other a new engineering marvel.

The pedestal sink. Pedestal sinks were once almost a given in a bathroom. They went out of favor for decades (the advantages of the vanity cabinet for storage are obvious) but have come back into vogue. They're not the answer for everyone, but they can be very handsome.

   As with virtually any household product, the price range is broad. With luck you may come across a slightly pitted but perfect usable sink at salvage for less than $100; new models start at about the same price. At the top of the line, you will find meticulously restored or newly designed models for $3,000 to $4,000! The choice is yours.

Low-flow toilets. Low-flow toilets are designed to use less water. While older designs used as much as 7 gallons per flush (gpf), low-flow models typically use a maximum of 1.6 gpf, the amount mandated first in Massachusetts then in California and subsequently in other states. Most of the low-flow toilets now on the market resemble conventional toilets, while matching their performance. Some of them, however, are loud, relying upon a plastic compression tank concealed within the vitreous china tank that uses the pressure in the supply line to force the water out of the tank, producing a whooshing sound. Even if you are not required by code to install low-flow toilets, it's an environmentally sound approach to do so.

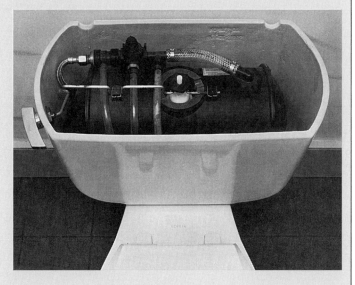

The compression tank in a low-flow toilet is usually hidden by the vitreous china top of the tank.

sure the plumbing lines are well supported (all pipes must be supported at least every 4 feet, either with clamps or hangers or some other fixing mechanism).

   The plumbing work at this stage probably won't look very familiar to you. There'll be no fixtures. You may also have no service to existing fixtures in the house for a time. But rest assured, progress is being made.

Indoor Climate Control

The work of adapting your heating, ventilation, and air-conditioning (HVAC) systems begins at this stage. When the walls are open, running new pipes, ducts, tubes, or wires is relatively easy. Ironically, deciding what to do can actually seem like the hardest part of the process.

If the system in place requires no modification, then the decision is easy. That also means there'll be fewer bills to pay and the overall cost of the renovation will be less. If you already decided no changes are necessary, you may want to skip to the next section of this chapter.

On the other hand, the systems in place may be insufficient to service the renovated spaces. Or you may decide that while the workers are on site that you want to update, perhaps by installing air-conditioning, adding radiant heating, or otherwise changing the systems in place.

When it comes to HVAC work, you will need to decide upon what the source of energy is to be (gas, oil, and electric are the traditional ones) and then the nature of the system (hot air, hot water, and so on). So we'll look at the choices: first, we'll talk about the energy, then we'll talk about the technology required to put it to use.

THE ENERGY OPTIONS. Two hundred years ago, heating systems were decidedly low-tech. If you wanted warmth, you lit a fire in the fireplace. If you were hot, you opened the doors and windows.

In the twentieth century, wood and coal, long the most common energy choices, have been largely superceded by oil, municipal gas, and electricity. Increasingly solar and geothermal energy are being used, too, often in conjunction with more traditional sources. The best choice for you depends upon many factors, including the nature of your existing system, the climate where you live, the relative energy costs in your area, and of course, your budget.

The choice isn't always obvious. In many parts of the country, natural gas is the least expensive fuel and the clear favorite. In some rural parts of the country, however, where there are no pipelines, liquefied petroleum (LP) is the substitute. It often isn't as economical as natural gas.

For many years, oil was the great energy bargain. Then in the 1970s, prices rose rapidly. As the cost of oil skyrocketed, countless homeowners in northern areas installed woodstoves, seeking to take advantage of a resource that was widely available, cheap, and renewable. But the rules continue to change. Today we think of burning wood as labor intensive and, particularly with older stoves that lack the latest advances, it's distinctly unfriendly to the environment. A woodstove sends up the chimney a range of unburned gases and releases particulate matter as well. In the meantime, oil prices have come back down, and today oil is, once again, favorably priced.

All of which is to say the right fuel isn't obvious. Your decision about which source you should use should be made in tandem to your decision about the heat distribution system.

THE DELIVERY SYSTEMS. Every approach has its advantages and disadvantages, whether you're talking about deciding among a furnace, boiler, heat pump, or space heater, and pipes, tubes, or ducts. Let's look at the options.

Forced hot air. Forced hot air is the most common and the fastest mode of heat delivery. The source of the heat may be an electric-, oil-, or gas-fired *furnace* or a *heat pump*. The heated air is then routed to the house through sheet metal, fiberglass, or plastic ducts, driven by a fan, emerging into the living spaces through registers.

The advantages of forced hot air are the speed with which heat is delivered to the house (these systems are significantly faster than, say, hot water systems) and the utility of the ductwork for other climate-control systems. Air-conditioning, filtration, and ventilation, as well as humidification and dehumidification, can all be done using the same system of ducts and registers. The disadvantages are the risk of heat loss through leaky ducts and added difficulty (and expense) in separating different parts of the house into distinct zones. Hot air systems also can be noisy, as the fans that drive the air are usually audible in the living spaces.

Hot water. Also referred to as *hydronic heat*, hot water heating systems consist of a *boiler* that heats the water and a pump that circulates the water through a system of pipes (hidden in the skeleton of the house) and radiators (in the living spaces). Typically the water is circulated at temperatures in the range of 130 to 180 degrees Fahrenheit.

Hot water systems are slower but quieter than hot air. They're easier to zone,

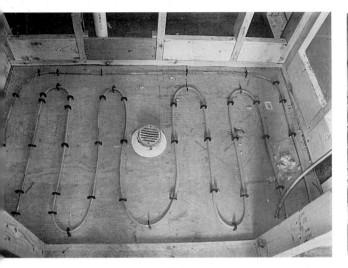

LEFT: The owners of this house will have warm feet when they step into their shower. The pan of this double shower will have radiant heat, with hot water pumped through the tubes to warm the masonry floor. RIGHT: Radiant heating can be used over larger areas than a bathroom or shower floor. Here a worker screeds concrete over the radiant tubing.

but cost more to install. The radiators also pose a challenge to interior design since their sheer bulk interferes with furniture placement. Hot water systems cannot be adapted for air-conditioning and other climate-control uses.

Radiant floor. Although variations on this same theme have been around for millennia, this latest incarnation has only returned to wide use in recent years. *Radiant floor heating* is the least obtrusive method of heating. As with hot water systems, a boiler provides hot water, heated to temperatures in the range of roughly 85 to 140 degrees Fahrenheit. The hot water is distributed to the house via a system of manifolds and controls that bring the heat to a complex network of plastic or rubber tubing that is hidden in the floor.

Three basic approaches are used in radiant floor systems. When a house is built on a concrete slab that sits directly on the soil, the radiant pipes are embedded in the concrete. The second approach utilizes a thinner

Beneath an existing floor, radiant plate heating can be retrofitted, as seen in this picture taken in the cellar, looking up at the floor joists above.

slab of concrete: once the tubing is fastened directly to the decking of a traditionally framed floor, a thinner slab of concrete is poured. The third uses aluminum heat-transfer plates that radiate the heat from the tubing. Tubing-and-plate systems can be installed on top of or below existing wood-framed flooring systems. The plate systems lend themselves to retrofitting; since they can be installed from below, the existing flooring needn't be disturbed. However, keep in mind that radiant heat isn't well suited to homes with wall-to-wall carpets and thick pads or multiple layers of plywood. These have high thermal resistance and effectively insulate the room to be heated.

The growing popularity of this technology is explained largely by customer satisfaction: homeowners with radiant heat report that it heats evenly, with fewer hot or cool spots and less stratification. Radiant heat costs more to install: it requires careful design and skillful installation. But it is easy to zone.

Electric baseboard. Mounted on exterior walls at floor level, electric baseboard heaters consist of sheet metal housings that protect wires inside that, like those in a toaster, warm and glow when current is run through them. The heating elements are lined with metal fins that heat the air around them; the housing then allows air to circulate in the bottom and out the top. Electric baseboard radiators are inexpensive to install.

Baseboard heaters are wired like any other electrical appliance. A feed line is run through the walls or floors from the electrical panel to the baseboard unit. Some baseboard heaters come with their own thermostats, but in a room where several radiators are required, a thermostat is mounted on an interior wall as a control system. This also means that electrically heated homes are easily zoned; for the added expense of a few thermostats, every room becomes its own zone, where the heat can be lowered when it's not in use.

Electric baseboard heat is inexpensive to install, but it's very costly to run. That's one reason it's often found in spec houses—the builder wants to save money up front and doesn't have to worry about bloated electric bills later. On the other hand, electric heat is quiet, clean, and quite unobtrusive (the baseboard units are modest in size and interfere little with furniture placement). I would not recommend using such systems for an entire house, especially in a cold climate. But for a small addition where the cost of enlarging an existing hot water or hot air system might be prohibitive, electric baseboard may be an appropriate choice.

Space heaters. There are other alternatives for heating individual spaces. Space heaters are direct heaters. Unlike systems where the heat is generated in one place and distributed another, these heaters are self-contained, directly heating the spaces where they are located. A fireplace is a space heater, albeit a very inefficient one. Others include woodstoves, gas and kerosene wall heaters, and freestanding heaters. The latter can be oil- or kerosene-fired or electric. Each of these has advantages—most are inexpensive to buy and fairly economical to run. But burning wood produces environmental pollution (particulate matter and unburned gases) and freestanding kerosene heaters in particular have a very mixed safety record.

Air-conditioning. In any refrigerant system—whether it's inside your refrigerator or an air conditioner—the key element is the cooling medium or *refrigerant*. The refrigerant is a gas at normal atmospheric pressures but, when compressed as by the compressor of a cooling system, it becomes a liquid.

With central air-conditioning systems, the refrigerant is passed through the coiled tubing in an *evaporator* located in the house. There a flow of household air is passed over the coil. As the pressure is released, the refrigerant returns to its natural gaseous state, absorbing heat from the air as it does so. The cooled air is then distributed to the living areas of a house via a network of ducts and registers. The refrigerant is then pumped outside to a condenser where the heat is discharged, the refrigerant recompressed, and the cycle repeats. A window air-conditioning unit functions in the same way, but its components are self-contained.

Heat pump and geothermal systems. These systems are near relations of central air-conditioning systems. They rely upon an electrically powered compressor that compresses a refrigerant from a gas to a liquid. In the process, heat is given off and, during the cool months of the year, that heat is distributed via ducts to warm the house. In warm weather, the process is reversed, and the system absorbs warm air indoors, releasing it outside.

One limitation of a heat-pump system is that it loses efficiency rapidly when

Not every piece of information can be memorialized on the architectural plans. As work progresses, the HVAC contractor installing a complex radiant system had to make ad hoc notes and a diagram as an easy reference for him and others.

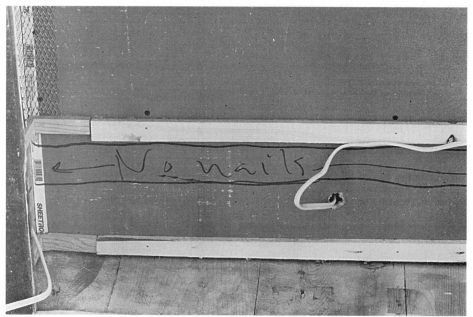

282

the thermometer drops below 40 degrees. As a result, in colder climates a *geothermal* heat pump system or *ground-source* heat pump may be used.

The earth's temperature 8 or 9 feet below the surface remains quite uniform all year round. That means that during the heating season, its temperature is warmer than the atmosphere's; during the hotter months, the earth's temperature is cooler than the air's. A ground-source heat pump puts that differential to work, again using a refrigerant and compressor system.

Because much of the energy is drawn from the environment, such systems are economical to run—typically, the electricity required to run them is roughly a third that of a traditional electric system. They're also clean. However, they're expensive to install, require annual maintenance, and typically their components have a shorter life expectancy than do traditional furnaces or boilers.

CHOOSING A SYSTEM. If you're considering a new system for your home, talk first to your architect or designer. Conversations with HVAC contractors will probably follow, although you or your designer may also want to consult a specialist, a heating engineer, in the event your remodeling presents unusual demands.

Talk through in detail exactly what your needs are. If your budget is tight, you'll need to identify essentials. If you can afford to think more broadly, consider the added comfort of, say, radiant floor heating. If you're unhappy with your present system or would like to add humidification or a filtration system, get bids for those costs. In most cases, extending your existing system or adding a smaller area heater will be the least expensive.

Here are a few other considerations:

■ The air-conditioning option. As a rule of thumb, if local temperatures rarely rise above 85 degrees Fahrenheit, you probably don't need central air-conditioning. On the other hand, central air is often regarded by realtors as a valuable selling point, so if there's a chance you'll be transferred to another region or are likely to put your home on the market for any reason in the near future, central air-conditioning may be a good investment. Top-of-the-market houses get top-of-the-market prices because they have all the bells and whistles. For people with asthma and other allergy problems, central air with its ability to filter and "condition" household air can also have health benefits.

> ## KEEPING A RECORD
>
> After the mechanical rough-ins have been completed but before the insulation goes into the wall surfaces, record the work with your camera and flash. Take a photograph of each wall that has wiring, plumbing, or ducts in it; take several of those areas where there's a lot going on.
>
> Keep the developed prints with your log book. You may never need the photographs. On the other hand, if you ever have a problem or if you later decide to make any changes, you won't have to open a wall to find out exactly what's where. It'll cost you about ten minutes and $10—but, in the future, this precaution could save you many times that.

■ Beware of oversize systems. Strange though it may sound, too much heating capacity will make a system *less* efficient. It will cause the system to cycle on and off frequently, producing excess wear and tear on the components. The system may never reach peak operating temperatures.

To be sure your system is suited to your home, ask your HVAC contractor, heating engineer, or whoever designed the system to walk you through the calculation. The process consists of determining what the *heating load* is (based on an arithmetical formula that factors in the size of your home, its insulation, and the local climate). The system capacity should be no more than 25 percent greater than the calculated heating load.

■ Simple is usually less expensive. Staying with your existing system is almost certainly the cheapest route. If your system has enough capacity that it can be extended to heat (or cool) new spaces, that approach will probably be less expensive than installing an all-new system.

■ Buy quality. Good shoppers don't always buy bargains. Buying durable boilers or furnaces that come with long warranties often costs more initially but, over the years, presents fewer headaches. Good furnaces often are guaranteed for twenty years, boilers for thirty, heat pumps for less.

■ Think locally. Don't buy equipment that no one in your area can service. If the only HVAC contractor who'll bid your job is a long-distance call away, you could be asking for trouble. These sophisticated modern systems require occasional checkups by service people familiar with their design, installation, and individual characteristics.

One industry study found that *half* of all service calls were the result of improper or insufficient maintenance.

The Insulation

Once the mechanical rough-ins are complete, insulation will be installed in the wall cavities. Insulation is relatively new—few houses built before 1940 had what we today would recognize as insulation. But in our energy-conscious age, insulation is a given.

Thermal building insulation resists the flow of heat: During the heating season, less warm air escapes and, during hot weather, less overheated air enters through properly insulated ceilings, floors, and exterior walls. Most insulation is made of airy, diffuse materials full of dead air spaces because air is a poor conductor of heat.

KINDS OF INSULATION. There are three basic categories of insulation that may be used in your home.

Batts and blankets. Thick blankets or *batts* of fiberglass, "glass wool," or cotton insulation are common in new construction and in retrofitting old where the wall cavities are open and accessible. The insulation, which comes in thicknesses of 1 to 13 inches, is stapled between the studs in the walls or the joists or rafters in the ceiling or floor.

Loose fill. Cellulose (typically made of recycled paper products), fiberglass, cotton, or even perlite or vermiculite are used as *loose fill* insulation. That means they can be poured by hand or machine blown into ceiling cavities or, in instances where the interior wall surfaces have not been removed, between wall studs. The loose fills tend to flow readily into nooks and crannies. A variation of this is a mix of loose fill with a binder or glue that enables the material to be pumped in and, when the glue hardens, to hold its shape. Foams like polyicynene are installed in the same way.

Rigid plastic boards. Typically of extruded or expanded polystyrene, polyisocyanurate, or fiberglass, *rigid plastic boards* are often used in new construction as exterior sheathing for walls or roof decks or interior masonry walls. Rigid insulation is available in a variety of thicknesses, from ¼ inch up to 10 inches.

The cellulose insulation is dumped into a bin and then, powered by a compressor, is fed into the pipes. Inside the home, the cellulose insulation is blown into the wall cavities. The excess that falls to the floor is quickly vacuumed and recycled.

As with any heating system, forced-air ducts decrease in size from main trunk lines to individual pipes that feed the registers.

INSTALLATION NOTES. Fiberglass batts or blankets must be firmly attached to studs or joists to hold them in place. The installer needs to work the insulation around electric wires in the walls by separating some of the insulation along its length and sliding it behind the wire. In the same way, the insulation must be carefully worked around wall receptacles. If the insulation is compressed, its insulation efficiency is greatly reduced.

When rigid plastic boards are used on interior surfaces, most building codes require that they be covered with a fire barrier, usually a ½-inch layer of drywall. This is necessary because, in the event of fire, the plastic boards give off toxic gases when ignited.

THE VAPOR BARRIER. Once the insulation is in place on the walls and ceilings, the vapor barrier comes next. Typically the barrier is a sheet of polyethylene film, asphalt-coated kraft paper, or aluminum foil. When a vapor barrier is installed in renovated portions of the house and there is no barrier in unrenovated areas, you may want to discuss with your contractor painting at least the ceilings in those areas with a specially formulated paint to form a vapor barrier.

The vapor barrier serves two purposes that are especially important in colder climates. The vapor barrier, as its name suggests, prevents moisture in the air of the home from traveling outward through the walls and condensing when it meets colder air. Moisture in the walls could reduce the effectiveness of the insulation, but more important, it could also lead to decay of the wood structure. The other value of the vapor barrier is to prevent the infiltration of cold air from the outside through any chinks in the walls.

Some Notes on the Mechanical Systems

The timing? Electrical, plumbing, and HVAC rough-ins should take roughly two to three weeks. The insulation will happen in a day or two. But delays are common at this stage.

If you are living in the house, particularly with young children, you need to be sure that all the tradespeople secure their tools, equipment, and overall work areas daily. Establishing a child- and pet-free zone is a must, but it's also a good idea for you to make it a habit after the workers leave each day to make an inspection—try to anticipate any hazards to you or your children, inside the zone and out. This means the work site should be clean and organized. If you have any safety problems or concerns, discuss them immediately with the general contractor or the subs involved.

The local building inspector will probably have visited during the foundation work, but he's guaranteed to come now. In fact, different inspectors may arrive to look at plumbing, electrical, and other work. Unless you're acting as your own general contractor, this probably won't be your responsibility. Your subs each should arrange for the inspectors to visit—and make sure their work passes the inspections.

You should also do your own inspections, just to be confident you're getting what you want. Among the items you might be concerned with are the following:

ELECTRICAL SYSTEM. Check the locations of electrical plug, switch, and light boxes. Is each where the plan says it should be and where you want it? According to many codes, there should also be a wall plug for every six feet of wall space and any small sections of wall two feet or wider (such as between doors, for example) should have their own receptacles.

Has a smoke detector been hard-wired into the system? Many building codes require them today and they are a sensible and inexpensive precaution.

Are there ground-fault interrupter receptacles on kitchen, bathroom, and exterior lines?

Are the phone lines and alarm systems properly located?

No one, of course, is perfect. The drywall guy who cut these holes missed, erring left, and had to cut another set to allow these stubbed off plumbing pipes through. No great harm done, however, as the plasterers will shortly cover his mistake forever.

PLUMBING SYSTEM. Are the stubs for the supply and waste lines all properly located, consistent with the plan *and* with your desires? Are there shutoff valves for each plumbing fixture? Have the lines been tested? If you had any special requirements, have they been incorporated: a dedicated electrical line for your computer, an extra plumbing line for that whirlpool you want to buy when you have the spare cash, whatever.

HVAC SYSTEMS. Does each room have the specified ventilation/heating/air-conditioning ducts or pipes? (Heating pipes are usually an inch or more in diameter, while plumbing supply pipes are typically smaller.) Are thermostats located on interior walls and out of direct sunlight? Does the insulation cover all the openings and chinks to the outside?

THE PAYMENT. Every job is different but typically when the rough-ins are completed, tradespeople expect to be paid. Many contracts specify a quarter or a third of the contract sum is payable at this stage. So get your checkbook ready.

And get yourself ready for the excitement to come. The time required for the mechanical systems may leave you feeling the process is proceeding very slowly, but from here on the finished product will begin to emerge.

Chapter 9

Finishing
the Job

For the novice renovator, one of the chief frustrations of the process is the hurry-up and slowdown nature of the work. At times, you feel like the job is progressing so well . . . but there's so far to go. Well, the finish work will provide pleasure *and* test your patience.

The finish work falls into two basic categories, the surface finishes and the mechanical installations. The walls get closed up, the plaster and trim are applied. The floor surfaces get put down. This is the time when plumbers put in your toilet and sink (it's called "trimming out" or "setting the fixtures"). The painters paint and the sanders sand. The electricians will install your dining room chandelier and your electric range. The plugs and light switches get tied in now, and the power comes on, too.

This pair of French doors, installed in wall pockets, allows light from the front room of this New York apartment to reach an interior space.
Photo credit: Hugh Howard

The mechanical work must be meticulously coordinated with the surface finishes: the toilet goes on top of the tile floor, so the tileman must do his bit before the plumber can do his. The order of things calls for the walls, ceilings, and floors to be finished, then for the bathroom fixtures to be set, along with the final electrical and HVAC work. After everything is tested and inspected the job is done. Except for those items on the punch list, of course. But we'll get to all that shortly.

I think of finish work as the hardest part. You look around you at the new walls and ceilings, knowing full well how much work has gone in already, and how many tasks have been completed. In reality, however, a remodeling job at this stage is only about half done: Finish work—which for practical purposes includes all the tasks that follow the rough-ins—takes a disproportionately long time.

Yet this is perhaps the worst time for impatience: Quality finish work, when executed just right, can make or break a job. Don't telegraph to the workers *I just want my house back!* That's the surest way to get them to slam-bam their way to completion. On the other hand, don't allow the carpenters and other tradesmen to come and go and finish at a snail's pace while they are working on other people's jobs. Keep your attention focused, be a little bit patient, and try to enjoy what's happening around you.

So let's see what's going on at the work site.

The Walls and Ceilings

The completed rough frame of the structure allows you to get a physical and visual sense of the new or renovated space, but it is only after the walls and ceilings are installed that you will get a clear sense of the final feel and dimension of the rooms. You will have decided long before this stage in construction what material is to be used for wall and ceiling surfaces, but the common options these days are gypsum board (a.k.a. drywall or Sheetrock) and wood paneling.

DRYWALL. The gypsum board comes in sheets, 4 feet wide and of various lengths, with 8-, 10-, 12-, 14-, or 16-foot sheets being generally available. If you're a home handyperson, you've probably "hung a little 'rock" over the years, so you may know the drill. If you don't, it's simply a matter of fastening the heavy sheets to the wall

If anyone tries to tell you plastering is easy, just refer to these two attaché cases full of tools. Every tool has a distinct purpose and each requires skill to use. And here are two key ones: The basic plasterer's trowel (right hand) and the hawk, used to hold plaster at the ready for application.

studs or ceiling joists using specially designed nails or screws. The heads of the fasteners are then recessed just beneath the surface of the gypsum board.

With the drywall in place, the volumes of the room have real definition. Often this is an emotional high point in a renovation: a great leap forward seems to have been made. When a professional drywall crew does the work, the change can take place in a matter of hours. On the other hand, if you have a one-person renovation crew, he or she may take a piecemeal approach and finish the rough framing, mechanical installations, and wallboard in one area at a time before going on to the next. That makes for a more gradual transformation.

Once the sheets of gypsum board have been hung, the next stage is the application of a plasterlike paste called *joint compound*. Joint compound comes in the big buckets that are ubiquitous at construction sites. It's a specially formulated mixture of gypsum, water, and additives that remains workable for several hours but dries overnight. It'll fill the nail or screw holes and, along with strips of tape, the joints between the sheets producing a uniform surface. Over a period of several days, three or more layers of compound will be applied, though with a crew of drywallers, they may use a rapid-drying compound, enabling them to do the job much more quickly. Gypsum board ceilings are done in the same way as the walls.

Not all drywall is the same. Most drywall is a dull gray color, but waterproof drywall, which is often required (and always a good idea) in kitchens and baths, is usually a greenish color. It contains a layer of fiberglass that is water resistant. In shower stalls, a cement board sometimes called tilebacker may be used. It typically comes in smaller, 3-feet-by-5-feet, sheets. This cement board is specially designed to withstand the dampness that can work its way between the joints in ceramic tile over time without becoming spongy and even collapsing as traditional drywall will when subject to prolonged dampness.

SKIM COATING. You may also decide to go to the added expense of skim coating the entire surface of the wall board with a thin veneer of plaster. If you do, the drywall sheets will have a bluish hue and the paper surface a toothier finish to enable the plaster to adhere. Skim coating typically adds considerably to the cost, often half again as much as the simpler tape-and-compound approach. However, it can add significant soundproofing, as well as a more durable, attractive finished surface.

TRADITIONAL THREE-COAT PLASTER. This was for almost two centuries the preferred method of creating a plaster wall. There are no sheets of drywall, but the bays between the studs were spanned with strips of wood *lath*; more recently, wide bands of wire mesh called expanded metal lath have come into general use. The next stages are the same whatever the lath, with the application of three separate of coats of plaster. First comes a rough or base coat of plaster mixed with sand that oozes through the gaps in the lath to form *keys*, which, upon hardening, hold the plaster surface in position. Next is a slightly finer plaster mix called a brown coat, and finally the smooth-as-glass finish coat. Obviously, this is a labor-intensive process requiring considerable skill. Therefore it is expensive, typically two to three times the cost of drywall. Is it worth the added cost? That's your call. To some people, the added soundproofing, durability, patchability, and finish are worth the expense.

PANELING. In the case of paneling, prefabricated veneered sheets are available, as are precut widths of solid boards. With the veneered sheets, the finish has already been applied: it saves time and money, but generally looks like it did, too. You, along with your designer and contractor, will have to resolve what gives you the look you want at a price you can afford.

There are ceiling alternatives as well. Ceiling tiles are a good option for some, while dropped ceilings may be suitable if the job involves remodeling an older home with ceilings that are judged for energy reasons to be too high. But once again, keep in mind the historical integrity of the building. More often than not, the high ceilings are crucial to the appeal of the room, and lowering them may leave the room with a feeling that something is amiss.

Flooring

Wood remains the most used flooring material. Its warm feel and appearance, affordability, and sheer variety probably account for its popularity. But ceramic tiles, carpeting, sheet flooring, and other options each have important uses.

If possible, it's always a good idea to see the flooring material you are considering having installed. That way you can assess the blend of colors and patterns with the other elements of the room. Different surfaces provide better service than others

KITCHEN CABINETS AND COUNTERTOPS

Often the two most expensive line items in a remodeling budget are the kitchen cabinets and the countertops.

Cabinets. Books have been written about making cabinets—and one could be written about buying them, too. But there are some key considerations and terms you should know. I'll try to give you in brief a few guidelines to help in your shopping.

New or refaced. Perhaps the least expensive option in a kitchen remodeling is to *reface* existing cabinets. This means the boxes that contain the shelves and drawers remain in place, saving demolition, construction, and purchase costs. Only the fronts of the cabinets are replaced, which usually involves new doors, face frames, and hardware. If you're happy with the layout and the number of cabinets you currently have but want to give them a new look, this may be the right way to go.

Material choices. Whether you're buying all-new cabinets or just refacing, you'll need to decide whether you want all-wood, wood veneer, or laminate doors and face fronts. With veneer cabinets, a thin ply of wood is applied to a substrate of plywood or a composite material like particle board (plywood is better, but more expensive). Laminate doors are often fabricated of polyvinyl chloride sheets that are heated, molded, and applied to a substrate to give a seamless appearance.

Buying the boxes. If you are buying all-new cabinets, you'll want to know of what materials the boxes are made. Solid wood cabinets these days are rare and expensive; even plywood boxes are becoming pricy and less common. More likely, you'll encounter *melamine*, a reasonably sturdy composite material made of resins. It will chip but is stronger than the lesser choices, which are little more than paperboard, sometimes surfaced with vinyl. When shopping for cabinets, ask to look at a cabinet box; a little visual examination will reveal how sturdy the secondary materials are. How well are the pieces fastened together? Are nails or screws apparent to the eye? It doesn't take a cabinetmaker's training to distinguish the wobbly and shoddy.

Look, too, at the construction of the boxes. Are the doors fastened directly to the sides of the box (*frameless*) or to an applied facing of horizontal and vertical members (*framed*)? Are the drawers dovetailed? Do the drawer bottoms flex noticeably when you put weight on them? What about the drawer slides? Do they work smoothly when you put a book or two in the drawer? Do the hinges and other hardware elements look well made and sturdy? Are they adjustable? (Look for slots and set screws.)

In general, the quality you get is a function of the money you're willing to spend. Solid wood cabinets cost more than cabinets made of composite materials. Hand-rubbed finishes, Euro-style hardware, mortise-and-tenon joinery, and other top-of-the-line qualities come only at added expense. Remember, too, that accessories can add both to the convenience and the price of your new kitchen: sponge drawers, lazy susans, gadget garages, glazed doors, recycling bins, and built-in pantries are only a few of the options available.

Countertops. There are choices, as usual, from moderately priced to expensive; there are natural surfaces and man made; the range is wide. The principal choices, from least to most expensive, are the following:

Laminate. This is the most popular category. Many colors and patterns are available, and the price is in the range of $15 to $40 per linear foot of countertop. Most consist of a core material with a surface veneer applied. Formica is one common brand name. The disadvantages are the surfaces can scratch or burn and are not easily repaired.

Ceramic tile. Like laminate countertops, ceramic tiles are available in a wide range of colors. In addition, tile comes in various sizes, textures, and finishes, and the grout that seals the joint between the individual tiles can also be tinted to add emphasis or highlights. Ceramic tiles can be installed by capable do-it-yourselfers, which can make them even more affordable. Costs vary from $10 a square foot or less to $50 or more, depending upon the tile selected and the installation costs. I'd recommend buying glazed tiles (they're less likely to stain or scratch) and an epoxy grout. Disadvantages are that tiles can break (though repairs are relatively easy) and the grout will need to be renewed periodically.

Wood surfaces. The range of colors is much narrower than with laminates or ceramic tile, but most people who opt for wood countertops do so because they like the color of a natural finished wood. Maple is most often used as a counter surface, but cherry, birch, mahogany, and other woods are other choices. Most often wooden counters are so-called *butcher-block* surfaces, consisting of glued up strips of solid wood. They can stain, dent, or burn, but usually sanding and resealing will restore a uniform finish. Wood is also vulnerable to variations in humidity (producing swelling and even changes in shape), so careful sealing near sources of water and moisture are critical. The surface should also be periodically treated with a wax or varnish suitable to food-preparation surfaces. Costs are moderate, in the range of $50 to $100 per linear foot, and do-it-yourselfers may well be able to install these surfaces successfully.

Solid surface. These synthetic surfaces are manufactured of polyester or acrylic resins and mineral fillers. They are available in many colors, textures, and patterns, some of which resemble other materials, including wood, stone, and even glass. Thicknesses vary, but $1/2$ inch is perhaps the most common. One advantage of such solid surfaces as Corian and WilsonartGibraltar, two of the common brand names, is that scratches and nicks can be buffed out using an abrasive pad. These surfaces are unlikely to stain, but can be scarred by knives or discolored by exposure to heat. Installation is best left to the professionals. The price range is broad, from roughly $50 to $200 per linear foot.

Stone. Granite is the most popular stone countertop, but marble, soapstone, and others are also available. Stone countertops are extremely durable, but also very unforgiving—one slip with that antique China teapot of Grandma's and it'll be reduced on contact to a pile of shards. Stone is unlikely to nick, scratch, or scorch, though coffee, cooking oils, and liquids with natural pigments can produce staining, especially with marble counters. Soapstone requires periodic sealing to maintain its good looks, so granite is the closest to being a care-free stone surface. While stone is a great option if you want your kitchen counters to last forever, it's also an expensive route to take, as the prices range from about $100 to $250 a linear foot installed. And the installation is best left to the experts.

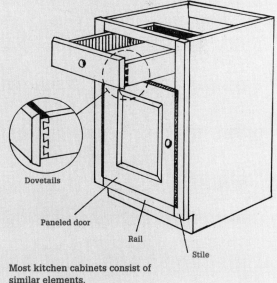

Dovetails

Paneled door

Rail

Stile

Most kitchen cabinets consist of similar elements.

297

in certain applications, so water-resistant materials like ceramic tile or vinyl sheet flooring are probably better choices than wood or carpet for a bathroom or kitchen. Cost is usually a factor, too, but keep in mind that a less expensive choice will probably be less durable: inexpensive carpets and sheet flooring may have to be replaced in a few years while a good hardwood floor will last for generations. But let's talk about the choices one at a time.

WOOD FLOORS. Traditional "floor boards" are just what their name suggests, boards that have been nailed to the framed floor of the structure. But today there are a multitude of kinds of floor boards on the market.

The most common option is called *strip flooring*. It consists of solid wood, typically cut to a face width of 2¼ inches, with tongues and grooves on opposite sides of each piece. *Plank flooring* is wider, typically 4, 5, or 6 inches, though in some pine species the width can be 11¼ inches or more. Oak, maple, cherry, ponderosa pine, Philippine mahogany, and numerous other species are milled into plank flooring. *Vintage* or *recycled flooring* has the same overall shape, but looks very different because it's made from recycled boards, typically reclaimed beams or roofers. It's characterized by variations in color, stains, and other signs of age that give it an antique character. *Engineered flooring* is still another option. Made of a thin ply of hardwood glued to a plywood substrate, engineered floor is very stable.

Which is best? Recycled flooring and wide plank flooring may match up best with an existing floor in an antique home. On the other hand, it's less stable, and

The first course of strip flooring is "face nailed," meaning the nails are driven through the top or face of each board. Those nails are subsequently hidden beneath the baseboard. Each course thereafter is "blind nailed," a technique in which the nails are driven through the tongues of each board so that the groove of the next course hides the nail heads from sight.

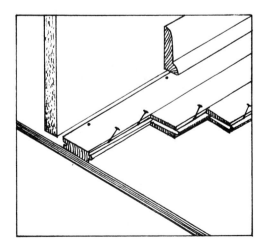

more likely to shrink and gap during the heating season. Most dwellings built in the twentieth century have strip flooring, which is highly durable, a very practical and perhaps the most economical choice. Engineered flooring is very stable and, when purchased prefinished at the factory, usually with an acrylic sealer, it saves time and mess during the final stages of construction. However, this also adds to the price. Your builder can tell you how much. In addition, the factory finish can get scratched or damaged in installation or in the other stages of completing the renovation process.

Finishing the floors. For a variety of reasons, including tradition, solid-wood flooring remains the most common choice. However, the quality of finish your new flooring will have depends upon many factors, among them the skill of the sander, the variety and grade of the finish used, the number of coats applied, and care with which it's finished.

There's an ongoing debate about whether water-based or oil-based finishes are better. One old pro I know who just retired from the business is convinced the oil-based finishes are still more durable (though he points out water-based finishes are rapidly catching up). Yet he also admits he almost always recommended water-base polys because the oil-base gave off more noxious fumes; from an ecological standpoint, water-based is friendlier, since it requires no chemical solvent. Oil-base also takes longer to dry, which meant that he, as a flooring contractor, had to revisit each job site more times when using oil-based finishes *and* got paid a week or more later than when applying faster drying water-based polys. One good way for you to make a choice is to finish a few scrap boards with the polys your flooring contractor recommends, then pick the one that appeals to your eye.

FLOOR TILES. There are a number of different types of flooring tiles. Ceramic tiles are made of clay that is glazed and fired at the factory; they are then laid on the floor with a special mastic or into a thin bed of mortar. Quarry tiles are unglazed variations on the same theme. They're installed like ceramic floor tile, though they usually need to be sealed and polished after installation. Marble and other stone tiles are available, typically for installation on mortar. Marble veneer tiles have also become popular in recent years, as a less expensive alternative.

All tile requires a very solid base to prevent cracking of the tiles or of the grout that is used to seal the joints between the tiles. Depending upon the product, the installer, and the expected traffic in the area being tiled, two layers of subfloor may be required, and the tile may be laid into a bed of cement, a thinset of mortar, or a mastic, epoxy, or cement-based adhesive.

Vinyl tiles resemble vinyl sheet flooring (see page 301) except that they have a latex backing and typically are self-adhesive and sold in 12-inch squares. Rubber and cork tiles are also available, though the cork usually requires sanding and sealing after installation.

First the tiles are carefully laid out—that way, when visitors eventually see the finished work, the impression is one of balance. Next the tiles, whether ceramic or stone, are set, in this case on a bed of mortar.

VINYL SHEET FLOORING. Sheet vinyl is the successor to linoleum. It's made from a flexible plastic, polyvinyl chloride (PVC), from which it also gets its name. It's manufactured in a variety of widths; your local supplier is likely to have rolls that are between 6 and 13 feet wide in stock. Vinyl flooring varies tremendously in pattern, texture, color, *and* price. Quality vinyls have a cushioned backing, which gives them added warmth, softness, and helps deaden sound.

Installation varies from product to product; some are simply laid in place, others must be glued with a special adhesive. While careful layout can often avoid seams, professional installations can match edges so precisely that the finished seams are virtually invisible.

LAMINATE FLOORING. A distant cousin of the plastic laminate often used as kitchen countertops, laminate flooring is a relative newcomer to the flooring sweepstakes. Laminate flooring consists of a moisture-resistant core (typically, fiberboard or particleboard) with a melamine-impregnated surface. The top wear layer also has a photographic pattern or image printed to resemble marble, wood, and other materials. The individual pieces are ¼-inch thick and are edge-glued, meaning the floor "floats." The floor can then expand and contract with the seasonal changes in humidity. It can also be installed on top of existing surfaces like vinyl, linoleum, tile, or wood. While not recommended for wet installations in bathrooms, laminate flooring has much the same life expectancy and serviceability of vinyl sheet flooring.

CARPETING. Carpets are made in one of three ways. *Woven carpets* are made with the tufts woven into the carpet backing. *Tufted carpets* have fiber loops (or *tufts*) inserted into a prewoven backing, while in *nonwoven carpets*, the tufts are bonded to the backing.

Carpets are made of wool, a blend of silk and wool, and cotton, as well as a wide variety of synthetic materials, including acrylics, nylon, polyester, and polypropylene olefin (for indoor-outdoor carpets). Wool carpets are expensive, cotton inexpensive, while the synthetics vary, depending upon the quality. Natural fibers tend to stain more easily than the artificial ones. Most good quality carpets, regardless of the fiber used, will hold their color and wear for many years.

Area rugs can be used in countless ways (for example, to define areas, add color or pattern, or to deaden sound). But the use of an area rug is really a design decision. Wall-to-wall carpeting, on the other hand, can be a principal flooring surface, and it's wall-to-wall carpeting that we're concerned with here.

Most wall-to-wall carpeting, regardless of its manufacturing process, is termed *broadloom carpet* because it leaves the factory in rolls of varying widths, typically 9, 12, or 15 feet. A padding is laid beneath the carpet, then the carpet itself is attached to the floor at the perimeter of room, most often using a tackless strip.

Carpet needs to be laid in a relatively dry setting, since all but olefin carpets tend to absorb moisture. But the decision about what kind of carpet to use tends to be a very subjective one. Many people feel expensive wool carpets convey prestige; others swear that top-of-the-line nylon is indistinguishable and more durable, too. I'd suggest you look at the options and arrange for estimates from a carpeting contractor. The balancing act of price, availability, texture, color, and pattern should bring you to your decision.

Paint and Paper, Fixtures and Fittings

With the finished walls, ceilings, and floors in place, the job may seem to be nearing completion. Once again, however, countless details remain. Carpenters will be applying casings around the windows and doors and doing other trim work, like finishing off the moldings at the baseboard and ceiling. Simultaneously, the cabinet guys may be installing your kitchen cabinets.

Meanwhile, the plumbers are waiting impatiently to put in the dishwasher, and the electrician and HVAC crew are elbowing each other in the basement. The floor sanding crew has just pulled into the driveway, as the painters are trying to back out.

There's a pile of boxes containing doorknobs, lock sets, and window latches that the UPS man just delivered. The alarm installer is on his way because somebody set off the alarm, and its incessant beeping has gotten the dogs next door barking their fool heads off. The fax line won't work, though, and you're on the phone with your designer, who has the bad news that the countertops aren't ready. You find yourself concerned about . . . well, just about everything.

Are you getting the picture? Your project may never be a madhouse like I've just described, but it might be. That doesn't mean, however, you should throw up your hands and give up. Actually, this is a time when your inspections are most important. You should be available to the workers, but not in their way. Often there are many questions that come up at the last minute, and if they know you are there to give them answers—or will be at a certain time—you're more likely to get what you want.

Among the many matters requiring your occasional attention will be the following:

THE WALLS AND CEILINGS. Before the painters arrive, check the work done with the joint compound or plaster. Is the surface flat and uniform, or can you see the dimples around the nail or screw holes? Can you see the joints between the sheets? How about corners, and if you are not planning on any moldings at the ceiling-wall joint, how do the surfaces look there?

After the painters have finished, are the painted surfaces smooth? Are there drips or missed spots? Are the paper or paneling seams straight and tight? Are the edges and corners tight to the wall? Do patterns align? Is there evidence on the surface of glue? Are paneling nails color-matched to the panels?

Check the holes for plugs and switches: the holes should be small enough that plate and switch covers will cover them.

If ceiling tiles, paneling, or wood strips have been applied, are the edges of the pieces parallel? Are they level or plumb? The longer the lines, the more obvious they will be to your and your guests' eyes if they veer up or down or to one side or the other. If there's a pattern, is it consistent?

ELECTRICAL WORK. Check electrical outlets and switches. Are they straight? Once the power is on, do they work? In particular, check three-way switches: Does each control the correct light properly? Check phone plugs, cable television, and other specialty wiring. Check any built-in units: Does the heater in the bathroom work? Any wiring trouble is less expensive and time-consuming to reroute before the final coat of paint or wallpaper goes on. Are new circuits on the electrical panel labeled?

PLUMBING WORK. Are the plumbing fixtures located where they are supposed to be? Do they sit securely fastened to the floor or walls? Once the water is on (it'll be one of the last things to happen, so don't be concerned if you can't check it until well into the process), do the drains work and is the hot water hot? Is the water pressure adequate?

HVAC. Are the registers or radiators located where the plans called for them to be? Are thermostats located on inside walls, away from sunlight and direct drafts?

THE FINISH TRIM. Check the moldings and other trim pieces. Is the fit tight and are the cuts even? Are there visible saw lines or hammer marks? If the wood trim is to be painted, then careless work is easily covered with wood filler and the paint that follows. However, if you are only sealing the wood, pay special attention to the care with which it was installed.

Doors involve multiple installation steps: the rough framing is hidden behind the casing, complete with jambs (on the inside of the opening) and the architrave (on the wall surfaces). Then the door is hinged and hung, the door and trim primed and painted or sealed, then the lock set or latch installed. Windows are easier (usually prefab units are inserted, then trimmed off). But the inspection is the same: Check the doors and windows to be sure they open, close, latch, and swing as they should. How do they look?

WOOD FLOORING, CARPETING, AND RESILIENT FLOORING. Are the joints tight? Does the floor surface sit flat? Are there bumps or gaps at the walls? Are there thresholds or transition strips where one surface gives way to another? Do the doors open easily over the flooring surface, or do they rub or scratch?

EXTERIOR. The outside of the house should be in good order, too. You should see neatly painted trim and other surfaces, the paint scraped from the windowpanes, and in general get the feeling the job has been done and done well. If your contract called for landscaping, grading, or plantings, have they been completed to specification? How about walks and patios and driveways?

Settling Disputes

So, you tried to anticipate everything. But the fact is, no one can plan for every exigency. So here are some ways to deal with the aftermath of a disaster. They do happen. Not often, but they occur. What do you do if something major does go wrong?

First things first. You ignore the pleas of your GC for partial payment and explain that everybody will get paid when the job is done. If the tradesman who is at

THE PUNCH LIST

As the end of the project approaches, enjoy the signs of completion as they emerge. At the same time, however, take careful note of areas where the work isn't quite done or done right. Like moldings that don't match up, a door that doesn't close, missing hardware, and other details.

Don't take it upon yourself to bring up every nit and pick with the nearest workman, or even with his boss. Instead, you should make a list. There's a term of art in the building trades for this final list of corrections.

It's called a *punch list*. The punch list isn't an hourly gift for your architect or contractor. Give it to him when you've got more than two or three items, and after he's had enough time to address the fixes you gave him on the last list. Keep copies for yourself, too, and follow up before you give him the next one to make sure what you asked for got done. If it didn't, find out why.

The punch list is a key part of getting the job completed. Always carry a small pad or notebook with you—it is critical to write things down. Don't trust your memory.

This is when that 10 percent of the final prices you're holding back comes in handy. You've got leverage now, so use it. Your contractor or some of the subs may complain and mumble under their breaths, but get the job finished before you pay.

---

fault has the GC on his case as well as you then the chances are much greater that he'll come back and straighten things out. One angry customer is an irritating inconvenience, but an angry contractor who will badmouth you to the trade is dangerous to one's professional health.

This doesn't always work, of course. Sometimes there is too little money left unpaid for the contractor(s) to be bothered. It's called cutting your losses. They figure you owe them a thousand dollars, it'll cost two thousand to fix the trouble so, what the heck, why don't we just make ourselves scarce for a while, aye?

If you checked your references thoroughly, this shouldn't happen. Contractors don't usually turn into bad apples overnight. But if they do?

Next you check what's in your contract. The contract will be at the beginning of any legal proceeding, so even before your dreams start featuring Perry Mason's rotund frame, look to your paperwork.

You should have negotiated some leverage there. Payment schedules are the best leverage but if you find yourself without sufficient monetary leverage, check with your lawyer to see what other options are available. There may be an arbitration clause, for example. In any case, the possible remedies open to you are several.

STATE, COUNTY, AND CITY CONSUMER OFFICES. In many areas, local governmental agencies have been established to help consumers who feel they have been wronged.

Start with your city's agencies first. If there isn't one or they cannot be of assistance try county or state departments of consumer affairs. Often you will find personnel there who know the local laws, and who may be able to advise you on what your next step should be. If you consult with any such consumer agencies, be sure you have your contracts and other records of payments with you.

SMALL CLAIMS COURT. Small claims court is an option if you are unable to get your complaint satisfied in other ways. Usually no lawyer is required, the paperwork simple and the results rapid. Small claims are usually inexpensive to pursue, and you may even be reimbursed for your filing fee if you prevail. Check at your local courthouse for hours and any requirements. You may find the small claims clerks very helpful in explaining procedures.

Small claims courts are, as the name suggests, for small claims. If the kitchen window you paid $400 to have installed leaks, small claims court may well be the right place to pursue your action. On the other hand, if the foundation on your brand-new $250,000 addition is riddled with cracks, go talk to your lawyer and get him to pursue it for you.

BETTER BUSINESS BUREAU. Many municipal Better Business Bureaus have programs for resolving disputes. Call your local Bureau and ask. Check the telephone directory for your local Better Business Bureau or write to the national headquarters, the Council of Better Business Bureaus, at 1515 Wilson Boulevard, Arlington, VA 22290 or telephone 703-276-0100.

Professional societies for electricians, plumbers, and other tradesmen may also have such a service in your area. Check them next. They are associations created to serve their memberships, but most are careful to be fair: they gain nothing in the long term from protecting the irresponsible, incompetent, or shoddy among their members, and at least some of them act as if they know it.

Professional arbiters are also available. Even if your contract does not include an arbitration clause, you may be able to get the contractor with whom you are hav-

THE DECORATORS AND THE LANDSCAPERS

When your job nears completion, you may want a couple of other pros to come in and help with the finish. I can't emphasize enough, however, that you should arrange for their services well in advance of the last broomful of sawdust being swept up and out.

One more point before you skip over these paragraphs: Decorators and landscapers are no longer just for rich people. On the contrary, they work mostly for middle-class folk who aspire to attractive settings, indoors and out, within which to live their lives. No, they're not essential. But I firmly believe good design always adds value and polish to a job.

The interior decorator. Your architect may be willing to consult with you on your interior decoration if you wish. He may be able to get you trade discounts, too. If the time involved is simply a matter of a session of "What do you think about this?" and "How do you think this fits with that?" then your architect is likely to regard it as part of his basic services.

However, if you want him or her to help you find what you want, to explore possibilities for you and with you, you should expect to pay a price. An hourly fee is probably best. Establish up front what the rate will be and what the estimated number of hours are.

You may do better with a specialist, an interior designer with specific training and experience. There's a great variety of designers out there, and the good ones have great skills at blending colors and textures and can do wonders on limited budgets as well as large ones.

Selecting one is quite like finding an architect, in that you must make a judgment that you can work with the interior decorator, that the decorator's tastes and yours are compatible. There are interior decorators who are in the business to satisfy themselves. That's fine, supposing your taste coincides with the decorator's. Get a decorator who comes well recommended, whose work you admire, and who seems inclined to listen to what you say.

Decorators are not licensed, but membership in one of the professional organizations like the American Society of Interior Designers (ASID) or the Institute of Business Designers does suggest some level of achievement in the business. Membership in those organizations requires three or four years of postsecondary education, at least two years practical experience, and completion of a written and design-problem examination given by the National Council of Interior Design Qualification.

Another reminder on timing: All too often interior designers arrive about the same time as the moving vans, when their appearance on the scene should be as early as possible. If you are planning to hire an interior decorator, he or she can be of maximum value to you if consulted before all the decisions are made on finish materials in the house. Most architects are quite willing to work with decorators, as their skills are compatible with one another. The earlier the interior designer is involved, the greater your chances of ending up with a carefully coordinated, coherently planned and decorated home.

The landscape architect. An experienced landscape designer, who may be a landscape architect or a veteran hands-on professional, can do for your site what the interior decorator does to the interior. He or she decorates, too, only the raw materials are bushes and trees and plants. He also has an architectural function in that he may advise you to add a stone wall, to regrade portions of the yard, or to make other topographical changes in its configurations.

A fully trained landscape architect will have studied horticulture, art history, and engineering; the experienced landscaper may have less book knowledge, but years of experience in what plant material survives in your climate and what doesn't. The landscaper's expertise will extend from which perennials will survive in the shade to the design and placement of retaining walls and drain lines and paved areas. The talk will be of hardscape, plantscape, *and* landscape.

A landscape architect, like an interior designer, is not a requirement on every job. If your home project involves only the interior, obviously the landscape architect isn't critical. Even if you are concerned with your yard, your architect or even a local nurseryman may provide you with the guidance and materials you need. But don't underestimate what a professional design consultant can do in making the most of your property.

While the finish work is going on indoors, the landscaping can be done outside. In this instance, a 'dozer is grading coarse gravel as a base for the layer of topsoil to follow.

ing your disagreement to agree to an arbitration proceeding to avoid your dragging him into court.

Arbitrations vary a great deal, but in general the idea is to get the parties to present their case to an impartial third party, who will then render a decision. Whether it is binding or not is a question of the paperwork (did everybody sign a written agreement up front guaranteeing compliance to the decision of the arbiter?). At the very least it is an opportunity to sit down in a room with a cooler head to try and solve the problem.

If none of these options works, you have two choices. Swallow your pride and get somebody else to fix it or get your lawyer on the case.

Some Final Notes on Finishing the Job

How long should the finish work take? That depends on the job, of course. When the job involves plastering and painting, each of those steps will take a few days. Given the work that comes before and after, finish work will require a minimum of two weeks. On big renovations, two months may be more reasonable.

Before your contractor has completed his job, he should clean up his mess. There shouldn't be chunks of wood left embedded in the soil (they're lures for termites). All tools and equipment and materials should disappear along with the contractors and their workmen. The bathtub shouldn't be left with a gritty layer of grout in it, and you should be able to see yourself in the mirror. There also should be no tools or materials tucked away in a corner of your basement or garage.

But let's suppose the paint is dry, the toilets flush, and the contractor's tools are finally gone. Even the bills are paid.

This is really the best part. By this point you will have made it through many sleepless nights, confronted some expenses that astonished you (and been surprised at the reasonableness of some others), and been struck dumb by one or more of the magicians who can take a pile of materials and turn it into a key part of your home.

Expect to have a few second thoughts. Having now lived in our Cambridge house for a couple of years, we're very happy there. But I have a few small com-

RECEIPTS AND RECORDS

Keep all your records together in a safe place. That means estimates, contracts, invoices, and especially canceled checks and receipts. Organize them into files if you wish, but at the very least keep an oversize envelope into which you toss all paperwork related to your renovation.

These records may be helpful in resolving any disputes and disagreements in the short term. When it comes to filing taxes for the year in which the remodeling was done, consult with your accountant regarding which expenses may be tax deductible. Among them might be certain closing costs; sales tax paid on large purchases (kitchen appliances, for example); and perhaps improvements that are work-related.

Later, when and if you sell your home, your receipts and check stubs will enable you to calculate the cost basis of your house for purposes of calculating capital-gains tax that may be due.

plaints. One is that our kitchen cabinets are too shallow to accommodate large serving platters and other bulky items. The approach our architect took is that such rarely used items ought to be stored downstairs in the cellar. But since we entertain often, that doesn't really suit our lifestyle. So I keep an heirloom nest of platters in the top drawer of a secretary in the front hall, just off the kitchen. We all adapt one way or another. I hope that your worst problem is no more serious than that.

So have a seat. Relax. Enjoy the feel and comfort of what you have wrought. And promise me something, okay? Don't even think about your next project. For at least a week.

Glossary

Adamesque. Architectural style based upon the work of Scottish brothers named Adam, in particular Robert Adam. In the United States, Adamesque with its delicate classical decorations is a subset of the Federal Style.

Allowance. Value of an item on the specification sheets; when a substitute material is used, the portion of its cost that is greater or less than the originally specified material shall be added to or deducted from the total price.

Amperes. Unit of measure of the power or flow of electricity. See also *volts* and *watts*.

Architect. Designation for a person or firm professionally qualified and licensed to perform architectural services.

ARM. Mortgage with an interest rate than may vary over the life of the mortgage. Acronym for adjustable rate mortgage.

Asymmetry. Not in balance. See page 117.

Awning window. A window that hinges at the top and swings outward.

Balance. An equilibrium that may be visual or physical. See page 121.

Bargeboard. Projecting trim board on the exterior of a house, typically covering the roof projection of the gable end. Term commonly used to describe the elaborated sawn or cut decorations along rooflines colloquially known as *gingerbread*.

Baseboard. Molding at the joining of the wall and floor; in England termed a skirting board.

Batts and blanket insulation. Insulation with the consistency of sponge cake, often of fiberglass, available in various widths and lengths to fill wall and ceiling bays.

In describing this handsome Greek Revival doorway, one could use dozens of handy architectural terms—among them, capital, column, Corinthian, cornice, fluted, lintel, pilaster, and sidelight.
Photo credit: Hugh Howard

Beam. Main horizontal structural member in the construction of a frame house. See also *post, joist, stud,* and *rafter.*

Bearing wall. Wall that carries some or all of the weight of the structure above. Also called a *structural wall.*

Blueprints. Architectural plans of a building. The name refers to a photographic print in white on a blue ground or blue on a white ground that is made of the architect's plans.

Boiler. Source of heat in a central heating system that uses hot water as the heating medium. See also *furnace.*

Bracket. Small, decorative projection that supports (or appears to support) an overhanging roofline or headpiece above a window or door. Common to many Victorian styles including the Italianate or American Bracket Style.

Building codes. National, state, and local regulations or statutory requirements governing materials, construction techniques, and building occupancy in the interests of safety, public health, and other considerations

Building inspector. Person authorized by your town or city to inspect buildings in progress for adherence to building codes and other regulations. See also *code enforcement officer.*

Building paper. The material, often asphalt impregnated tar paper, that was traditionally applied to the sheathing prior to the application of the finished siding or roof material; also called felt.

Building permit. Legal document issued by the building department in your city or town granting permission for construction work. A fee is usually charged for issuing a permit.

Capital. Head of a column.

Casement window. Window that hinges at the side and swings outward.

Casing. Molding used to trim door and window openings. Also called a *surround* and an architrave.

Caulk. Puttylike sealant used to fill gaps between two hard surfaces for weather-proofing or cosmetic reasons. Caulk is made of soft materials (typically silicone, acrylic with latex, butyl, neoprene, or oil-based compounds) that remain flexible.

Certificate of insurance. Document each contractor should provide certifying appropriate insurance coverage in the event of personal or property loss.

Certificate of occupancy. Legal document issued by your city or town certifying that your dwelling is fit for habitation. In most jurisdictions, a new C. of O. will be required upon completion of a renovation.

Chair rail. Decorative interior molding located at waist height that also protects wall surfaces.

Change orders. Contractual amendments signed by owner, contractor, and, in some cases, the architect, during construction that specify material, labor, and/or cost changes in a job from the original specifications or schedule.

Chase. Wall or ceiling channel through which wiring, plumbing, or vents pass.

Classical. Building styles or elements that have been derived from the Roman or Greek buildings of classical antiquity. In practice, such revival styles as Georgian, Federal, Greek, and Renaissance Revival are classical; in contrast, Gothic Revival, Romanesque, and Queen Anne Styles allude to medieval (rather than classical) archi-tecture.

Closing. Meeting at which the legal formalities of a real estate sale are completed, including the transfer of the deed from the seller to the buyer; also called settlement in some regions.

Code enforcement officer. Building inspector; the person authorized by your town or city to inspect buildings in progress for adherence to building codes and other regulations.

Construction budget. Sum allotted for construction costs, from bidding through the completion of the project.

Construction documents. Drawings and specifications created by the designer that detail requirements for the building project.

Construction manager. Architect or other expert hired to supervise a construction project for a fee or a fixed percentage of its cost.

Corner board. Vertical boards at the corners of traditional wood-frame buildings.

Cornice. Decorative horizontal finish that projects at the crown of an exterior or interior wall.

Cost-plus contract. Agreement in which the homeowner and contractor agree in advance on a percentage of the total construction cost as a fee for the contractor's services. See also *lump-sum contract*.

Covenant. Restriction specified in property deeds, typically regarding land use, subdivision, changes to the house, or other limitations.

Crawl space. Cellar area of insufficient height for standing.

Dedicated circuit. Electrical line that services one receptacle or appliance. Typically used for furnace, hot water heater, or other larger appliances and, more recently, for computers.

Detail sheet. Architectural rendering that indicates special construction details of a house, such as for a staircase, kitchen cabinetry, or molding details.

Double-hung window. Window that slides up and down within its frame.

Draw. Method of payment in which a contractor will be paid on a periodic basis for work completed.

Drywall. Finish material for walls or ceilings that consists of a layer of gypsum sandwiched between two layers of paper. It is applied dry (unlike plaster, whose finish it resembles). Also called *gypsum board*.

Ductwork. Network of round or rectangular pipes or ducts for the distribution of warm or cool air.

Easement. Strip of land inside the boundary of a piece of property that must be left free of construction. Easements are usually mandated by local ordinance, often for drainage or utility uses. See also *setback*.

Elevation. Architectural drawing that indicates the two-dimensional appearance of completed interior or exterior wall; the point of view is of an observer looking from a horizontal vantage. See page 118.

Ell. A building addition at right angles to the main axis of the original structure.

Equity. Difference between the value of a property and the owner's total remaining indebtedness.

Fabric. Physical material of a building.

Fascia. Flat, vertical boards that form a band around the edge of the roof. See also *cornice* and *soffit*.

Fenestration. Arrangement of openings (windows and doors) in a building.

Firebox. Portion of a fireplace or furnace where the fire or flame is located.

Fixed-price contract. See *lump-sum contract*.

Fixture risers. Vertical plumbing pipes that carry the water, hot or cold, to each fixture.

Fixtures. Any of the various parts of the plumbing or electrical systems that are installed permanently in a building, such as bathtubs, basins, toilets, and wall or ceiling lighting fixtures.

Flashing. Sheet metal (copper, aluminum, or lead) or other material used in roof and wall construction to protect the joints in a building from being penetrated by water.

Floor plan. Architectural drawing that shows the location of the rooms in a structure, drawn as if from the point of view of an observer looking from directly above the building. Separate floor plans for each story of the building indicate outside walls, interior room configurations, wall openings (windows and doors), appliance and plumbing fixture locations, and other details. See pages 188–195.

Footing. Rectangular concrete mass set below grade level onto which the foundation wall or piers are set. The purpose of the footing is to distribute the weight of the building evenly onto undisturbed earth around the foundation. See page 243.

Footprint. The perimeter and inside area of a house foundation.

Foundation plan. Top-view drawing that indicates the outside dimensions of the house and the specifications for grading, excavation, and footing and foundation wall construction.

Frame construction. Construction in which the structural parts are wood or depend upon a wood frame for support (as in a brick veneer wall).

Framing. Process of assembling the skeleton of a building, typically consisting of the lumber elements. See also *stud, joist, beam,* and *rafter.*

Frost line. Depth the frost penetrates into the earth in a given location, a determining factor in how deep the foundation footings must be set.

Furnace. Source of heat in a central heating system that uses hot air as the heating medium. See also *boiler.*

Gable. Triangle at the top of an end wall of a building formed by the eave line of a double-sloped roof.

General contractor. Person who manages the construction process, handing financial, scheduling, materials, and personnel matters pertaining to a building project.

GFI. See *ground-fault interrupter.*

Gingerbread. Sawn or carved exterior decoration found in many Victorian styles, characterized by spindle work and turned posts on porches and bargeboards on rooflines.

Girder. Major horizontal beam.

Ground-fault interrupter. Safety device that functions as a secondary fuse to shut off power to the outlet and prevent electrical shock in the event of a fault in the electrical ground.

Ground sill. See *sill.*

Gypsum board. See *drywall.*

Hardscape. Wood, stone, and other fixed elements in a landscape, including walls, fences, driveways, walkways, terraces, and decks.

Header. Wooden beam positioned over a door, window, or other opening to bear the weight of the structure above. See also *lintel*.

Heating load. Amount of heat required to heat a structure that is determined using an arithmetical formula that factors in the size of the structure, its insulation, and the local climate.

Heat pump. HVAC system that uses compressed refrigerant to concentrate the relative heat of the air, ground, or ground water for heating or cooling. See also page 278.

House wrap. Membrane applied to the exterior of the house that prevents the infiltration of air but allows water vapor to escape.

Hydronic heating system. Term synonymous with hot-water heating.

HVAC. Shorthand term for *h*eating, *v*entilation and *a*ir-*c*onditioning.

I-joist. Prefabricated structural member made of laminated veneer lumber. In section, it resembles the capital letter I. See also *joist* and *laminated veneer lumber*.

Infiltration. Flow of air that enters the house through gaps around windows, doors, electrical boxes, and other exterior openings.

Insulation. Materials used in walls, ceilings, and floors to prevent heat transmission. See also *R-factor* and pages 54 and 261.

Jamb. Side or head lining of a door, window, or other opening.

Joint compound. Premixed, plasterlike substance applied with a putty knife to cover nail holes and joints between sheets in gypsum board construction; also known as mud or spackle.

Joist. One of a series of parallel beams laid edgewise, often of lumber of nominal 2-inch thickness, that support floor or ceiling loads. Joists are, in turn, supported by beams or bearing walls. See pages 157 and 250.

Kitchen triangle. Design guideline regarding the location of the sink, refrigerator, and stove; according to the rule, each of the three elements is set into a point of a triangle whose perimeter is not more than 22 feet with sides 5 to 9 feet in length. See page 57.

Laminated veneer lumber. Structural lumber manufactured of thin layers (veneers) of wood glued together to form joists, beams, or headers.

Light. Individual panes of glass in a window sash.

Lintel. Horizontal member, usually of metal or stone, that supports the load over an opening, such as a door, window, or fireplace.

Loggia. Roofed, open gallery, often with a row of arches or columns.

Lump-sum contract. Agreement in which the homeowner and general contractor agree in advance on a total price for a job; also called a *fixed-price contract*. See also *cost-plus contract*.

LVL. See *laminated-veneer lumber*.

Masonry. Brick, concrete, stone, or other materials bonded together with mortar to form walls, piers, buttresses, or other masses.

Mass. Three-dimensional bulk of an object, such as a house. See page 118.

Millwork. Wood components that are finished and assembled at their place of manufacture, often including windows, doors, and paneling.

Molding. Strip of wood (or occasionally of plaster or other material) used for finish or decorative purposes. A molding has regular channels or projections, and it may be flat, curved, or both. Moldings are used as transitions from one surface to another and for visual appeal.

Mullion. Large vertical bar between separate window units. See also *muntin*.

Muntin. Wooden elements, also called glazing bars, that separate the panes of glass in a window sash.

Or equal materials. Goods, typically finish materials such as carpeting, light fixtures, or tile, that may be substituted for equivalent items listed on the spec sheets. The term "or equal" also implies that the substitution may be done at no cost to the homeowner if the alternate choice is priced the same as (and thus equal to) what was specified. Also called *allowances*.

Outline specifications. Preliminary listings of materials and instructions to be used for estimating purposes. See also *specifications*.

Palladian window. Three-part window consisting of a central arch flanked by two shorter flat-topped windows. Named after sixteenth-century Italian master Andrea Palladio.

Picture molding. Interior molding located immediately below the ceiling that is used for attaching hooks to hang picture frames.

Pier. Masonry column used to support the structure of a house.

Pilaster. Flattened or half-round column projecting from a wall.

Plantscape. Vegetative components of a landscape, including the trees, shrubs, flowering and fruit-bearing plants, and ground cover.

Plate. See *top plate*.

Plot plan. Top-view drawing that identifies the boundaries and other significant aspects of the land on which the structure is to be built as well as the structure itself. See page 38.

Plumb. Precisely vertical.

Pointing. Filling of open mortar joints between masonry units (brick, stone, block). See also *repointing*.

Post. Main vertical structural member in the construction of a frame house. See also *beam, joist, stud,* and *rafter*.

Preservation. Conservation of original architectural fabric. See page 7.

Program. Outline of needs, expectations, budget, and design inclinations that define a design task. The program will guide the designer in creating a structure that satisfies the homeowner's objectives, site and other limitations, building regulations, and any other constraints.

Proportion. Relative size of different elements to one another, often expressed in ratios.

Punch list. List of final problems to be corrected when a construction job is approaching completion.

Rafter. One of a series of inclined structural members that support the roof, running from the exterior wall to the ridgepole or ridge board. See page 250.

Rebar. Steel rods set into concrete to add strength; shorthand for reinforcement bars.

Rehabilitation. Modification of original structure or elements for adaptation to new uses. See page 7.

Repointing. Renewal of deteriorating mortar between masonry units (brick, stone, or block) by removal of old, crumbing mortar and the tooling in of fresh mortar. See page 47.

Restoration. Act of returning a structure or object to its original appearance. See page 7.

Retainage. Payment scheme in which the homeowner retains 10 percent of each interim payment until substantial completion of the job, when the withheld monies are released.

R-factor. Measure of insulating ability; the higher the R-factor, the greater the insulating value. Also referred to as *R-value*.

Ridgepole or Ridge board. Horizontal member at the peak of the roof to which the top ends of the rafters attach.

Right-of-way. Legal right of passage over another person's property, usually specified in the deed to that property.

Riser. Vertical board that closes the space between the treads of a stairway. See also *tread, stringer*, and page 125.

Rough-in. Preliminary stage of electrical, plumbing, or HVAC work where the wires, pipes, or ductwork that will eventually be obscured by finished walls and ceilings are installed.

Rough opening. Unfinished opening in a building for a window or door.

Sash. Wood or metal frame in which the glass lights of a window are set.

Scale. Relative height, width, depth, and size. When applied to a drawing, the size of the drawing in relation to a full-size structure, usually expressed in ratio such as ½ inch = 1 foot. See page 159.

Sheathing. Layer of boards or plywood over the supporting structure of the house but beneath the final siding or roofing material; called "sheeting" in some regions. See page 255.

Sheeting. See *sheathing.*

Sheetrock. Proprietary name for sheets of plasterboard. See also *gypsum board.*

Section. Drawing or model of a part of a building that has been cut vertically or horizontally to reveal the interior or profile; a floor plan is an example of a section, where the cut is made through all the doors and windows so as to best show the construction.

Setback. Minimum distance specified by local ordinance that a building must be located (or "set back") from its boundaries. See also *easement.*

Siding. Finished surface of exterior walls, commonly clapboard or shingles.

Sill. Lowest member of the wood framing of a house, the sill rests on top of the foundation wall. Also referred to as *sole, sole plate,* and *ground sill.* See page 250.

Site Plan. See *plot plan.*

Soffit. Underside of a roof overhang or cornice.

Sole. See *sill.*

Sole plate. See *sill.*

Specifications. Series of sheets attendant to the architect's drawings that specify standards of performance for a job as well as schedules of the materials to be used.

Stair carriage. See *stringer.*

Stringer. Sides of a staircase onto which the risers and treads are attached. Also called the stair carriage. See page 125.

Structural wall. See *bearing wall*.

Stud. One of a series of vertical wood or metal structural members, usually (in the case of wood) of nominal 2-inch thickness, used as supporting elements in walls or partitions. See page 250.

Subfloor. Layer of plywood or boards laid over the floor joists on which the finished floor is applied.

Supply pipes. Plumbing that delivers clean water to the fixtures. See also *waste pipes* and *fixtures*.

Surround. See *casing*.

Survey. Document prepared by a surveyor that delineates the extent and position of a tract of land.

Symmetry. Proportionally balanced, as in a building in which the elements on either side of a central line correspond in size, shape, and position. See page 116.

Takeoff. List of materials required for a particular job, usually derived from the spec sheets (see also *specifications*); used in cost estimating.

Top plate. Horizontal framing member to which the lower end of the rafters are fastened. Also referred to as the *plate* or *wall plate*.

Tread. Horizontal boards of a staircase colloquially known as the step. See also *riser, stringer*, and page 125.

Trimming out. Stage of construction at which the final trim elements are installed by the various trades.

Upset price. Agreed upon maximum price for a job specified in a cost-plus contract. See also *cost-plus contract*.

U-Value. Measure of the heat loss through a window.

Valley. Joint between the planes of two inclined roof surfaces that form a runoff for rain water.

Vapor barrier. Layer of plastic or other watertight material applied to the inside of exterior walls to prevent inside moisture from condensing within the walls and to limit air and water infiltration from without. See page 54.

Variances. Exceptions granted by local authorities to zoning regulations. See also *zoning* and *easement*.

Veneers. Thin sheets of wood (typically an ⅛-inch thick or less) used for finished surfaces in furniture and, when glued up in multiple layers, to form plywood and laminated-veneer lumber.

Vergeboard. See *bargeboard*.

Volts. Unit of measure of the rate of an electrical current. See also *amperes* and *watts*.

Volume. Interior space of an object. See page 136.

Wall plate. See *top plate*.

Waste pipes. Plumbing that drains the water and other waste from the fixtures. See also *supply pipes* and *fixtures*.

Watts. Unit of measure of the rate of the power actually used by an electrical appliance. See also *amperes* and *volts*.

Weatherstripping. Lengths of metal, plastic, felt, or other material used to line the sides, top, or foot of doors or windows to prevent infiltration of air and moisture.

Wet wall. Bathroom or kitchen wall containing plumbing lines.

Wing. A section of or addition to a house that extends out from the main part of a structure.

Zoning. Local ordinances specifying the restrictions in a given area (or zone) regarding the use of that land.

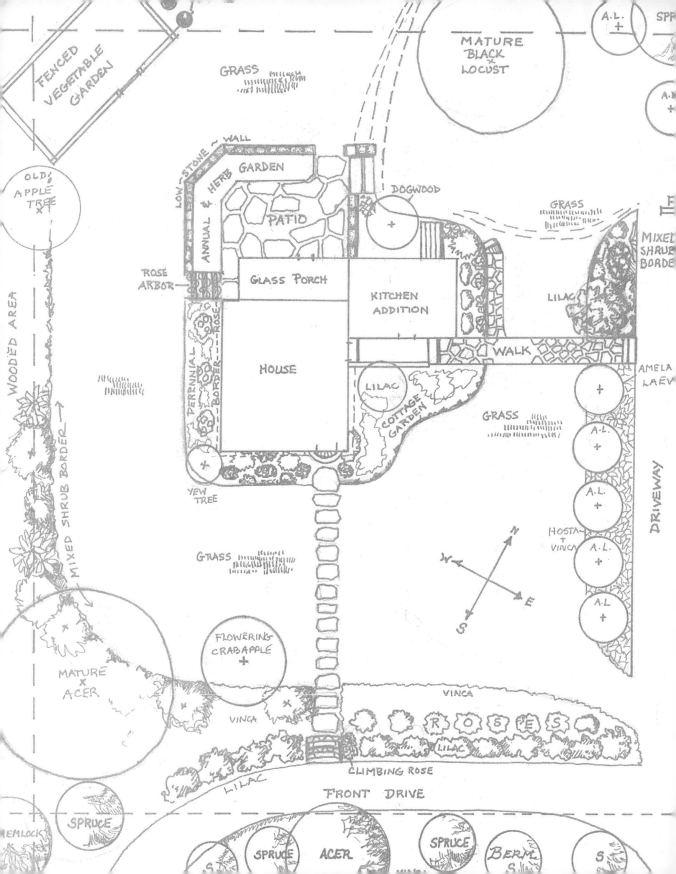

Index

Page numbers in italics refer to photographs and illustrations.

DATE			